P9-EEP-614

Date Due

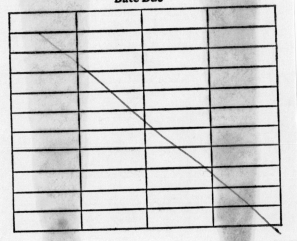

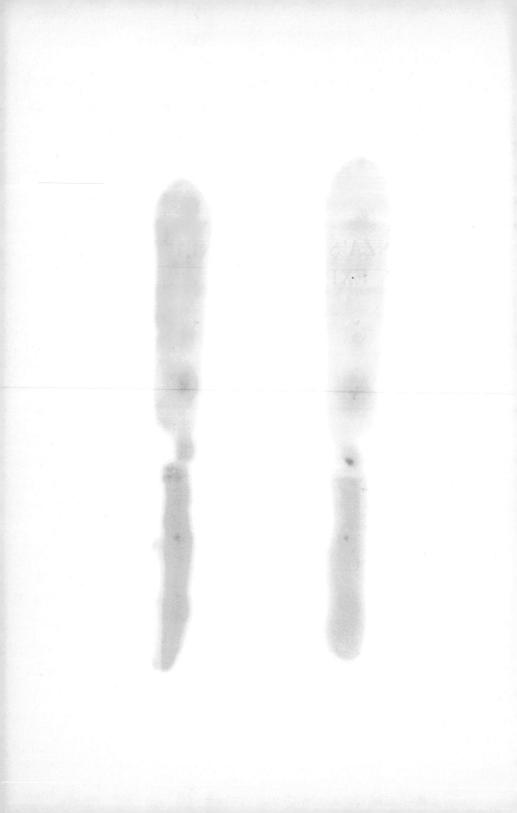

ANZA'S CALIFORNIA EXPEDITIONS

VOLUME II

Diario de la Ruta, i Operaciones, q.e Io el Infrascripto Capitan de
Cavalleria de el Real Precidio de tubac, en la Provincia de Sonora, practico
en Solicitud de abrir communicacion de d.ha Prov.a á la California Setemptrional por los Rios Gila, y Colorado, â cuia expedicion
soi commicionado por el Ex.mo S.r theniente General D.n Antonio Maria Bucareli y Ursua, Virrey Governador y Capit.n General de la Nueva España; como consta de mi Superior Orden de dies y siete de Septiembre de mil setecientos setenta y tres años.

Individuo, q.e se comprehenden, y baña d.ha expedicion.

Commandante de ella, D.n Juan Baptista de Anza 1
Padres Predicadores de Propaganda fide del collegio de la Cruz de Queretaro, Frai Juan Dias 1
Frai Fran.co Garzes 1
Veinte Soldado, voluntarios, de el mencionado Precidio incluso
un Cavo 20
Uno d.to remitido de Mexico de Orden el Ex.mo S.r Virrey por
practico de los caminos de la california 1
Un Natural de la mencionada Peninsula, q.e el dia veinte, y
seis de diciembre ultimo anterior, salio de ella de los Pueblos
de la Pimeria alta, y Precidio de el Altar 1
Un Interprete de el Bioma Pima, por supuesse se deriben
de el los intenciones 1
Un Natural de el Precidio de mi Congo, con el destino de Carpintero 1
Cinco Arrieros, y dos sirvientes mios 7
                                              total 39

Se conducen treinta i cinco Cargas de vivones, municiones de
Guerra tabaco, equipages, y otros utiles necesarios para
terrenos ignorados.

First page of Anza's Complete Diary.

ANZA'S CALIFORNIA EXPEDITIONS

VOLUME II

OPENING A LAND ROUTE TO CALIFORNIA

DIARIES OF ANZA, DÍAZ, GARCÉS, AND PALÓU

TRANSLATED FROM THE ORIGINAL SPANISH
MANUSCRIPTS AND EDITED

BY

HERBERT EUGENE BOLTON

NEW YORK / RUSSELL & RUSSELL

1966

"No historical narrative is quite so good as the raw material of which historical narratives are made."

—Duffus.

PREFACE

In this volume are printed the diaries of the first Anza expedition. They are eight in number, no one of which has been printed hitherto in any language. In addition I have included the Brief Account by Father Garcés, which, though written in the form of a letter, is essentially another diary. Besides these narratives, I have inserted Father Palóu's diary recording the exploration of San Francisco Bay made by himself and Rivera to look for mission sites. This journey was a link between the two Anza expeditions, and Palóu's account belongs with the Anza diaries.

Anza left three diaries of the first expedition. The first, listed here as B, covers the distance from Tubac to San Gabriel. This was sent to Mexico from San Gabriel by Valdés, the courier. The second (C) covers the ground from San Gabriel to Monterey, and back to Tubac. Anza combined these into a complete diary (A). A and C were carried by Anza to Mexico and there delivered by him to the viceroy in person. The original of the first of these diaries (B) is in Anza's own delicate and beautiful hand. The others are in the letter of a scribe, but are signed by Anza.

Father Díaz wrote two diaries of the expedition, one (D) covering the journey from Tubac to San Gabriel, and the other (E) narrating the return journey from San Gabriel to Tubac. Of D we have the original; of E a certified official copy. D was carried to Mexico from San Gabriel by Valdés, and E was sent from Tubac.

Father Garcés wrote a diary (F) for the journey from Tubac to San Gabriel and back to the Yuma junction. While in California he went from San Gabriel to San Diego and there wrote to Bucareli a letter (G) which covers the expedition from Tubac to San Gabriel and carries his personal story to San Diego. This Brief Account was sent to

PREFACE

Mexico by way of Lower California. Garcés awaited Anza's return to the Yumas, and with him ascended the Gila River to the Gila Bend. Instead of continuing with Anza to Tubac, he now turned northwest and visited the Jalchedunes on the Colorado River in the vicinity of Ehrenberg, whence he returned to Gila Bend and San Xavier del Bac. Of this journey to the Jalchedunes Garcés wrote a most interesting diary (H) which was sent to Mexico from San Xavier del Bac. Of diaries F and G we have the originals and of H an official copy.

Because Anza's diary A covers the whole expedition and is the most complete single account, I have inserted it first in the volume and have edited it more fully than the other diaries. In editing these others, to avoid giving inconvenient cross-references, in some cases I have repeated, in briefer form, data found in the notes to diary A.

Don Juan was a good chronicler. He was busy with the tasks of leadership, and he would be excusable for failure to make a first rate record. His was the duty to assemble mules, stock, men, provisions, and equipment, and on the road to keep things moving. Yet he had the energy and the skill to write excellent diaries. His record deals with the things of first importance from practical considerations —distances, directions, landmarks, water, pasturage, the strength and disposition of tribes, the features of the trail, sites for settlements.

Anza's style was more involved and less practiced than that of Díaz, who was simple, lucid, and logical. To Garcés, writing was a weariness. His hand was crotchety and his spelling bad. He was always apologetic for his awful chirography, and out of kindness to his readers, whenever possible he employed a copyist. Yet he was a keen observer, and his experience on the Colorado River frontier was more extensive than that of any of his associates. His four accounts of the two expeditions are indispensable.

PREFACE

LIST OF THE DIARIES

FIRST EXPEDITION

A. Diario de la Ruta, i Operaciones; q.e Yó el Ynfrascripto Capitan de Cavalleria de el Real Precidio de Tubac en la Provincia de Sonora practico en solicitud de abrir comunicacion de dha Prov.a á la California Septemptrional por los Rios Gila, y Colorado, á cuia expedicion soi commicionado, por el Exmo S.r Theniente General D.n Antonio Maria Bucareli y Ursua, Virrey Governador, y Capit.n General de la Nueva España; como consta de su Superior Orden de dies y ciete de Septiembre de mil setecientos setenta y tres años. Tubac, January 8, 1774–Tubac, May 27, 1774. Original. Archivo General y Público, Mexico, Historia, Tomo 396. Signed by Anza but written in another hand. On November 13, 1774, in Mexico, Anza delivered to Bucareli this document together with the "map hereinbefore mentioned," namely that of Father Díaz. On December 24, 1774, a testimonio of this document was made to send to the viceroy. A beautiful copy is in A.G.P.M., Provincias Internas, Tomo 23.

A contemporary copy of this diary, not in Anza's hand, is listed in Maggs Brothers' *Bibliotheca Americana, Catalogue No. 465*, pp. 280–287 and plate XLI (London, 1925), and offered for sale for £1250. The dealers justify this price by "the very few data concerning this expedition, which are extant in the printed works on the early pioneer work in California."

B. Diario de la Ruta y Operaciones q.e io el Ynfrascripto Cap.n de Cavallería y del Re.l Press.o de Tubac en la Provincia de Sonora Hago y practico en solicitud de Abrír camino de dha Provinz.a á la California Setemptrional; por los Rios Gila y Colorado á cuia Expedicc.on

PREFACE

procedo por Comicc.^{on} del Exmo Sor Thte Gral D.ⁿ Antt.^o María Bucareli y Urzua, Virey Govr y Cap.ⁿ Gral de la Nueva España como consta de su Orn de Diez y siete de Septiembre del Año prox.^{mo} pasado de Mil setec.^{tos} setenta y tres. Tubac, January 8, 1774–San Gabriel, April 5, 1774. Written and signed by Anza. Original in the Archivo General y Público, Mexico, Correspondencia de los Virreyes, II. Série, Bucareli, 1774. Tomo 38/55. Del N.º 1421. A certified copy made in Mexico June 26, 1774 is in the Archivo General de Indias, Sevilla, 104–6–15. Another copy is in the Archivo General de Indias, Sevilla, 104–3–4.

C. Continuacion del Diario del Capitan del Presidio de Tubac D.ⁿ Juan Bautista de Anza Commandante de la expedicion destinada á descubrir camino por tierra desde Sonora á Monte Rey que empieza en el dia 6 de Abril de 1774, que se hallaba en la Mission de S.ⁿ Gabriel primera de los Nuevos establecimientos, y comprehende su regreso hasta el expresado Presidio de Tubac. San Gabriel, April 6, 1774–Tubac, May 27, 1774. Archivo General de Indias, Sevilla, 104–6–15. This is a certified copy made in Mexico, November 26, 1774. Another copy is in the Archivo General de Indias, Sevilla, 104–3–4.

D. Diario que forma el Padre Fr. Juan Díaz Missionero Appco del Colegio de la Sta Cruz de Queretaro, en el Viage, que hace en Compañia del R. P. Fr. Fran.^{co} Garces, para abrir Camino desde la Provincia de la Sonora a la California Septentrional, y puerto de Monterrey por los Rios Gila, y Colorado, por encargo del Exmo Sor Then.^{te} gral. D.ⁿ Antonio Maria Bucareli, y Ursua, Virrey, Govr y Cap.ⁿ gral. de esta nueva España, su decreto en 17 de Sept.^{re} de este año proxime pasado de 1773. Tubac, January 8, 1774–San Gabriel, April 8, 1774. Original. Archivo General y Público, Mexico, Historia, Tomo 396. A copy certified in Mexico September 26, 1774, is in the Archivo General de Indias, Sevilla, 104–6–17.

PREFACE

E. Diario, que formó el P. Fr. Juan Dias Misionero App.º de la S.ᵗᵃ Cruz de Queretaro en el Viage, que hizo desde la Mision de S.ⁿ Gabriel en la California Septentrional hasta el Presidio de S.ⁿ Ygn.º de Tubac del Govierno de Sonora en Compañia del S.ᵒʳ Cap.ⁿ D.ⁿ Juan Baptista de Ansa Comandante de la Expedicion. San Gabriel, May 3, 1774—Tubac, May 26, 1774. Archivo General de Indias, Sevilla, 104–6–17. This is a certified copy made in Mexico, September 26, 1775, and transmitted to Spain by Bucareli on that date with letter No. 1521.

F. Diario de la entrada que se practica de orden del Exᵐᵒ Sr. Vi Rey Dn Antonio Maria Bucareli y Ursua producida en Junta de Guerra i real acienda a fin de Abrir camino por los Rios Gila y Colorado para los nuebos establecimientos de Sn Diego y Monte Rey el Cpn. Comandante Dn Juan Baptista de Ansa. Tubac, January 6, 1774–Junta de los Rios de Sn. Dionisio, April 26, 1774. Original. Archivo General y Público, Mexico, Historia, Tomo 52. Del No. 2705. A copy certified in Mexico September 26, 1774, is in the Archivo General de Indias, Sevilla, 104–6–17.

G. Brief Account of the Anza Expedition from Tubac to San Gabriel. Written by Fray Francisco Garcés from San Diego, April 2, 1774. Expediente formado á consequencia de Representacion de el P.ᵉ Fr. Francisco Garces con que acompaña el Diario de su expedicion á los Rios Gila y Colorado: en que expone su dictámen sobre fundacion de Misiones en estos parages. Archivo General y Público, Mexico, Provincias Internas, Tomo 23.

H. Diary of Fray Francisco Garcés from San Simón y Judas de Uparsoytac to the Jalchedunes. Uparsoytac, May 22, 1774–San Xavier del Bac, June 8, 1774. Expediente formado á consequencia de Representacion del P.ᵉ Fr. Francisco Garcés con que acompaña el Diario de su expedicion á los Rios Gila y Colorado: en que expone su

PREFACE

dictámen sobre fundacion de Misiones en estos parages. Archivo General y Público, Mexico, Provincias Internas, Tomo 23.

I. Diario de el Viage que de órden de el Exmo S.ᵒʳ B.ᵒ Fr. D.ⁿ Antonio Maria Bucareli Virrey de esta N. E. hize yó Fr. Francisco Palou, por el mes de Noviembre de 1774 a las cercanias del Puerto de S.ⁿ Francisco en la costa del Mar pacifico de la California Septentrional, afin de ócuparlas con nuebas Missiones encomendadas a mi App.ᶜᵒ Colegio de Missioneros Franciscanos de la regular óbservancia de Propaganda fide de S.ⁿ Fernando de la ciudad de Mexico. Monterey. November 23, 1774–Monterey, December 14, 1774. Archivo General de Indias, Sevilla, 104–6–16. This is an official copy in an excellent hand, certified by Peramás in Mexico, May 27, 1775, and transmitted by Bucareli to Spain on May 27, 1775, with letter No. 1823.

ABBREVIATIONS

In these volumes, the following abbreviations are used:

A. G. P. M.: Archivo General y Público, Mexico. Of this archive various sections are cited, as Historia, Correspondencia de los Virreyes (Cor. Vir.), Californias, Provincias Internas, etc.

M. N. M.: Museo Nacional de México.

A. G. I.: Archivo General de Indias, Sevilla. Different sections of the archive are cited by audiencias (Mexico, Guadalajara, etc.) or by other large divisions. The main divisions of this archive are arranged in estantes, cajones, and legajos (cases, shelves, and bundles). Thus the citation A. G. I., 104–6–17 means: Archivo General de Indias, estante 104, cajon 6, legajo 17.

B. L.: Bancroft Library, University of California.

S. B. A.: Santa Barbara Archives.

CONTENTS

LIST OF ILLUSTRATIONS

ANZA'S COMPLETE DIARY

1774

(*A*)

DIARY OF THE MARCH AND OPERATIONS WHICH I, THE UNDERSIGNED CAPTAIN OF CAVALRY OF THE ROYAL PRESIDIO OF TUBAC, IN THE PROVINCE OF SONORA, AM UNDERTAKING FOR THE PURPOSE OF OPENING COMMUNICATION FROM THAT PROVINCE TO NORTHERN CALIFORNIA BY WAY OF THE GILA AND COLORADO RIVERS, FOR WHICH EXPEDITION I AM COMMISSIONED BY HIS EXCELLENCY, THE LIEUTENANT-GENERAL DON ANTONIO MARIA BUCARELI Y URSUA, VICEROY, GOVERNOR, AND CAPTAIN-GENERAL OF NEW SPAIN, AS IS SHOWN BY HIS SUPERIOR ORDER OF SEPTEMBER 17, 1773.

Tubutama.

Ruins of Mission Santa Theresa.

FROM TUBAC TO CABORCA[1]

PERSONS COMPRISED IN AND GOING ON THIS EXPEDITION:

The commander, Don Juan Baptista de Anza......	1
The father preachers de propaganda fide of the College of the Holy Cross of Querétaro[2]	
Fray Juan Díaz...	1
Fray Francisco Garzés	1
Twenty volunteer soldiers from the presidio named, including a corporal.............................	20
A soldier sent from Mexico by his Excellency the Viceroy because he knows the California roads[3]	1
A native of that Peninsula who, on the 26th of last December, came out from it to the towns of Pimería Alta and the presidio of El Altar[4]	1

[1] Diario de la Ruta, i Operaciones; q°. Yó el Ynfrascripto Capitan de Cavalleria . . . practico en solicitud de abrir communicacion de dha Prov^a ã la California Septemptrional. A. G. P. M., Historia, Tomo 396. The division headings in this document were inserted by the editor.

[2] The Franciscan College of the Holy Cross was founded in the later seventeenth century at Querétaro, a city some two hundred miles north of Mexico. From it went a great many missionaries to Texas and Coahuila. When the Jesuits were expelled from Pimería Alta in 1767 a band of friars went from the College of the Holy Cross to replace them. Fathers Garcés and Díaz were members of this group.

[3] This soldier was Juan Bautista Valdés.

[4] The Indian was Sebastián Tarabal. He played an interesting part in the explorations of the next few years.

An interpreter of the Pima language, because it
is thought that from it the interior tongues
are derived 1
A native of the presidio in my charge to serve as
carpenter 1
Five muleteers and two of my servants................. 7

34

There are carried thirty-five loads of provisions,
munitions of war, tobacco, equipage, and other
things necessary for an unknown country.
Item, sixty-five beeves on foot.[1]
Item, one hundred and forty mounts, counting those
which it is planned to get later in the pueblo of
Caborca.[2]

1774   *Summary of Leagues*

Saturday, the 8th of January, 1774, all the foregoing being ready, Mass was sung in the morning
with all the ceremony which the country permits, to
invoke the divine aid in this expedition, and the
Blessed Trinity and the mystery of the Immaculate
Conception of Holy Mary were named as its patrons.
This having been done, at one in the afternoon the
march was begun, and having traveled a league
we made camp for the night at the ford of San
Xavier del Bac.[3]

[1] These cattle were driven for food on the way.

[2] It is not certain just how many mounts were actually taken,
because Anza was unable to get his full quota at Caborca.

[3] Diary B adds here "to the north," without which the route
would be puzzling. The march was begun to the north in order to
get round the end of Tumacácori Range, which lies immediately west
of Tubac.

Sunday, January 9.—At eight o'clock in the morning we set out to the south-southwest over the highway for the towns of the Pima tribe which we call the Pimas of the West, and for the presidio of El Altar, which is in their midst and is the presidio of the province of Sonora the most advanced toward the Gulf of California.

It was not necessary to make the journey through these regions, because the port of Monte Rey or its environs must be sought toward the northwest of the presidio in my charge, and there is doubtless a road to it by way of the Gila and Colorado rivers.[1] However, I was forced to depart from this plan, which I had always wished to adopt, for the following reasons:

First, in order to take as the safest route the direction or road followed as far as the Pimería by a native of California who fled from the new mission of San Gabriel which, according to his report, is midway between the ports of San Diego and Monte Rey, and whence he set out for the rivers named. From these rivers, if possible, I shall go straight to the last-named port, if it is indicated or is learned through any tribe of Indians that in that region there is the same abundance of pasturage and water which this native says he noted in the region which he crossed, as I have informed his Excellency.

Secondly, because a large number of Apaches, on the 2d of last month, attacked the horse herd of

[1] Anza started out with a very definite intention to go directly from Yuma to Monterey, without touching at San Gabriel.

my presidio and stole from it about a hundred and thirty saddle animals, including many of those destined and reserved for this enterprise. This loss it is not possible to repair in my presidio or its environs, nor can I delay any longer under the circumstances, since those which escaped are exposed to a greater loss, and since the best season for this journey is passing. For this reason, and because there is better opportunity to replace a part of my losses in the towns named, I have decided to go that way, and I have begged the governor of the provinces to give his order that when I pass through them they shall provide me the number of animals which I need to complete my equipment.

Finally, I decided that it was well to test immediately the road through the part of Pimería next to the Gulf of California, because this is the best and only one by which to provide the Peninsula[1] with what it needs, not only from the Pimería and the provinces of Sonora, but also from those which follow as far as Mexico. Indeed, along the coast the raids of the Apaches do not occur, an important advantage which will not be obtained so readily by any other route over which a road may be opened.

At vespers on this day the march was concluded, we having traveled eight leagues, as far as the site of La Aribac,[2] a place which was occupied by some

[1] He probably refers here to California in general, and not to what we now call the Peninsula.

[2] Arivaca today is about twenty-four miles from Amado, but it is southwest instead of south-southwest. Three miles east of Arivaca

cattle ranches and Spaniards until the end of the year
1751, when it was abandoned because of the general
uprising of the Pima tribe, which killed most of its
inhabitants. The battle with the rebels themselves,
which took place right here the year after the uprising, is memorable. For, having come more than two
thousand strong, led by their captain-general, to
attack the Spanish force composed of eighty soldiers
and commanded by Don Bernardo de Urrea, now
captain of the presidio of El Altar, the army of the
enemy was completely put to rout, with many deaths
on their side, from which resulted the pacification of
this tribe.

This place has the advantage of good gold and
silver mines which were worked until the year 'sixty-
seven, when they were abandoned because of greater
persecution by the Apaches. From that time hence-
forward grains and good-sized nuggets of pure gold
have been found in the neighborhood, for I have
seen them. It also has most beautiful and abundant
pastures, and a number of permanent springs in the
interior of the mountains. The chief one where the
settlement was, is now running, although not with
great abundance.

Monday, January 10.—At nine in the morning
we set out toward the south-southwest, passing vari-

is Arivaca Ranch. I conclude that the whole Arivaca Creek valley
was then called Arivaca, and that Anza camped on the upper waters
of the creek not far from Oro Blanco Mine. The region today is
just as beautiful as he describes it. Numerous mines have been
opened in the district in recent times, and some are operating now.
I stopped at Arivaca on the night of December 28, 1927.

ous ranges on our right and left, and having traveled about seven leagues we halted to pass the night at the site of Agua Escondida,[1] so-called because the spring is about a quarter of a league off the highway on the right.—From Tubac to Agua Escondida, 16 leagues.

Tuesday and Wednesday, the 11th and 12th, we remained in this place, because it had been raining and snowing incessantly since the night of the 10th.

Thursday, January 13.—Today having dawned clear, at eight in the morning we mobilized our train and set forth to the south-southwest and marched seven leagues, until the end of the afternoon, when we halted for the night in the pueblo of El Saric.[2]— From Tubac to El Saric, 23 leagues.

This is a town of Pimas Altos and the first of the Pimas of the West, when coming from the north. It has forty families, and like all the rest of the towns of this tribe it is administered in spiritual affairs by the fathers of the College of the Cross of Querétaro. The fertile country around this pueblo, its own abundance of water, and the vast irrigable lands which it enjoys in superabundance, would provide crops enough to support two thousand citizens. They likewise would be able to raise and maintain any kind of stock which they might wish, since there are

[1] Hidden Water. This day's march took them over the Sierra del Pajarito to its southern slope, overlooking the Altar Valley.

[2] Saric, called by the natives Sáriqui, is on the west bank of the Altar River. It is now a town of some five hundred inhabitants. Few or no full-blood Pimas live here. The Pimas Altos were the Upper Pimas.

advantages for every species, as well as for obtaining good timber of various kinds, all of which are unused because at present this is one of the places most plundered by the Apaches.

About seven or eight leagues to the northeast of this pueblo is the site of Arizonac,[1] or of the celebrated nuggets, so-called from the nuggets of virgin silver which were found in the year 1736, some weighing as much as a hundred and fifty arrobas.[2] This story has been doubted, but it is well authenticated, because there are still living many persons who possessed them, and I could likewise give documents which prove the story. Besides, my father, upon the advice of persons learned in the law, sequestrated them because it appeared to him that they belonged to his Majesty, and while his proceedings were not entirely approved by the council in the City of Mexico, they were sustained by the royal council of Castile.

On the information of men versed in mining I have heard it surmised and said that they failed, and have still failed, to discover the mother lode from which those nuggets came, and that their value, although great, did not compare with the profits that might be obtained from the many and good mines which could be worked with quicksilver. But this

---

[1] It is from this famous mine that Arizona got its name. The mine was in Sonora, just over the border, some ten or fifteen miles southwest of Nogales. The story of the rush thither is well told in Chapman, *The Founding of Spanish California*, chapter II.

[2] An *arroba* is twenty-five pounds.

process has not been introduced into this province of Sonora, to the very grave injury of its inhabitants and of the royal exchequer. Indeed, the lack of this practice is the reason why this prodigious site has been abandoned, and why it is suffering increased risk from the Apaches, who have made their road right through it.

Friday, January 14.—At seven in the morning we continued the march south-southwest down the river of El Saric. This river rises in the spring of El Búsani,[1] which is about a league and a half to the north of El Saric. Having traveled about four leagues we halted at La Cuesta, or La Estancia, because thenceforward for several leagues there is no pasturage.[2]

Saturday, January 15.—About seven in the morning we set forth to the southwest, still following the river. Having traveled along it for two leagues, we passed through the pueblo of Tubutama,[3] which is inhabited by the Pima Indians, of whom it has

[1] Búsanic was formerly a Jesuit mission. Built on a high plateau, it overlooked springs that are still famous. The pueblo is entirely abandoned now, but the ruins of the old church are visible by the roadside some four miles north of Saric.

[2] La Cuesta means the ridge or grade. The place is just twelve miles by automobile from Saric, and still bears the same name. La Estancia means the ranch or grazing place.

[3] Our speedometer registered seven miles from La Cuesta to Tubutama. Tubutama is an idyllic spot. Standing on the left bank of the river, it overlooks a beautiful vega or bottom-land. Dominating the rest of the pueblo are the bell towers of the old mission church founded by Father Kino in the seventeenth century, the first in the Altar Valley. Today Tubutama is somewhat larger than Saric.

about thirty families. A league and a half farther on is the pueblo of Santa Teresa with twenty families, and two leagues beyond that place is San Francisco del Ati, which must have thirty families.[1]

These pueblos along this river enjoy good and plentiful lands for irrigation, sufficient to support by their crops as many as three thousand families of Spaniards, who might also raise some stock, although not on a large scale, because from Tubutama to Ati the pasturage decreases greatly. All the pueblos as far as this last one, and those farther downstream, suffer from the Apache persecutions, although they do not equal the depredations at El Saric by a long shot. Just before reaching the pueblo of Santa Theresa the road turns, inclining now to the west and west-southwest. Halfway between Santa Theresa and Tubutama placers[2] have recently been found, and still more recently another very large one was discovered right close to El Ati, where we passed the night.—From Tubac to Tubutama, 29 leagues. From Tubac to El Ati, 33 leagues.

Sunday, January 16.—At eight o'clock in the morning we began the march, going west, and having gone about six leagues along the same river we

[1] Santa Teresa is entirely abandoned, but the ruins of the mission church stand at the right of the road four and one-half miles below Tubutama. Nearly six miles below Santa Teresa, in a flat country, is Atil, now a place with some five hundred inhabitants. The ruins of the old church stand beside a new and inartistic one.

[2] The placers were doubtless in the Altar River near the little mountain which stands half-way between Tubutama and Santa Teresa.

halted in the pueblo of Oquitoa,[1] which is inhabited by
thirty families of the tribe already named, and where
also live twelve families of Spaniards. This pueblo
is as well provided as the foregoing with irrigable
farm lands. It enjoys nearby, up the river, a beautiful marsh with much pasturage, and in the same
region there are silver mines which in another country, free from the plague of Apaches, would afford
their workers some advantages.—From Tubac to the
pueblo of Oquitoa, 39 leagues.

Monday, January 17.—Having traveled two
leagues[2] to the west, downstream from Oquitoa, a
halt was made at the presidio of El Altar, because it
threatened to rain and since it was necessary to give
time to arrange for the exchange of some saddle
animals which had arrived here almost used up,
for others in better condition. The exchange was
effected in the best manner possible, the greater part
being contributed by the captain, Don Bernardo de
Urrea. This presidio has a regular force of fifty

[1] Oquitoa is only twelve miles from Atil. Anza's estimate is liberal here. The place occupies a picturesque site near vast vegas, and
is overlooked by a high hill on which the old mission church stands,
alone. A quaint old water power grist mill stands on the main street.
Oquitoa is larger than the towns above it.

[2] Our mileage from Oquitoa to Altar was seven miles. This place
is considerably larger than any of the towns above it, is better built,
and has a fine plaza. Altar stands on a barren flat or playa, resembling a beach or river bottom. Mange tells us that the place gets its
name from a rock that looked like an altar, but the natives whom
I talked with never heard of it, though they had various other fanci-
ful explanations. In the mountains northwest of Altar I saw a peak
resembling an altar and wondered if it were the one told of by
Mange.

men, including two subalterns, like all of those depending on the government of Sonora. Of all the interior presidios this is the least troubled by the Apaches, who rarely reach this place and who seldom, and less often severely, attack the pueblos which follow down the river. This stream, although it takes its course toward the Gulf of California, does not empty into it, partly because from the presidio of El Altar forward the volume of water decreases, and partly because the land is now spongy and sandy and absorbs a large part of the water.—From Tubac to the presidio of El Altar, 41 leagues.

Tuesday, January 18.—Because morning dawned with signs of rain, which were partly verified, it was not possible to travel today.

Wednesday, January 19.—At the regular time we continued the march, going west-northwest, somewhat apart from the river, and having traveled rather more than five leagues, camp was made in the pueblo of El Pitic.[1]—From Tubac to Pitic, 46 leagues.

Thursday, January 20.—Having traveled two leagues in the same direction and along the same

[1] Our speedometer recorded fifteen miles from Altar to Pitic (now called Pitiquito), going essentially over Anza's trail. Nearing Pitic one comes to a range of mountains (Sierra del Rajón) over the northern end of which the road runs through a charming pass. From the top one looks down on the thriving town of Pitiquito, which has electric lights (the first seen in the valley) and an electric power grist mill. The old church stands on a hill to the west, with its back to the new and its face toward the old town, where stood the village which it served.

river, we halted in the pueblo of Caborca, which has ninety families.[1] We stopped here because it was necessary to travel a part of the afternoon, in order to make the next journey with some convenience, so that by marching a part of the night and the next morning we may reach the only water which intervenes.[2] We had to stop, also, to obtain in this pueblo some mules which we lack, in order to have those necessary for the journey and to get which, as was said in the beginning, we decided to come this way. —From Tubac to Caborca, 48 leagues.

In this pueblo, in that of Pitic, and in that of Vísani,[3] distant [six leagues] from here downstream to the west-southwest, are found assembled the Pimas who surrendered as a result of the expedition which was made against them and the Seris, their

[1] Our speedometer registered six miles to the old Caborca mission church. The road runs through rich fields and palm groves, crosses the river to the south, then winds through a low ridge (the Gamuza Range), drops down, and crosses the river again at the church. The old town and the new are somewhat apart. Altogether the place is one of some two thousand inhabitants. The church stands on the river's edge, part of it having fallen into the stream bed. Here it was that Father Saeta was murdered in 1695 and Father Tello in 1751. Here Crabb's filibusters fought and died. On the church front is a plaque telling of that battle of April 6, 1857:

"Humble tribute of gratitude to perpetuate the memory of the defeat inflicted by national forces and citizens of this town upon the North American filibusters on April 6, 1857, this temple having served as a bulwark for the defenders of the Fatherland.

"Caborca, Sonora, April 6, 1926. The Committee of 1925–26."

[2] He means in order to reach Arivaipa.

[3] Vísani still stands on the same site, some eighteen miles below Caborca. By a slip Anza's diary reads west-northwest.

allies, in the years from 1768 to 1770,[1] people in whom one now sees nothing which would suggest revolt. At four leagues from Vísani, and the same distance from this pueblo of Caborca, are found good-sized silver mines, which would be more esteemed if the people of this country had devoted themselves to working them with quicksilver; but this method not being practiced and these mines having a mixture of copper in abundance, by extracting the dross with fire they likewise lose what is valuable in the process. Twenty-five leagues from the same Vísani, right on the Gulf of California, are found abundant beds of crystallized salt, although the very purest usually becomes scarce in years when it rains.

Friday, January 21.—By order of the governor of the provinces and of Captain Don Bernardo Urrea, two small droves of mules were shown to me, but whereas I had flattered myself that I should leave this pueblo amply supplied with the mules which I needed, I saw only stacks of bones which the animals torpidly moved. I caused others to be shown me, but, although our need was extreme, we were able to get only two very poor ones. As a means of supplying myself I finally had to take advantage of the very few possessed by the missions of this river, which were three, but with these I remained in almost the same need as before.[2] Although this was to me a

---

[1] Anza took part in that campaign. The MS. is polillo eaten here and I have followed the copy in A. G. P. M., Provincias Internas, Tomo 23.

[2] This failure to get mules was a great handicap to Anza, as will be seen further on.

matter of great sorrow, because of the lack which I
might experience on a long journey, yet I yielded to
the situation since there was no other recourse and
no means of remedy. No march was made on this
day because our muleteer, who left us at the presidio
of Altar to go to the mining camp of Cieneguilla to
get shoes for his mules, did not arrive with them as
he had agreed.[1]

1 Cieneguilla (now called Ciénega) is still on the map in the same
place, south of Altar.

THROUGH THE PAPAGUERIA

Saturday, January 22.—At twelve o'clock we set forth toward the northwest over a good country, traveling at first a short distance from the river of Caborca. Then, having gone about four leagues, we paralleled on the right the medium-sized sierras of Piast and Buccomari, names in the Pima language, and some small peaks on the left. Having traveled two more leagues between them, we camped on a flat which has plentiful pasturage, the first found after leaving Caborca. Here the rest of the night was passed, and the place was called San Ildephonso.[1]

Sunday, January 23.—Raising our train, we set forth at eight o'clock in the morning, continuing on the same trail that we followed yesterday. Having traveled northwest and north-northwest over good terrain for eight or nine leagues, we arrived at Baipia or Aribaipia, as the Pimas variously call it. In our language the name means "Little Wells." In front of them ends the Sierra de Buccomari, making

[1] Anza's route was close to the road used today, perhaps a little to the east of it. Exactly twelve miles out from Caborca mission begins a small range (Sierra La Zorra), two and one-half miles long, on the right side of the road, which evidently constitutes the small hills to the left mentioned here. Anza apparently passed on the east side of it. San Ildefonso was near the foot of Cerro Babura. Sierra de Buccomari was the one now called Sierra de Chupurate.

between it and another a pass leading to the valleys
of the Papaguería.[1]

This Baipia or Aribaipia, in which our men have
been several times, is known to them by the name
of San Eduardo. Its water is found in wells and is
scarce, but the natives say that even so it never fails.
Its pasturage is sparse and very bad. About three
leagues before reaching this place, between some
small hills through which the road runs, there is so
good an opportunity to make a dam that with a small
amount of labor and almost without cost a plentiful
supply of water could be assured for everybody who
might wish to travel through here.

[1] The wells or pozos of Aribaipia were the typical pozos dug in
the sand. Arivaipa is still on the map and well known in the vicinity,
but it is entirely uninhabited, the place being marked only by three
rude shacks and the crossing of Arroyo El Coyote. The stream bed
here is probably a hundred yards wide. Except after a rain the sand
is dry on the surface, but by digging a foot or two the water wells
up rapidly. When we crossed on December 31, 1927, both of our
machines bogged down and were pulled out by a team composed of a
mule and a horse, which by good luck happened to come along. This
crossing is on the old Pápago trail, and we probably crossed by the
same ford that Anza used. Anza's Sierra de Piast was the present
Sierra de la Basura, which ends nearly east of Arivaipa. Through
the gap of the pass mentioned by Anza runs Arroyo El Coyote and its
tributary Arroyo de Cubo. Half way between San Ildefonso and Arivaipa, at Tajitos, Anza crossed Arroyo de Cubo at the forks (or possibly twice crossed El Coyote, as does the road today), and thus got
between the two branches. Here at Tajitos, just above the junction,
Arroyo El Coyote runs for a short distance through a narrow gorge
where "with a small amount of labor" a dam could be made. This
evidently is the place to which Anza refers, although it is somewhat
more than three leagues from Arivaipa. At Tajitos in December,
1927, a little gold mine was in operation by the old arrastre process,
by which the ore is crushed by a stone dragged around by a horse
attached to a sweep.

Altar Valley below Saric

A view of Quitobac.

Site of old Sonóita Mission. Photo by Bolton

Looking south from Sonóita Mission. Photo by Bolton

In this place we met two families of the Pápago tribe, who in language and customs are the same as the Pima tribe, the only difference being that these are too barbarous to be reduced to mission towns. Most of the Pápagos who enjoy this benefit have been persons who either voluntarily or through the chastisement of the political government have come down to the pueblos. With these, from the year 1756 down to the present, I have seen both the northern and the western Pimería repopulated, and indeed if it were not for them neither district would exist today with such towns as they have.[1]

These Pápagos are not the people most hostile toward us, as we have experienced on the few occasions when they have revolted, and at such times as they have done this, stimulated by the example of the Pimas, they have paid dearly before the fury of our arms.[2] Because of their nearness to our settlements, both of Spaniards and Indians, the Pápagos frequently live in them, especially in the winter, in which season they almost completely desert their own country.

This is one of the most unfortunate regions that can be imagined, for even water necessary for their support is very scarce, and they are never sure of having any.[3] For lack of it the only crops which they

[1] That is to say, the Pima missions were inhabited largely by Pápagos.

[2] The principal Pápago uprising was that of 1751, already mentioned by Anza.

[3] The country is indeed a difficult one from which to wrest a living, but to a well equipped traveler it would be hard to find a more charming and interesting region to journey through in January.

raise are a few calabashes, watermelons, and musk-melons, which they trust to the seasonal rains, and if the rains are not unusually good the crops are entirely lost. In this region the only places known where they might make use of irrigation are Sonói-tac, through which we pass, and two others which have less permanent water, and never sufficient for crops of any consequence. In spite of all the unhap-piness and the infelicities which have always been experienced in the land of the Pápagos, it has never been possible to induce them to settle amongst us, notwithstanding the advantages of the lands which have been offered them.

I estimate that the country which they inhabit must be sixty or seventy leagues from north to south and thirty or forty from east to west.[1] This space they occupy according as there is more or less rain, but only for the time that this lasts, and there are few villages which maintain themselves in consider-able numbers. For this reason, although I have been through most of this country, I cannot say, nor can anyone with certainty say, what are the habita-tions of these people. The estimate of their num-bers is also extremely variable. Indeed, some have said there are six thousand, and others less, but in my opinion they number only perhaps twenty-five hundred souls, for the war and epidemics have greatly reduced their number during the last sixteen years.

[1] That is, between the valley of the Altar and the Gila.

These people, among whom are found both heathen and Christians, occupy the space that lies between the pueblos of our possessions and the Gila and Colorado rivers. Generally speaking, all this region is so sterile that neither shade trees nor roof timber[1] are seen in it. However, if its inhabitants were given to industry and labor, they might without great difficulty store the rainwater and irrigate good-sized pieces of land.[2] This Pápago tribe reaches to the Gila River, but the people living along that stream and in three or four other pueblos in which they are congregated are considered true Pimas. These are the only ones who have fields of maize, wheat, cotton and other crops, for which, in addition to the fertility of the land, they avail themselves of tapping the river. From this it may be inferred how easy it is once they have undertaken it. These Pimas, as well as the Pápagos, maintain communication with us and render obedience as best they can.

Monday, January 24.—Having watered the horses at the wells which had been opened the day before, we set out from San Eduardo at one in the afternoon, going northwest over good country and an open road, the chain of low hills of yesterday continuing on our left, until at vespers we reached the Pool

[1] Arboles para techos.

[2] Here and there through the country there now are a few families of residents, as at Tajitos, east of Arivaipa, and at Temporales, Cozón, and Costa Rica, where dams have been made and small fields are under cultivation. These inhabitants are Mexicans, not Pápagos.

of San Juan de Matha,[1] distant from San Eduardo four leagues, where we camped for the night. This place is in a wide plain with an abundance of pasturage, and the water which it now has, although assembled from the rainfall, is plentiful, and it would be possible by means of an earthen dam which could be made in a few hours to gather enough for the whole year. Here we found four families of Pápagos, natives of the village of Quitobac, through which we shall pass.—From Tubac to San Juan de Matha, 67 leagues.

Tuesday, January 25.—At one in the afternoon we set out from San Juan de Matha toward the northwest over open road, the hills continuing on the left and others on the right though farther away.[2] Having traveled four leagues those on the left come so close that the road passes along their skirts, and right there they end. Two leagues back a trail

[1] San Juan de Matha was about at Temporales (Temporal Llamarada). Anza gives the distance as four leagues from Arivaipa. Our speedometer registered 11.8 miles. Here at Temporales crops are now raised by seasonal rains—that is what temporales means—and earthen dams in the rainy season form wide, shallow ponds. A family lived here in January, 1928.

[2] Receding in the distance on Anza's right was Sierra de la Campana. Keeping west of Arroyo El Coyote, he gradually got closer to the Cozón Range on his left, with Cerro de Cozón rising boldly above its fellows. On this stretch of the road one now passes Cozón, where there are two or three ranches, nine miles from Temporales, and Costa Rica, two and one-half miles further northwest. Just beyond here the range ends in a conspicuous isolated peak or small mountain. Anza's camp was in a brushy flat some five miles beyond Costa Rica and three beyond the terminal peak. Our mileage from Temporales to this place was thirty miles. Anza called it ten leagues.

branches off to the left, and leads to a well which has a small amount of water. Passing the hills mentioned, and continuing into the night, we traveled two more leagues and halted in a flat with little pasturage. A short distance before reaching the flat there is a trail branching off from the road and leading to a well like the other.

Wednesday, January 26.—At eight in the morning we continued the journey toward the northwest for a little more than a league, to a place where there are some small hills with a well of water like the last ones. Leaving the hills to the left, and continuing to the north about another league, one turns again to the northwest; going in this direction another league and a half one turns finally to the west-north-west, and going in this direction two and a half leagues and skirting the hills on the left one reaches the village of Quitobac.[1]—From Tubac to Quitobac, 78 leagues.

A short time before we reached the place its justice and governor came out to meet me in a very friendly manner, and in the same way I saluted him

[1] Anza estimates the distance to Quitobac as five leagues. Our speedometer registered only twelve miles, but his directions correspond to the turns in the road today. We reached the hills on the left, near Chujubabi Ranchería, at three and one-half miles from the place marked for his previous camp site. Thence to Quitobac it was eight and one-half miles. Quitobac is approached from the southeast over a long, slow rise of ground. The town of two hundred persons, composed of Mexicans and Pápagos living at opposite ends of the place, stands at the foot of a conspicuous, high conical peak. The springs have been dammed and a good sized lake made. Here again we saw gold ore being worked by the arrastre process.

and four families who are living in the village. The rest of the people, he told me, were partly in the missions and partly in the neighborhood seeking the few herbs and fruits which they customarily eat. One of those which is very usual is the fruit of the abrojos, which they scald, taking off the spines. From this may be inferred the poverty in which these miserable people live, having no recourse such as others have to any kind of game, for the sterility of the country deprives them of everything.

This place is surrounded by hills on all sides, except on the east and north. It is one of the best of all the Papaguería, because it has five springs of water, by no means the worst, which they gather and use to irrigate some small pieces of very sandy land where at most half a fanega of maize can be planted; but some cattle and horses could be raised, although not more than five hundred head, because the pasturage would not provide for more.

This Quitobac was called by the Jesuit fathers San Luís de Bacapa, but of this name the natives have no recollection, nor of the arrival here, of which the fathers tell, of the religious from New Mexico,[1] but they do preserve the name of San Luís and the addition of Quitobac, by which name it is known to its inhabitants and to other tribes. Likewise it appears to me that there are not as many leagues between here and Caborca as those fathers say.

Thursday, January 27.—At twelve o'clock today we set forth toward the north by the road which

---

[1] The reference is to Friar Marcos de Nizza, who in all probability never saw Quitobac.

leads from San Luís de Quitobac to San Marcelo de Sonóitac, over the good country which lies between the many hills which are near by on all sides. Having made about five and a half leagues, we halted to pass the night on the skirts of a hill which has some pasturage, and in which toward the south there is a tank which gathers rain water. Another like it is found about a league and a half before reaching this one, to which leads a trail that branches off to the left.[1]

Friday, January 28.—About eight in the morning we set forth on the same road toward the north-northwest, along the skirts of the hills on the left, for a distance of three leagues. These finished, the road turns to the north for two more leagues, when San Marcelo de Sonóitac is reached.—From Tubac to Sonóitac, 88 leagues.

This place is situated in a good plain surrounded on all sides by cliffs and hills very close by, and some high peaks farther away. The country is open only to the north and northeast, in which direction

[1] Leaving Quitobac, Anza went a little east of north nearly fifteen miles, then swung round the point of Sierra de Cubabi, and camped not far from Piedra Parada. Next day he continued northwest along the skirt of the sierra, then turned north over the hills to Sonóita. The old trail followed by Anza is still used as a horse trail, the distance being just about what he estimated. Our road continued north-northeast from the neighborhood of Piedra Parada till we struck the road from La Nariz to Sonóita, when we turned west-northwest.

The old Jesuit mission of Sonóita was a mile and a half east of the new town. There is nothing left to mark the site except the holes made by perennial diggings for treasure. The new town of Sonóita has a population of a few hundred, and has some importance as a port of entry into the United States.

there is to be seen about six leagues away a large range which the Pimas and Pápagos call El Cubot.[1] It is of medium height, black in color or very dark, and in the middle of it a pass is visible. In the same northerly direction is the watering place, which is a sort of marsh, like which the water tastes. Although it is muddy it is very abundant and is the largest to be found in this country. It runs for a little more than a league and a half. It is sufficient for planting in the moderately good land about a fanega of maize. It lacks roof timber but it has pasturage enough to maintain as many as a thousand head of stock.

Of all the missions in the Pimería maintained by the Jesuit fathers, this was the last and most advanced to the northwest. They had just established and founded it in the middle of the year 1751, when it was destroyed on the occasion of the general uprising of the Pimas and Pápagos, who with cruel and prolonged torture murdered its missionary as well as one of the people of the country who kept him company.[2] Notwithstanding that this place is unquestionably the best in all the Papaguería, I did not find in it more people than some six families, because the rest were engaged in the same occupations as those of Quitobac.

Today, upon leaving the hills which we have had on our left, the country was observed to be mineral

[1] The Ajo Mountains and the Cubo Hills lies northeast of Sonóita.

[2] The mission was first founded by Father Kino near the end of the seventeenth century. It was abandoned soon afterward, and refounded in 1751, as Anza says. The missionary killed was Father Rhuen.

bearing, and to have in it an abundance of rock which they call tepustete, this being the rock which indicates gold placers. I caused some portions of the ore to be dug out and loaded, to see if it showed any grains of that metal, and although we did not succeed in seeing any, yet there were all the indications that it would be found if greater efforts were made. And I shall not omit the labor of making the same experiment in any place that may appear to me to give promise of having any kind of metal.

Saturday, January 29.—At half past eight in the morning we set out down the arroyo of Sonóitac, on the road to El Carrisal, which most of the way runs[1] straight west over fairly good country. We traveled in this direction eight or nine leagues, until nightfall, when we halted at El Carrisal, which is on the same arroyo of Sonóitac. This stream has plenty of water, but it is drinkable only for want of any other, besides which defect the place suffers from a lack of pasturage.[2]—From Tubac to El Carrisal, 96 leagues.

[1] The page is polillo eaten here, but the missing words are supplied by the text in A.G.P.M., Provincias Internas, Tomo 23.

[2] Camp was at Agua Salada. The road now follows essentially along that taken by Anza. On the way from the old Sonóita mission today one passes the town of Sonóita, Santo Domingo Rancho, Quitovaquita, Agua Dulce, Carrizal (23 miles) and comes to Agua Salada (24 miles). Evidently Carrizal extended to Agua Salada in the old days. At Quitovaquita, which is exactly on the international line, there lives a prosperous Pápago family, who take advantage of the springs there. They live in a substantial house, and grind their flour with an arrastre by pony power. We saw no other inhabitant along the entire stretch between Sonóita and Yuma, one hundred and twenty-five miles away.

A league and a half after leaving San Marcelo, and at the same distance off the road which we have been following, on the right side, there is a round peak, conspicuous for this shape, for it is the only one among several in whose midst it stands, and it is composed of salt, or has veins of salt. I have heard of this for many years, and now the natives have confirmed the story, pointing out the hill to me and telling me that they use the salt, and that because of its extreme hardness they are able to get it only by prying it out with stakes in the rainy season, because this is the only time when it softens somewhat.[1]

Sunday, January 30.—Because the next watering place is far away and very difficult to reach for watering the riding animals, I decided to march to it in two divisions, both setting out in the afternoon. For this purpose I left the pack train here at El Carrisal with a corporal and seven soldiers. With the rest of the riding animals, the cattle, and the equipment that is necessary to use in reaching it, at twelve o'clock today I took the road which leads to it, going north-northwest for about three leagues and then three more to the northwest, with numerous hills always on one side or the other; then going through a good pass, after nightfall camp was made in a flat, although there was no pasturage here, as was true of all the country traveled over this afternoon. For

[1] There are round peaks in the vicinity indicated, but my guide, Antonio López, who had lived over half a century in the region, had never heard of the salt deposits, nor had other residents whom I consulted.

this reason the animals ate only some mesquite sprouts.[1]

Monday, January 31.—At half past seven in the morning, setting out in the same direction, we took the road and began our march for El Aguaje Empinado. Having traveled about a league we reached the skirt of a medium-sized range on the right, which is of bare rock, and for that reason has neither pasturage, tree, nor bush, either large or small. The ground over which the road runs is fairly good, and having traveled over it five or six leagues in all, I arrived at the canyon where the water was, but to reach the place where it is found it was necessary to go on foot, or rather more on my hands than on

[1] After leaving El Carrizal Anza's animals had not another drop of water for fifty-four miles and forty-six hours. At Agua Salada the trail turns sharply northwest, with Sierra de la Salada on the right. For two and a half miles the road runs through hills, a spur of Sierra de la Salada, then it opens out into a flat, ocotilla and hediondilla covered plain. Twenty-five miles to the west-southwest rises Sierra del Pinacate, with its three conspicuous domes, and with flat playas in the foreground. Nine miles out the international boundary line is crossed. Just before we reached the line Sierra Pinta loomed fairy-like in the afternoon sun, one part light, the other dark, hence the name Pinta or spotted—like a pinto horse. The next eight miles are through level but rough country, with many washes and arroyos, part of the way over *malpais*, till one passes through an easy gap in O'Neill Hills, Anza's very "good pass," called by Garcés a "white pass" or "puerto blanco." The pass is just north of La Playa Dam or Represo, near boundary marker 179. On January 2, 1928, we camped at Represo, after going through the "white pass." About five miles before reaching the pass a road to the Represo branches off and runs a little to the south of the Camino del Diablo, which Anza took.

my feet.—From Tubac to El Aguaje Empinado, 108 leagues.[1]

I saw at once that there was not enough water for all our animals, and that if it were given to all of those which I was taking ahead, it would leave the pack train exposed to death, this being the part of the train that can advance least rapidly because of the load which it carries. For this reason I decided to go on to the next watering place and leave this one free. So I set out for it about two in the afternoon, and having traveled three leagues west-northwest, in addition to the six already covered, I camped for the night among some small hills where there was found a little pasturage, although it was bad.[2]

Tuesday, February 1.—At eight in the morning we set out on the road on which we had spent the night. Going northwest, immediately we climbed some small hills which must be hollow, because when the horses walked over them there was a sound simi-

[1] Breaking camp, Anza continued northwest six leagues along the Sierra Pinta, to Aguaje Empinado, or the "water high up in the mountain." This was Heart Tank, in Sierra Pinta. It was Kino's Aguaje de la Luna. It is located high up in the canyon (la quiebra) a short distance north of the line that is formed between the light and the dark parts of Sierra Pinta. It is called Heart Tank because at certain levels the surface of the water makes a heart-shaped figure. Eldredge, never having gone over the trail, erroneously identifies Aguaje Empinado with Cabeza Prieta Tanks eighteen miles northwest. See p. 154.

[2] Anza's three leagues west-northwest took him nearly west across the plain and into the gap between Tule Range and Cabeza Prieta Range, northeast of Tule Well. The hills are quite open here.

lar to that of an underground cavern.[1] Having passed these hills, which lasted for a league, and then traveled two more over better terrain, the water was reached.[2]

This watering place is found in the midst of a number of hills whose opening is towards the east. It has six tanks of very good rain water. In the first the animals drink. It is easily filled from the tanks above by climbing up and emptying them through the natural channel in the living rock which connects them all. In them there is a large supply of water, and as much more could be supplied if they were cleared of the rocks and sand with which they abound. All the animals were well provided with water and when pasturage was sought it was found at a short distance.

These tanks, the one farther back, and another which is ahead of us, are inhabited by the Pápagos

[1] Eldredge, being one lap ahead of Anza here, assigns this phenomenon to Lechuguilla Desert, west of Cabeza Prieta Range.

[2] Anza now swung northwest into Cabeza Prieta Range, evidently striking the trail that runs from Tule Well. Aguaje de la Purificación was Cabeza Prieta Tanks, seven miles northwest of Tule Well. Eldredge erroneously identifies Aguaje de la Purificación with Tinajas Altas. No one could give a more graphic description of the characteristic features of the tanks than Anza gives here. There are six main tanks, and several smaller ones higher up. The tanks are round pot-holes in the solid rock, the largest being about eleven feet in top diameter and six or seven feet deep. In them the water remains nearly all summer. They are placed in a series at different elevations like stairs, and all are fed by a common channel or spout worn in the bare rock, so that by dipping the water out of the upper ones it runs down into those below, as Anza says. I visited the tanks on January 3, 1928, walking from Tule Well, where we were in camp, repairing a broken automobile spring. Tule Well is a modern dug well.

in the height of the dry season and as long as the water gathered in them lasts, through their desire to hunt mountain sheep there. These animals, as to skin and other characteristics, are like large deer, differing only in their horns, which are thicker than those of the largest ox, but in shape and position are like those of common sheep. They live among the cliffs that are highest and most difficult to scale. They are native to dry and sterile regions. Their flesh is better than that of deer. They multiply very slowly, and almost never run in the level country because of the impediment of their horns. These horns the Indians are careful not to waste. Indeed, whenever they kill the sheep, they carry the horns to the neighborhood of the water holes, where they go piling them up to prevent the Air from leaving the place. Those who, like ourselves, do not practice or do not know of this superstition, they warn not to take one from its place, because that element would come out to molest everybody and cause them to experience greater troubles.[1]

Wednesday, February 2.—I named these tanks La Purificación. While here I learned that the pack train had reached El Empinado greatly fatigued and with some of the mules worn out. I therefore decided to await the pack train here, and to send the relay muleteer to it with the few mules which I

[1] I saw a few wild sheep horns scattered about in the vicinity of these tanks. On the way up the canyon to the tanks one sees piles of stones heaped up by passersby in the course of centuries, it is said, for some religious purpose.

brought to carry my necessary baggage and other indispensables, and they set out today.—From Tubac to El Aguaje de la Purificación, 114 leagues.

Thursday, February 3.—In the middle of the day the pack train arrived, indeed completely worn out, and for this reason I thought it best not to march until tomorrow.

Friday, February 4.—About half past eight in the morning we set out west-northwest on the road which leads to some wells. Going over good terrain, passing hills on both sides, and traveling five leagues, the wells were reached. I immediately had them opened, and it was seen that the water ran in quantities sufficient for all our animals, and that there was pasturage. Camp was therefore made at these wells for the night and they were named Pozos de en Medio.—From Tubac to Los Pozos de en Medio, 119 leagues.[1]

[1] To get out of Cabeza Prieta Mountains Anza could have swung slightly to the south or slightly to the north, and then found an open road between the hills and out into the plain. He seems to have emerged by the northern route. Lumholtz's map is distorted at this place, showing Cabeza Prieta too far north. Pozos de en Medio were Coyote Water, or wells in the same arroyo, to the east-northeast of Tinajas Altas. Eldredge, hopelessly at sea here, puts Pozos de en Medio indefinitely west of the Gila Range, instead of east of it.

From Tule Well we swung west 2.9 miles to Tule Tank, then into a pass, which lasted four miles, when we entered the vast plain. At our right we had Cabeza Prieta Range, and striped Tordillo Mountain. As we crossed the plain we closely paralleled Anza's route. Ahead of us was Sierra de las Tinajas Altas and its remarkable tanks, Tinajas Altas, made famous by Kino, but where Anza did not stop.

Saturday, February 5.—At half past seven we set out along a made road toward the west-north-west, and having traveled seven leagues, continually passing hills on both sides, we reached the watering place which, on account of its long distance from the road, we inferred must be the one which the Jesuit fathers called Agua Escondida.[1] Here with much difficulty we succeeded in watering the horses and mules only, for, because the flow decreased[2] and of the great inconvenience, the cattle could not be watered by nightfall, so this was left until tomorrow. —From Tubac to El Agua Escondida, 126 leagues.

[1] Anza's entry here would be inconclusive if it were not for supplementary statements of the other diaries. Garcés and Díaz tell us that from Pozos de en Medio they went through Tinajas Pass, just north of Tinajas Altas, and up the west side of the Gila Range. Agua Escondida was a well in Arroyo San Albino, near Albino Tank. This is made plain by Anza's account of how he left Agua Escondida, next day. Eldredge ventures a guess that Agua Escondida was at Telegraph Pass, near the Gila River. This, of course, is impossible, because it would take Anza leagues beyond the Gila in the next two days' march.

On January 4, 1928, we left Tinajas Altas, went two miles to Tinajas Pass, another to the top of the pass and two more to the plains on the other side, making five miles. At 16.4 miles from Tinajas Altas we reached the spur of mountains at Arroyo San Albino, which I shall call San Albino Point. Anza went three or four miles farther than we to get to Tinajas Pass, followed closer to the Gila Range, and found water some four or five miles up the arroyo above San Albino Point, thus making his distance of eight leagues. Anza was mistaken about the Agua Escondida of the Jesuits. Kino, at least, always went up the east side of the Gila Range, and his Agua Escondida was Tinajas Altas.

[2] This shows that the watering place was a well in the sand, not a tank.

Photo by Bolton

The Puerto Blanco, looking east.

Photo by Bolton

Looking northeast from Sonóita.

Tinajas de la Purificación.

Sierra Pinta, looking east from Camino del Diablo. Aguaje Empinado
is beyond the little hill in the foreground.

THROUGH THE YUMA COUNTRY

Here at this place we found a Pápago, a native of the pueblo of San Marcelo de Sonóitac, with his family. He was a Christian called Luís, and was returning to San Marcelo from the rivers Gila and Colorado. Having already learned of my coming to the rivers,[1] he had set out from there the day before to warn me that I should advance to them with caution, saying that part of the people, and especially those living some distance above the junction of the two rivers, had decided to prevent me from crossing the streams, intending to kill me, the fathers, and others who were with me, in order to possess our horses and other things which I brought. He added that the captain of the Yumas whom we call Palma (I saw him last month at the presidio of El Altar, and told him of my coming) had not been able to dissuade these people from their intention; but that he had declared that he was always favorable to me, as were all of his nation and his allies down the river, and that his friendly attitude was being supported by two other chiefs or head men. The Pápago said that these two and Palma were checking the disturbers, chiding them for their

[1] A blank here has been caused by polillo, and I have supplied the words from the copy in A.G.P.M., Provincias Internas, Tomo 23.

bad conduct, and warning them of their peril, saying
that the soldiers were sufficient with their valor and
their weapons to cope with many more if they should
provoke us, but that if they did not do so we were so
well disposed that without any pressure we would
make them presents of whatever we were bringing
and they might desire, as we had done with Palma
himself when he went to our settlements, where he
and those who accompanied him were treated kindly.

This report, although it gave me no great anxiety,
served as a warning, so that in case it might have
some foundation I might provide the means to frus-
trate the plan completely. Indeed, any inquietude
on the part of these chiefs would be prejudicial to
us. And since the prevention of such unrest was
one of my first cares and one of the first aims of
the orders of his Excellency the Viceroy, and of the
Council of War and Exchequer, I prepared to proceed accordingly. For this purpose, consulting the
reverend fathers who accompanied me and who
agreed with me, I set about learning with certainty
what foundation this story had, and since nobody
could tell us better than the same Captain Palma,
I thought it best to talk with him before taking
for granted the report about the disaffected Indians.
To put this into effect I decided to send for him,
before reaching the rivers, by the bearer of the story
himself, promising him a horse and presents. He
replied that he would gladly go the next day, but
that he was tired now, and he knew that there would

be time to come with the Captain to meet me the following morning, on my arrival at the rivers.

Sunday, February 6.—At eight in the morning I sent the messenger named on a good horse, and he again promised to meet me on the road the next morning. An hour before this we had commenced to water our horses, in order to be free in the middle of the day to set forth to reach the rivers. Indeed, it was not possible to remain here any longer, because of the scarcity of the water and the still greater scarcity of pasturage.

And so at two in the afternoon we set out over a traveled road toward the south,[1] to round the little range which contains the Agua Escondida. On its skirts we traveled in this direction about a league and a quarter, then, leaving it behind at the right, the road turns to the northwest,[2] in which direction we traveled five leagues more, until nine o'clock at night, when camp was made in a place that had plentiful pasturage.

On the march of this day and that of yesterday we have had on our left the sand dunes through which the Jesuit fathers made their way to the Rio Colorado and which cost them the failure of many of their journeys. This transit, so difficult, unless we

[1] This is the clinching statement regarding the location of Agua Escondida. To get water Anza had ascended Arroyo San Albino, and to get on the trail again he swung south and back-tracked nearly four miles, with the Sierra de Agua Escondida (San Albino Point) on his right. Doubling this, he again took the trail for five leagues, camping between Fortuna Mine and Yuma.

[2] By a slip Anza wrote *sudueste* for *norueste* here.

are mistaken, they never would have made except
with the idea that only by crossing the Colorado
near where it empties into the Gulf they would find
the passage which they sought.[1]

Monday, February 7.—Shortly after sunrise we
set forth over the road on which we had camped for
the night, always skirting the sand dunes described
on our left, although for a distance of about two
and a half leagues some small patches of them are
crossed before reaching the Gila River.[2] At that
distance from the river, at eleven o'clock this morning, the messenger whom I sent yesterday came out
to meet me with one of the headmen of the Yumas,
because Captain Palma was absent from his village.
This headman is a subject of his, and immediately
he told me that Palma and all his people had good
hearts, and desired to know us, and that we should
go to their houses to accept their hospitality, and
that in faith of this we must go at once, for the
rumors of unrest, as I already knew, had been dispelled by him and his captain, Palma, who would
tell me the same when I met him, which would take
place today.

This headman came with an escort of eight of
his subjects, with no other arms, clothing or baggage than a firebrand in his hands. The others,
as naked as he, carried bows and a few arrows,

[1] Fathers Kino and Salvatierra tried to reach the head of the Gulf
by way of Sierra del Pinacate and the sand dunes.

[2] The route from San Albino Point seems to have been rather
directly across the sand plains to the Gila River.

and were mounted on good mares. As soon as he
had finished his speech I answered him tenderly,
telling him to dispatch one of his followers to tell
his people to come to see me, with the assurance that
I loved them all, and that I would neither injure nor
incommode anybody. He did so at once, although
in truth it was not necessary, for from here forward
all the country swarmed with people, most of them
unarmed.

About three in the afternoon we descended to
the Gila River, having traveled five leagues.[1] I was
now followed by a company of more than two hundred men, all of them overjoyed at our coming,
which they celebrated with cheers and smiles, at the
same time throwing up fistfuls of earth into the air
and with other demonstrations expressing the greatest guilelessness and friendship. At this hour a halt
was made in the first pasture and good terrain which
was found, and here every minute assembled more
and more people of both sexes, who the longer they
looked at our persons, our clothes, and other things
used by us, the more they marvelled.—From Tubac
to the Island of La Santíssima Trinidad on the Gila
River, 138 leagues.

At five in the afternoon Captain Palma arrived
at our camp with more than sixty persons in his
company. As soon as he dismounted he begged me
to embrace him, which I did. With every sign of

[1] This camp was just above the branch of the Colorado forming
the east side of the island, and a short distance above the forks of
the Gila and Colorado, at Yuma City.

affection, I had him sit down and given some refreshments, after which he spoke as follows:

He was sorry not to be at his village when I
arrived, in order that I might have come to it at
once today; he had already reprimanded his people
because they had not invited us; the reason why he
had not come out to receive me sooner was that when
he arrived at his house my messenger had departed
and was already several leagues away. The disturbances due to some opposition to us, of which he
supposed I already knew, had not succeeded. Those
who had caused it did not dare to do anything; they
were not his people, but lived a long way from his
house up the river. As soon as the rumor went forth
he expelled them from his jurisdiction, therefore I
must not pay any attention to it. Indeed, he and
all of his people were rejoiced at our passage by his
residence, to which, as he had promised me at the
presidio of El Altar, he had notified his people to
come to see me, giving orders that they must not
steal anything or molest us in any other way. I
must let them look at me and touch my belongings
without being offended, for they wished it, especially
those who never had seen us, who were the majority,
so that they might know what we were like and
might serve us with the things with which we
clothed ourselves and used.

While he was making this speech the captain
noticed that the soldiers were going around with
swords in their belts, keeping the horses ready, with
other signs of vigilance on the part of the troops.

He begged me that they all should be put at rest and break ranks, with confidence in their friendship, because there was no danger to fear. I replied that such a disposition of the soldiers was indispensable to us wherever we might be, entirely apart from any risk, which was lacking within the presidios where, as he knew, guards were established daily, just as if they were in front of the enemy. With this he was satisfied. I then answered his first speech, eulogizing him warmly for his friendship and fidelity, saying to him that with full confidence he must tell his people to come and see me freely and whenever they might wish, and that they would be humored in everything just like my children and my friends, for such they were, since he was.

In view of the fidelity which this Indian professed for us, and realizing how important it was at all times and for all events to keep his friendship, I thought it well to confer upon him some honor to distinguish him from the rest, and to give him a present to correspond with his good conduct. I therefore told him to assemble all his people near my tent. When they had come I asked them if they recognized him as their chief and superior, to which they all answered "Yes." I then told them that in the name of the king, who was lord of everybody, I was confirming him in his office, in order that he might rule legally and with greater authority, and be recognized even by the Spaniards, who would respect his rights; that I was decorating him, as I did, with a red ribbon bearing a coin of his Majesty,

of whom that image seen on it was a likeness, an
honor which I was conferring upon him as a sign
of the obedience which he must render to the king.
He promised to comply, and after I had hung the
coin around his neck I embraced him. With both
the medal and the embrace he was pleased, and the
hundreds of his people marvelled at the gift, and
at my demonstration of affection, manifesting theirs
with unbounded joy.

Noting the appreciation which the chief showed
for his insignia (for he had not eyes enough with
which to look at it or words in which to express to
me his gratitude, though he did manage to say I was
his master), I took the opportunity to tell him, in
the presence of two of his subalterns, that there was
only one God; that He was the one who created us,
the heavens, the sun, the moon, the stars, and everything there is on earth, including a master, the king,
who was subject to God, and that all the Spaniards,
who were more numerous than he could imagine,
were subject to both; that God had given to the king
all these lands and many more, in extent unknown,
full of Spaniards, and that he therefore ruled all of
us; that we not only obeyed him but revered his
orders; that it is because the king loves us so much
that we have plenty of horses, clothing, iron, knives,
and all we possess; that for all this they thanked
him sincerely, for indeed he had provided his realm
with much more, so that like them, with our labor we
might acquire maize, wheat and other crops, for he
who does not work does not have them; but that

even without labor the king provides many things free of cost, as he had seen in the pueblos of the Pimas, for he supports the fathers, the churches, and other things.

I told him that the king, who is liberal with all, is so in greater measure with them and all other Indians, from whom he asks nothing and takes nothing; that he had commanded all the Spaniards to call them brothers, and because he loved them all he had sent me through this region, enduring toils, in order to visit them and give them peace in his name, without injuring anybody, and in order through my report to learn about them; that if they should suffer any damage in the smallest trifle from the men in my command I should deal with them severely; that in the name of the king I should go on regaling them as I passed through their villages; that the king does not ask from them any other thing than that they return the love which he feels for them, by rendering him vassalage and obedience, and living without killing one another; that God also commands this; and since we are all children of both God and the king, and just as none of them like to have their children killed, and if any of them should die the father would grieve, just so it is with God and the king. I told him that I was saying all this to him so that he might tell it to his people. To everything he listened attentively, saying that he had never heard any words more welcome, and that he would make them known to all who were under his rule.

Soon after this speech the captain asked me for my cane. Taking it in his hands he called to his people, and in their midst commenced an harangue which lasted more than an hour. From time to time we observed that those assembled very frequently covered their mouths, in sign of surprise. Having finished, he ordered them all to go to their huts, but very few of them did so. Indeed, most of them remained to spend the night with us, with as much confidence as if they had dealt with us for years. Palma came to tell me that he had repeated to his people what I had told him; that they had all listened with pleasure; and that he would do the same in other villages as we passed through them, as far as he went with me, and of these matters he would speak also to other tribes, his allies.

Tuesday, February 8.—At the usual hour we set forth down the Gila River, and having gone half a league along its bank we came to a ford to which Captain Palma guided us. Here I gave orders to unload in order to take over the cargo, which this captain offered to have carried across on the heads of the strongest and tallest of his men. Seeing the willingness with which they offered, and there being nothing to cause mistrust, I consented to it. Nevertheless I first crossed over with half of the soldiers.[1] Immediately afterward followed the horse herd and the cattle, and then the cargo was taken over. The crossing having been finished with entire success,

[1] The crossing was just above the junction and two or three miles east of Fort Yuma Indian School.

at three in the afternoon, and in the presence of
more than five hundred persons, we halted in a convenient spot where we unloaded, because there was
not time enough to continue to the Colorado River.
And so we remained to finish this day between the
two rivers, which unite a short distance away.

Right here a beautiful island, which I named La
Santísima Trinidad, is formed by a branch of the
Colorado River which enters the Gila before it unites
with the former, and is the residence of Captain
Palma of the Yumas. More than six hundred persons, ranging from eight to fifty years of age, of
both sexes, having assembled on the island, I arranged to give presents to them all, to see if they
would leave us in peace for a while, because since
daylight it had been nothing but get near us, touch
us, and ask us about everything we use, and other
impertinences of this nature. To prevent any one
from twice getting the little gift of beads and
tobacco which was given to each one, and which they
greatly esteemed, I stood them all in a row. Their
captain then made them an harangue similar to the
one described before, commanding them to give
thanks for the gifts and to go away till next day,
so that we might rest. Some of them obeyed, but
many remained till nightfall, when we began to prepare a little food, for hitherto it had not been
possible with the disorder caused by so many people,
for there was not a thing at which they did not
marvel, for which reason the utmost patience and
tolerance has been necessary today.

While I was engaged in the distribution, an Indian, naked like all the rest, came groaning so pitifully that it seemed that he was suffering the greatest affliction and grief. He gave three groans to each person, touching him on the shoulder, and so he went amongst them all. I asked what the man was suffering from, for in truth he won my compassion, and they replied "Nothing;" that he was from one of the villages down the river; that he brought the news that his father had died, and accordingly he had come to invite all those present to go and weep while they were burning the body of the deceased, which was the kind of funeral they customarily held.

Wednesday, February 9.—Observing the same precautions as yesterday, at nine o'clock today we began to cross the Colorado River by a special ford to which Captain Palma guided us. The crossing was effected with all success in the presence of more than six hundred men, most of whom, and even the women and children, assisted lest we should stray from the places where they told us it was the shallowest. With this help we all succeeded in crossing on horseback without wetting anything of importance. In celebration of the crossing, which could not have been done with the same facility in any other part of this river, and because this was the first time it had been done by the arms of the king, I had a salute given by firing off some rockets. This volley pleased the Indians, although the roar frightened them so that on hearing it they threw themselves on the ground.—From Tubac to the junction of the Gila and Colorado rivers, 138 leagues or a little more.

After this ceremony I measured the present width of the Colorado River at the place where the Indians told me it was its regular width at the height of the dry season, as is now the case. It is ninety-five fathoms wide and a little more than five palms deep on an average, the branch which forms the island whence we set out today being smaller at this point. The Gila I did not measure, because at the place where I could have done so it had already been joined by this branch of the Colorado mentioned, but according to the report of the Indians it may be estimated as half the size of the Colorado in every way, except that in the quality of the water the Gila surpasses the other, although that of neither river is of the best, because both are a little salty.

After all the foregoing I caused all our train to halt in the very place where these rivers unite,[1] and, after joining, pass between two small hills of solid rock. To this place the Jesuit Fathers gave the name of San Dionicio, and from the hill on the other side they observed the latitude, which they say is thirty-five and a half degrees.

To the hills on this side I gave the name of the Pass of Concepción.[2] From them one gets a very

[1] In the flat two or three miles northeast of the Southern Pacific Railroad bridge across the Colorado at Yuma.
[2] At the Indian School.

delightful view, having in sight the confluence of the rivers, and the immense grove of willows and cotton-woods which cover the banks both upstream and down and as far as the eye can reach, all useful for beams because they are so straight. One also sees a sierra close by, through an opening in which the Colorado River comes from the north-northwest. In the same direction one sees a large peak, which because of its size and form I named the Giant's Head.[1] To the east-northeast there is another open-ing in a sierra that is cut by the Gila, and likewise another peak, smaller than the other, which I called the Bell[2] because it is shaped like one.

This day was no less troublesome than yesterday because of the assemblage of more than eight hun-dred persons. I regaled them with a beef, glass beads, and tobacco. They appeared more confident today than yesterday, and remained to spend the night amongst us in much larger numbers than last night.

Here I talked with an Indian of the Soiopa[3] tribe who told me that three days' travel up the Colorado where he lives it divides. He said that the larger stream was this one, and that the smaller branch turned to the north to join another river larger than this Colorado, and that there its water is even redder than that of this river, and of whose disemboguement

[1] Cabeza del Gigante, now called Castle Dome.

[2] Sierra de la Campana, or El Bonete, now called Chimney Peak.

[3] The Mohaves.

into the sea, he said, they are ignorant.[1] Likewise another told me that three days' travel down this Colorado River the natives who inhabit it told him that five days beyond them there was a road traveled by Spaniards, who we presume must be those of the port of San Diego, but that to reach it there was a great scarcity of water even in the rainy season. I have inquired whether or not this river has any fall, and they assure me that between here and the place where it empties into the sea there is none, and that they do not know that it has any above in the many leagues concerning which they have information.

There seems no doubt that it is twelve days from here to the province of El Moqui,[2] for according to the reports which I have acquired there intervene only three or four tribes. The blankets of black and blue wool that come from that province are seen in abundance among these Yumas, who acquire them through the Soiopa tribe already named.

Thursday, February 10.—Raising our train, shortly after eight o'clock we set out down the river toward the west-northwest with a following of more than six hundred persons, who insisted on showing us the best trails, clearing them of little brush or reeds which obstructed them, and with the same vigor volunteered to drive the pack mules, horses and cattle, each animal having at its side five or six men

[1] This story is in keeping with an old belief current in Mexico in Anza's day.

[2] The Moquis are now commonly called Hopis.

who had the satisfaction of guiding it along. Having traveled about four leagues in this direction, we passed along the skirt of a hill which we called San Pablo, and going beyond it to the west for another league, halt was made for the night on the banks of the river at a place where there was some pasturage and many habitations of Yumas.[1]

At this place a larger assemblage gathered than at the preceding ones. I regaled them with glass beads, tobacco and a tired-out beef. Someone among the multitude who remained to pass the night amongst us, now entirely disarmed, stole from us a lance and an adz just to furnish one of those mishaps that are bound to happen. When I reported and complained of this theft to Captain Palma he denounced it severely and promised that on our return he would have the articles restored and punishment administered.—From Tubac to San Pablo on the Colorado River, 143 leagues.

Friday, February 11.—At eight in the morning we continued the march downstream toward the west with the same crowd, which stayed with us until about a league before reaching the place where we camped for the night. Only some sixty persons came to the camp, including those who lived in this place, which must be about six leagues from the foregoing camp, and is on the farthest boundary or

[1] Cerro de San Pablo was Pilot Knob, just north of the international line. Camp one league beyond was at the village called San Pablo by Fathers Díaz and Garcés. A mission was founded here in 1780. In 1771 Garcés visited a village which he called San Pablo across the river from the camp site.

Photo by Bolton
Looking west at Cerro de San Pablo.

Photo by Bolton
Looking east from Tinajas Altas. Pozos de en Medio are in the plain.

jurisdiction of Captain Palma and the place where the Yuma tribe ends.[1]—From Tubac to the same river, 149 leagues.

I have not said anything in particular about this tribe because, since I had to travel through the country which it occupies, I wished meanwhile to observe more closely both the land and the people, in order to speak of them with more foundation. The people in general are very robust and more than eight palms[2] tall. Their temperament is the best to be found among Indians, for they are very festive, affectionate, and generous. Their color is not as dark as that of other tribes and they are less painted than some. They have naturally good features, but they make themselves ferocious by painting all the body and especially the face.

The men go entirely naked, without the least sign of shame for their manhood, and to go partly covered they consider womanish, as they themselves

[1] Camp was made at a small lake near the river at the end of Palma's jurisdiction, and near the place where Garcés in 1771 came out from the sand dunes and the Well of Rosario and crossed the river. The place was a little above the west end of the line between Arizona and Sonora.

All four of the diaries give the day's march as six leagues west, but the direction was undoubtedly southwest, by about the course now followed by the river. On this assumption the whole itinerary from here forward fits the map, otherwise it fits nowhere. To read west instead of southwest would require that the river at that time ran twenty miles along the international boundary line west from Pilot Knob, a manifest impossibility.

[2] A palm is nine inches. Father Kino tells us that at Yuma he met the largest Indian he ever saw. For a sketch of the Yuma tribe see Hodge, *Handbook of American Indians North of Mexico.*

have told us. They have good heads of hair, which they do up in many and diverse ways, with very fine mud, upon which they scatter a powder of such bright luster that it looks like silver. In order not to disturb this coiffure they sleep sitting up. It has already been said that the men paint their faces excessively with black and red colors, and this applies also to the women. The men have their ears perforated with at least three holes, five being the most common, and in all of them they wear earrings. They also perforate the nose, or its cartilage, and through it thrust a cluster of feathers, or more commonly a sprig of palm as long and thicker than the largest bird's quill, wherewith they succeed in making themselves not only ferocious but horrible.

To arms and warfare they appear to be little inclined. They rarely have a quiver. Few have as many as five bad arrows, and their bows are worse. In this way about a third of them go armed, the other two-thirds carrying merely a lance four yards long, an instrument for a game, while the old and aged men carry clubs. At the first touch of cold in the morning or in the afternoon, those armed with bows and arrows generally lay them down wherever they happen to be, and take a firebrand which they generally put in front of their stomachs or behind their backs to warm themselves. The reason why they sleep only three hours out of the twenty-four in a day is the slender shelter they have, especially when they are outside of their villages, for in the villages they at least have their little huts in the soft earth, into which they crawl and assemble all that make up a family. Their language is easy to pronounce, and it seems to me that it would be easy to write. They pronounce Castilian as plainly as we do.

The women are like the men in robustness and height. Their features are generally medium, as Indian women go. I have seen no horribly homely ones here such as are seen among other tribes, nor anyone particularly handsome in this respect. They go clothed or half covered only from the waist to the thighs or knees, with little skirts which they make from the inner bark of the willow and the cotton-wood, divided in two pieces, wearing the shortest in front. From the same kind of bark and from that of the mesquite they make some wide fabrics which, although they are more closely woven, are nearly as coarse as the cloth which in the kingdom we call *guangoche bruto*. These fabrics they have for clothing, and the women who wear them might be called rich, and much more so those who acquire pieces of skins of beaver, hare, and other fur-bearing animals. Both men and women go entirely bare-footed.

From those I have seen and from what I have heard of the rest I judge that there must be 3,500 people in the Yuma tribe, and this is the estimate given me by Father Garcés, who before now has observed these villages more at leisure. The number will not be much more or less than this estimate.

In the country which I have seen from the junction of the rivers to here, at intervals there are fields sown with wheat without irrigation, but so good and well sprouted that the best irrigated wheat in our country does not equal it. One sees also the places where they plant maize, beans, calabashes, melons, and muskmelons, all in such abundance that we have marvelled, and wished that the Indians whom we have reduced would devote themselves as industriously to agriculture as these. This fertility of the land, which they say is the same upstream and better downstream, is greatly aided by the annual overflow which the meadows receive after the coming of spring, as a result of the melting of the snow in the interior, while it does not destroy or carry away the trees; and the meadows are silt covered for at least half a league on each bank, and many persons tell me that the waters spread out to even a greater distance. This fertility is enjoyed by both rivers, considering them separately, for it is known that the tribes who inhabit them gather equal harvests.

From all that I have seen of these rivers, especially from the junction downstream, this place seems to me to be very suitable for planting vineyards and many other kinds of fruit trees, for the crops would be obtained without irrigation, and in view of the climate, which is so mild that we have scarcely felt any cold at night, the fruit would not be exposed to danger from frosts.

At the hills at the Pass of Concepción, according to my limited knowledge, I judge that two irrigating ditches could be made, one on each side, safe and very long, to run the water to the firm land, with which the crops would be assured in every way; and even without these ditches crops can be gathered here beyond one's imagination. This river is short of pasturage, but it does not lack what is necessary to maintain small numbers of cattle. Most of the pastures are of bottom land, and they abound in carrizo, on which cattle thrive, and in the rainy season, although they tell me the rains are light, there must also be other grasses which serve the same purpose. The horses which these natives have, keep very fat, although it may be that this is because they do so little work, which must be the case, because the people, going naked and not providing the least trapping on which to ride (indeed, only Captain Palma was seen mounted on a very poor blanket), it follows that the bodily heat of the animals prevents the Indians from undertaking any great exertion on horseback.

Because everything pertaining to the jurisdiction of the Yumas ends at this place, and because some persons of the tribe which lives next beyond had come to meet me, I asked them who lived between here and the Gulf, and how many leagues it is to the mouth of this river, and they tell me that it may be thirty or forty leagues. They say that on the other side of the river live the Quiquimas, a tribe distinct in language from the Yumas and less numerous, though they extend clear to the mouth of the river; and that on this side clear to the mouth and to the mountains near the river dwell the Cojat tribe, which is much more populous than the Yumas, and whose idiom is the same except that they speak so rapidly that they are not the most easily understood. Up to a short time ago the Yumas have been at war with both of these tribes, but now they are at peace and have become related, as they say, by means of many intertribal marriages which they have made.

I have noted that the Yumas do not marry when very young, nor, according to what I have learned, is there much polygamy. I have seen no woman pregnant or with a child who did not appear to be twenty-five or more years old, and when I have asked the men about their late marriages they have replied that it is not profitable to marry young girls, because they do not know how to work.

Saturday, February 12.—At half past eight in the morning we renewed the march down the river, leaving it a considerable distance to the left, traveling to the southwest and sometimes to the south according as the brush required it; and having gone about four and a half leagues camp was made on the bank of a lake with much water and pasturage, to which I gave the name Santa Olaya.[1] It is one of

[1] This lake of Santa Olaya was some distance apart from the river. It became a strategic point in Anza's itinerary. Its precise location is one of the hardest problems of the whole journey. Father Font's diary supplements Anza's in an important way. A careful study of all the data makes it clear that Santa Olaya was twenty-five or more miles from Pilot Knob, six or seven miles west of the old bed of the Colorado, and not far above Pescadero Dam. Recently the Colorado left its bed and now flows through the channel of the Rio de las Abejas. It is probable that Laguna de Santa Olaya was in the channel of the Abejas or one of its affluents. Near Pescadero

several lakes which the river forms when it overflows its channel. Soon after we started many people of the Cojat [1] tribe came to meet me, asking me
to pass through their villages. I declined with
thanks, saying that I was very sorry to separate
from them, but that if they wished to see me and
did not live far from the place where I was going
to camp they might assemble there as the former
people had done. With this explanation they were
satisfied, and a few hours later they came in hundreds, and I regaled them with glass beads and
tobacco.

I made efforts to find out from this tribe, as I
formerly had done among the Yumas, what form of
government they had, and where their ruler lived.
All replied that they lacked both of these things, for
each head of a family ruled his own. Captain Palma
ridiculed this want of government, saying to me that
since this tribe were not so manful as his people they
imitated the Spaniards in nothing.

Dam there is an old lake bed which answers to Font's description of
Laguna de Santa Olaya (more detailed than Anza's), and since it is
in the locality indicated it may well be the very one. With Mr.
V. E. Stanley as driver I went over the ground from Yuma to Pescadero Dam in November, 1928. At Paredones Main Camp (No. 9) I
was shown fine hospitality by Mr. Frank G. Will, who went with us
over the ground between camp and Pescadero Dam. I was assisted
also by Mr. Sawnie Robertson and by Mr. Tony Mansir, an old
timer in that region.

[1] More commonly known as Cajuenches. Father Garcés explains
the different names of these people. ''The Pimas call them Cojat;
those who live in the sierra call them the tribe of the mescal sandals
or more properly guaraches; and the Yumas call them Axagueches,
but they themselves say that their tribe is the Cajuen,'' hence
Cajuenches. See p. 325.

These Cojat people, whose idiom, as has been said, differs from the Yuma in velocity, in fact are different from them in few respects. Generally speaking they are not so tall. They are somewhat darker colored, and for lack of tints are less painted. But in their lack of arms, their nakedness, the dress of their women, and other customs they are identical. They told me that the lands which they plant are as rich and fertile as those above, and that there is a greater abundance of pasturage. This tribe does not possess as many horses as the former, which is the one kind of wealth in which the Yumas surpass them.[1]

[1] An extended treatment of the Yumas will be found in the forthcoming monograph by C. Daryll Forde, *The Ethnography of the Yuma* (In press, University of California Press, Berkeley). In language the Cajuenches are closer to the Cócopas than to the Yumas.

ACROSS THE DESERT

Sunday, February 13.—With some individuals of the Cojat tribe guiding us to a suitable watering place, we set out from Santa Olaya at nine in the morning, going west-northwest and at times northwest. On the road which we followed we found two pools of dirty salt water without any pasturage. Traveling until sunset, and covering only about seven leagues, because today a number of the loaded mules became tired out, camp was made at an arroyo which I called El Carrizal,[1] the only one which was found with water fit for the animals to drink. It has an abundance of water but it is as bad as that of the foregoing places.

[1] El Carrizal was on Paredones River, and camp was some twenty miles from Santa Olaya. Díaz and Garcés say nine leagues instead of seven. Two-thirds of the way to El Carrizal they passed the Green Well of El Rosario, which Father Garcés recognized. Here he pointed out to his companions San Xacome "to the west-southwest by west," which gives a clue to the location of El Rosario. In November, 1928, I followed or closely paralleled Anza's route (in sight of it all the way) from Pescadero Dam and Rodríguez's store (at Old Saiz Levee) to Cerro Prieto. At Delta Canal Camp I was given charming hospitality and generous aid by Mr. D. A. Blackburn, engineer in charge.

Eldredge's map of the route across the Colorado Desert, while giving a general idea of the itinerary, is drawn with little regard to the diaries. Anza states clearly that the sand dunes where they turned back were only four leagues from Cerro Prieto, and they reached this place after a short march in the afternoon of the 15th. Eldredge places El Carrizal and Pozo de las Angustias on Alamo River, which is much too far north to answer the conditions given by the documents. They were clearly on the Paredones River.

Salvador Palma, the captain of the Yumas, remained at the place from which we set out today. The last proof which he gave us of his love and affection is noteworthy. Having apologized to me several times for not being able to accompany me forward because we were already in the country of his enemies, when he bade me adieu he could not refrain from tears, and while the rest were telling him goodbye he wept. This action appears to me to be the strongest proof, and most praiseworthy in a heathen Indian and in a class of people amongst whom such a thing is not done even on the loss of children and relatives; for, indeed, although it is true they do make such demonstrations they are feigned and transparent. Shortly before this incident occurred he voluntarily told me that by the time I returned to his house the great flood of the river already would have arrived, but that I must not worry about crossing, for he would begin at once to assemble timbers to make rafts, and would take me over to the other side in perfect safety.—From Tubac to Arroyo del Carrizal, 161 leagues.

Monday, February 14.—At nine o'clock we took up the march toward the west, guided by only two Cojat Indians, for although several had come as far as El Carrizal they turned back today, saying that they were already close to their enemies. After we had gone a short league the two guides took me down to the same arroyo whence we had set out,[1]

---

[1] That is, they had been traveling parallel to the arroyo, which was Paredones River.

saying that they could not cross it for the same reason which the others gave. They added that from this watering place, where we opened wells with better water than that of the last one, and to which we gave the name of Pozos de en Medio,[1] we could easily reach the next one, near the sierra, to which led an open road, and moreover, they pointed out to me its location. These notices were given more by signs than by any other means, signs being the language by which from here forward we shall make ourselves understood, since the Yuma tongue which we have hitherto used is now ended, and there is no other means of understanding those who follow. Because of this well and there being, according to reports, no pasturage beyond here for the animals, I decided to halt for the day here, where there is some carrizo, and also because the pack mules arrived in a most disastrous condition, notwithstanding that the day's march had been very short.—From Tubac to Pozos de en Medio, 162 leagues.

Tuesday, February 15.—At seven o'clock in the morning the march was begun toward the west-northwest along the trail by which the Indians said we should arrive at the watering place near the sierra,[2] whose existence I did not doubt for the foregoing reasons and because we had seen smoke in that direction. After going a little more than a league

---

[1] Half-way Wells. B says the distance was a league and D says two leagues.

[2] This sierra was Signal Mountain.

we found a pool of very salty water. From here we went on another league through a sand dune and found another well of water very limited in quantity,[1] but more potable than the foregoing. Having examined this we went forward by the trail mentioned, but it led us into some very dense sand dunes and we became lost entirely, because the wind moves the dunes about and carries the sand in various directions.[2]

For this reason it was now necessary to leave half of the load at the last well mentioned, since we knew it was impossible to complete the day's march with it all, on account of the worn-out condition in which the mules arrived. On ordering that this should be done and that a sufficient guard should remain with it, I suggested to the two fathers who accompanied me that, since it was now entirely idle to think of going forward with all the packs because of the weakness of the mules, it would be best to send back half of the load and half of the soldiers, to the village of the Yumas, in view of the fine welcome which they have given us, to await us on the return; and that with the other half, less embarrassed, we should be able to effect our arrival in Northern California. I said that I would decide on this division very gladly, because it would have the best results, and that if either one of them

[1] This became known as the Deep Well of Little Water.

[2] In the summaries are not included twenty-five leagues which were traveled from this day until the 19th, when we returned to the Laguna de Santa Olaya, for which reason from the lake forward the summary will be continued. [This note is a part of the document.]

wished he might remain, since with his presence and their respect for him it was to be supposed that neither Indians nor soldiers would be guilty of any misconduct that would disturb the tranquillity which we have experienced in our crossing of the rivers. I said also that I would make this decision in the present circumstances if I might take with me an officer in whom they had confidence.

This proposal did not meet the favor which I had expected, especially from Father Garcés, who did not consider the division of the forces prudent, nor that it was so necessary as I and Father Díaz thought. I therefore decided to point out to him more clearly what might otherwise happen. Nevertheless, I did not wish to insist upon my opinion because, since this father was considered experienced in these matters, if my plan should turn out ill-advised I should be held responsible and considered capricious.

All this having taken place, we again took up the march, and at half past eleven, after having crossed many sand dunes we came to another, larger and higher, which it was necessary to cross in order to reach the small range where they told us the water hole was. It appeared that the range was about five leagues away, and that in the weak condition of the riding animals they would not be able to get over the sand dunes, and much less the loaded mules. Therefore, because another peak was visible toward the south and nearer, in which direction it was seen that the sand dune might be circumvented, and because Father Garcés assured me that very close to it there was a large village where he had been two years before, having an abundance of water and pasturage and which he called San Jacome, I decided to go to it.[1] So I sent orders to move forward the pack train and the riding animals which were coming behind.

Heading toward San Jacome[2] and aiming to reach it, after sunset we found ourselves in front of the little peak which is near it, but upon reaching it and even having passed it we saw no track, trail, or other sign leading us to think that there was any habitation of people nearby, a very unusual circumstance in any class of Indians, because of their wandering nature. Being skeptical, and since some soldiers had arrived on foot because their horses were so tired out, I decided to halt while seeking the village in the direction where Father Garcés had found it. He, with his companion and two soldiers, went on this errand, but they returned after nightfall without finding it. Father Garcés decided to look for it again, believing that he would find it this time, since it could not be more than two leagues distant.[3]

[1] B gives the distance to the turning back place as five leagues. Díaz gives it as six and Garcés as five. The turning back place was southwest of Sesbania and east of New River channel.

[2] Anza in diary B gives the distance to the hill as less than four leagues south. Garcés gives the direction to San Xacome as south-southeast. The Cerro de San Xacome was Cerro Prieto. Its identity is fixed by Garcés's exploration of 1771. In his diary of this expedition he calls it the "Black Hill" (Cerro Prieto).

[3] This helps to fix the distance of San Xacome from Cerro Prieto. It was about two leagues to the southeast.

For this purpose I furnished him the only soldiers whose horses would stand the journey. He traveled that distance and more, but after midnight he returned without finding any San Jacome in the region where he thought it to be. The fact that it was not where he had supposed is not surprising, for in lands little traveled and without prominent landmarks, like this, it is not strange that one should make a mistake, for this happens even on roads that are very much traveled.

Finding myself uncertain of a place nearby affording water and pasturage and what I needed to recuperate our animals, and since the pack train and the extras did not arrive the whole night through, I decided to return to the nearest as well as the most certain camp, for if next day another should not be found, which was doubtful, all this expedition would be exposed to entire loss, as has happened in similar circumstances.

Wednesday, February 16.—At daylight I began to retrace my steps, and shortly after sunrise I met the pack train,[1] the horses, and cattle. The corporal told me that early the night before all these animals had become tired out in the crossing of the sand dunes, and for this reason he had decided to halt a few hours to give them some rest and to

---

[1] Anza did not start straight for the place where the half-load was left. On the 15th the pack train was behind when Anza turned south, and messengers were sent back to turn it south to San Xacome, wherever they might be met. So Anza set out north to meet them and then swung northeast to Las Angustias, or Deep Well of Little Water.

continue the march at daybreak for their greater alleviation, but after all he was unable to move from the place where he had camped six saddle animals and three cattle which were completely worn-out. I ordered him to follow me, after gathering up all the worn-out stock, with which he ought to arrive at night, as he did, but with only four head, because all the rest had died.

Going at a very slow pace we arrived at two in the afternoon at the well where the half load had been left, worn-out by hunger and thirst and all the animals used up. For this reason and for other trials which were endured, the soldiers called this well Pozo de las Angustias,[1] which indeed they all suffered. So, convinced that with this setback the expedition would be frustrated, from here I sent back our cattle to the wells called Pozos de en Medio,[2] because they had plenty of water and some carrizo which they might eat, although not much.

Thursday, February 17.—Seeing the generally disastrous condition of all of our riding animals and the impossibility of continuing the march with them, I decided to return to rest them a few days at the lake of Santa Olaya, as a place very near by and convenient, and with a view to sending for Palma, captain of the Yumas, to entrust to his care a part of the cargoes as well as the animals which would embarrass me in going forward. For, besides their leanness when they set out and the bad

[1] Well of Tribulations.   [2] Half-way Wells.

Cerro Prieto.

A pack train struggling through sand dunes

places on the march, they have become seriously ill from eating an herb which abounds in these parts, for lack of grass, causing them excessive slobbering of black color and evil scent.

Apropos of the foregoing setback, and of our having undertaken the march by uncertain roads and watering places, it may be remarked on little reflection that since I brought with me, as has been said at the beginning of the diary, a native of California who came out of it by the Colorado and Gila rivers, we ought to have taken his road or trail. But this plan, which would seem so proper to have followed as the surest, it was impossible to carry out because the native mentioned came out lost, through the immense sand dunes, to the villages of Captain Palma. And in these sand dunes such hardships and lack of water were suffered that his wife perished from these causes and he and a brother of his just escaped the same fate.

For this reason it had been decided to go as far as one or two marches beyond the peak toward which we were headed on the fifteenth of the month just past.[1] For, notwithstanding the reports given us by the last Indians, who did not wish to accompany us to it, we had formerly received other reports, all of which assured us that we could reach that peak without any great inconvenience. And there is no doubt that we should have succeeded in doing so if our animals had been more serviceable and if the

[1] Signal Mountain, or Cerro Centinela.

wall of sand dunes, for such it appeared to us, because of the worn-out condition of the horses, had not interposed.

Today, after noon, with a half load, for in this way only is it possible to reach the lake of Santa Olaya, following our own trail, we returned to the Pozos de en Medio to spend the night. As a result of starvation and illness we lost four riding animals today, and three others died yesterday afternoon. For this reason, the loss of the other horses, and because most of the soldiers had made the march on foot, I gave them a little talk in order to animate them in such a situation. They replied that in order that the purpose of the expedition might be achieved they would not flinch, even if all the horses should be lost, from making the whole journey in the same way. This good will I applauded, promising to keep them in mind to recompense them for the devotion which they were showing for the royal service in so far as it might be in my power.

Friday, February 18.—At seven in the morning I sent back all the mules that were able to carry anything, to the Pozo de las Angustias, where the half load had remained, in order that they might bring it to this well and from here in the same way to the lake of Santa Olaya, for which purpose I left in charge a corporal and eight soldiers. At twelve o'clock on the same day, by the same road and trail which I had followed to these wells, I went toward the lake named with the horse herd, the cattle, and some mules loaded with the most necessary goods, in order that the stock might more quickly reach good pasturage and water, and halted with them at nightfall at a place which had no other pasturage than the leaves of some mesquite trees.

Saturday, February 19.—At sunrise we set forth on the road and trail mentioned, and at half past eight reached the lake of Santa Olaya. A short time afterward a Yuma arrived. Having made him a gift I charged him to send a message[1] from his house, whither he was bound, to the villages farther on, to tell Captain Palma to come to see me with his Pima interpreter.

Sunday, February 20.—Many people assembled to see us, showing the greatest satisfaction. Among them came an under-chief of the Yumas saying that Palma, his companion and friend, was not at home, but that he had already sent messengers requesting him to come, and that meanwhile he would fill his place, and accordingly I might command him at my pleasure. Late in the afternoon there came an Indian who, near the place where we were camped, had run upon the trails of two of our mules, which we inferred must have fled from those which had remained behind, and the under-chief offered and went immediately to look for them.[2] At eleven at night the pack train arrived with a half load, but they were so worn-out that I considered it wise to let them graze and rest all the next day.

[1] *Recado,* omitted here, is supplied from B.
[2] This under-chief was Captain Pablo.

Monday, February 21.—At four in the afternoon the Yuma under-chief returned with one mule, telling me that the other had been killed by the people of the other side of the river, the Quiquimas. He said that, not being able to restore it or punish the Indian who took them and killed one, he had taken revenge on the wife of the thief by killing her with an arrow. He showed me the arrow and even wished me to take it in my hands. This deed was repugnant to me, and I disapproved it as its barbarity deserved, but as soon as I turned my back he said very serenely that one life was of little consequence, and that as for the one which he took, he was only sorry that I did not approve it. From this incident may be inferred the little weight and scruple attached by these unhappy people to killing one another. And thus it is seen that in a small space of country most of them are at war, without any self-interest or any grave cause. For this reason I exhorted all of those present, urging peace with one tribe and another, and told them with some severity that I should be angry with anyone who should make war or kill after I had ordered in the name of God and the king that all kinds of war should cease. To this they replied that they would not fail in the future.

Tuesday, February 22.—At five in the afternoon I dispatched the pack train to go and bring the half load which was lacking.

Wednesday, February 23.—At ten o'clock at night the pack train arrived with the half load which had remained behind.

Thursday, February 24.—Everybody was allowed to rest. Early in the afternoon Palma, the captain of the Yumas, arrived. He showed inexpressible joy at seeing me, signifying deep sorrow for my troubles, and because he did not know the roads by which I wished to go forward so that he might tell me about them. But the thing for which he showed the most grief was the death of the riding animals, thinking that in them we had lost our greatest wealth and treasure.

The same afternoon Father Garcés decided voluntarily to go to visit the nearby villages which are downstream from here, in which he says he was two years ago, hoping to acquire in them helpful notices concerning our route. I charged him to return within four or five days, this being as long as we could wait before continuing our march.[1]

Night having fallen, I began to sound out this captain of the Yumas to see if he gave any cause for withholding from him the confidence which I felt. Not finding in him any ground for mistrust, I told him of my intention to leave part of the loads and of my men in his care, because I was unable, for the reasons already set forth, to take them forward, and so that they might await me at his house till

[1] The diary of Father Garcés tells of his journey down the river.

I should return in a little more than a month. I told him that on hearing that I was coming and that I was returning with most of the soldiers, or if others should come to his house from the direction from which I had come,[1] as might happen, because of my delay in getting back home, he must give them news of me and tell them to await me at his house. To this he replied that he was agreed; and he promised to take good care of everything just as he had done by Father Garcés when he came alone, and by the native of California when he came out at his village last year, personally conducting him to the presidio of Altar; and that in order that the mules might reach his house he would transport the cargo on the backs of his men. It cost me no small effort to persuade him to forego this labor, as well as to convince him of the reasons which I had for trusting his good heart and good conduct, without any misgivings whatsoever.

In order to get more complete assent, I communicated the foregoing to all the men of the expedition who were present, and in one voice they told me that they embraced the plan as the only one that would make possible the necessary efforts to carry out the desired enterprise. This, they said, being a matter of the service of God and the king and of the honor of everybody taking part in it, ought to prevail over everything else, even though the risk of losing all that we might wish to leave behind should

1 He means from Tubac.

be patent; but this ought not to be expected in dealing with an Indian who so manifestly respected and loved us, of which there was an excess of evidence, including his care of our dependents, as already related, and the communication and commerce which he had maintained for many years past with our towns and those of the Pápagos and Pimas, who are subordinate to us. And since these lived near and came to the Yumas frequently, it would not be easy for the latter to attempt any outrage, for even if the Pimas could not restrain them, the Yumas, on the other hand, could not prevent them from reporting to our people, whom the heathen fear so much. And finally, there was nothing else to do. Therefore, they again repeated their pledge, in order that the expedition might be carried out, and promised their best efforts whatever might happen, saying that in case the horses should all be lost or worn-out, they would undertake the march on foot until they achieved their goal. But they felt sure that this loss or wearing out of the mules would not happen, because now they would be reinforced and relieved by not having to drive mules or herd the cattle, and that on the few mules left in fair condition small packs could be carried with supplies for a month, and we must come out by that time at the latest to some of the new establishments of northern California. This general opinion I promised to accept, whereupon we all were satisfied.

The time from Friday the 25th to Monday the 28th was devoted to rest. No disturbance occurred nor was there any sign of any among the hundreds of Yumas, Cojats, and Quiquimas who assembled to see us, with such confidence that he was very conspicuous who carried a weak bow and arrow to hunt animals. They stayed with us in these numbers day and night, not requesting anything except that we should play for them a violin which the soldiers brought for their diversion. They became so extremely attached to it that they gave up their own pastimes, and in their stead learned the customs of our men, particularly the women, who constantly wished to be dancing the seguidillas which the soldiers taught them, and in whose steps they became proficient. They also learned to salute us, both sexes, each time they saw us, by saying "Ave María, Viva Dios y el Rey." They learned these praises without much difficulty because of their facility, which I have mentioned before, in pronouncing the Castilian language, and because of a few beads and a little tobacco.

Tuesday, March 1, was spent in the same way as the preceding days, and awaiting Father Garcés, who returned without bringing any news favorable to our journey.

Wednesday, March 2.—As was agreed on the 24th of last month, I left in charge of Captain Palma, in order that he might conduct it to his house, the greater part of our cargo, with the necessary mules for carrying it. There are remaining likewise the extra cattle and saddle animals which are unable to go forward, three trustworthy soldiers of good conduct and tolerance, three muleteers, and one of my servants, all admonished to comport themselves with the greatest harmony amongst these tribes, and with various instructions for whatever adverse event may happen; likewise two Pima natives under pay, in order that they may be at the orders of the foregoing, so that through them they may be understood by the Yumas.

By two in the afternoon the division had been made, and at that time I set out on the march with the rest of the troop, the best horses, and ten mules of the same quality, with supplies for a month. I went west-southwest[1] along the meadow down the Colorado River, having on our left many beautiful groves of willows and cottonwoods which grow along the branches that overflow this large-volumed river at the time of its highest flood. This afternoon I have passed through many villages of the Cojat tribe, being obliged to do so by the reports which I have had that by going down the river a little further it will be easier for me to reach the sierra which I formerly attempted. At nightfall, after having traveled about four leagues, we camped in a good field of maize and bean stubble, very close to several villages of the tribe named. For this

[1] B and D give the direction as west, A says west-southwest. F says west with some declination to the southwest. The stop was made at Laguna del Predicador or, de la Merced (Diaries B, D, F).

reason many persons came to see me, and I exhorted
them to maintain perpetual peace with the Yumas.
This place was named Laguna del Predicador.—
From Tubac to the Laguna del Predicador, on the
Colorado River, 166 leagues.

Thursday, March 3.—At half past seven we set
out on the march, continuing along the same meadow
to the west-southwest, and having traveled about
three leagues we camped at another lake like the
preceding one,[1] in order to acquire more exact information concerning the road which I wished to open
from here to the sierra, to which two members of
this Cojat tribe offered to guide me. They proposed
to me that I should set out tomorrow afternoon, in
order more easily to make the journey, which they
have always told me is very long for a bad season
like the present. We agreed to this plan, and I
remained today in this place.

Farther back I have said that this tribe spoke
a language different from that of the Yumas, because the latter had told me so, but having today
seen them communicate with each other, I have no
hesitation in saying that their language is the same,
and that there will be the same difference from the
nearby Quiquima language. Neither is there any
doubt that the lands from the lake of Santa Olaya
downstream are better than those preceding, with

---

[1] B says about a league and a half. C, A, and D say three leagues.
Camp was near Volcano Lake. In November, 1928, I examined the
region southeast and west of Cerro Prieto, along the line of Anza's
march.

more pasturage, more crops, and more people. All this proves that this tribe is larger than the Yumas, as has been said.—From Tubac to another lake on the same river, 169 leagues.

Friday, March 4.—At one in the afternoon we took up the march to the west-northwest, guided by one of the two Indians who promised to lead us to the sierra. Having traveled six or seven leagues[1] he proposed that camp be made for the night, with the certainty that tomorrow at midday we should arrive at the watering place. He affirmed this three times and we therefore decided to camp here for the night, although there was no pasturage for the riding animals.

Saturday, March 5.—Starting shortly before daybreak, we went west-northwest for about six leagues, having on our left a medium-sized range,[2] toward which we traveled three more leagues to the northwest. Then we went between some medium-sized hills which make a good pass, after which one turns to the west to go around some sand dunes near them. In this direction one travels a little less than two leagues, during which the sand dune is doubled. After this one turns again to the north-northwest for about a league and a half, coming to some wells

[1] B and D say it was seven leagues west-northwest. A says six or seven. F says they went west-northwest a little more than four leagues to the abandoned village of San Xacome, then three more in the same direction. This fixes the route. D says they halted near Cerro Prieto, that is, northward of it. By placing Santa Olaya too far north, Eldredge takes Anza north of Volcano Lake on this stretch.

[2] Cocopah Mountains.

of fair surface water, and some pasturage. We reached the edge of the wells about vespers, and I named them San Eusebio.[1] The journey made to this place in the manner described did not turn out so favorable to us as we had flattered ourselves it would, because of the prevarication of the guide.

On doubling the sand dune mentioned one comes out to an estuary of the sea. At least we inferred that it must be an estuary, because we found stranded an infinite number of fish of kind and size appropriate to the sea and not to lakes and rivers, however large they may be. Whether or not this lake is of live water I am not able to say with certainty, but I do know that it is water depending upon the Gulf, from which it must be distant about thirty leagues, if not more. This estuary is the one which appeared to Father Garcés two years ago to be the Rio Amarillo which he mentions or cites in his diaries, because it did not occur to him to test what it really was, for he did not taste the water.

Within a few hours during the night such good water as flowed from the wells was completely ex-

[1] This day's march took Anza through the Lower Pass of Cocopah Mountains and across the head of the Laguna Salada to camp at San Eusebio. B reads six leagues west-northwest; three more through the pass; then three more, crossing a large estuary, to the well of San Eusebio. A reads west-northwest six leagues, then three northwest into some hills which make a good pass; then west a little less than two leagues to go around some sand dunes to the estuary; then north-northwest one and one-half leagues to the well of San Eusebio. D reads ten leagues west-northwest to the top of Sierra de San Gerónimo, descending by a dry arroyo one league to the southwest and across a sand dune, then west and west-northwest across a wide, dry, lake to the marsh of San Eusebio, where there were wells. F says ten

hausted, the new which came in being so salty that not even the animals could drink it, although more than half of them, which had not yet been watered, were greatly in need of it. All this trouble and care was added to the hard journey which we had made today.—From Tubac to San Eusebio, 188 leagues.

Sunday, March 6.—To add to our ills, in the morning we learned that our guide had fled, leaving us his poor weapons as signs at the place where he had slept. For this reason, and for the lack of water which we were suffering, I sent six men with a corporal to look for the watering place which our runaway guide had said was nearby. The corporal bore appropriate instructions in case he should find heathen there or in any other place and to report to me whether or not he had found the water.

At two in the afternoon I set forth with all our train toward the west-northwest over the trail of the six explorers. When I had gone about three leagues two soldiers met me and reported for the corporal that they had found a good watering place in the middle of the sierra and near it a heathen In-

leagues in the same direction (west-northwest) then one and one-half along an arroyo through a sierra, and past a sand dune to a dry lake, then two more across the lake. On its banks they found a well of fresh water at San Eusebio. This place was at the head of Laguna Maquata, or Laguna Salada. Garcés in 1771 called it Laguna Maqueque. This lake sometimes dries up completely, but when Anza camped there it must have been at about the same level as when I saw it in November, 1928. At present the road from Mexicali to Tiajuana crosses Cocopah Mountains by Upper Pass, two or three miles north of Lower Pass, through which Anza went. San Eusebio, where Anza camped, was west of the lake, at the left of the road and a mile or more distant as one goes west past the head of Laguna Salada.

dian boy. Guided by these two soldiers we arrived at nightfall at the place where the water was, distant from the preceding one a little more than four leagues.

Immediately the corporal, who was here, told me that soon after he had seized the Indian boy mentioned an older Indian came down with great timidity and gave him to understand that the boy was his son, and that he should be given up to him. To this the corporal replied that they must not run away, because he would do them no harm, but in spite of this they insisted on leaving, which they were permitted to do after they had been regaled, in keeping with my orders, for I have always impressed upon the minds of all the soldiers with me that they must not use force upon any heathen, even in minor matters, except in cases of extreme necessity, in order that we may not acquire a bad name at first sight.

This watering place I gave the name of Santo Thomás.[1] Besides five small springs of bitter water which are here, there is one of very sweet and clear water, and there is also some grass but of bad

---

[1] Santo Thomás was in Pinto Canyon, on the highway from Mexicali to Tiajuana. A says it was in the main California sierra. B says they ascended a running arroyo (Arroyo Pinto). From San Eusebio Anza went west-northwest across the valley, at first a little southward of the highway and then close along it. Reaching Pinto Canyon, he followed it southwest, as does the highway now. Santo Thomás was some five miles up the canyon, near the bottom of the corkscrew grade on the way to Tiajuana. On November 8, 1928, with Mr. Stanley, I followed Anza's trail over this day's march. Returning

quality. It is situated in a sierra which we infer must be one of those which form the California chain.—From Tubac to Santo Thomás, 192 leagues.

Monday, March 7.—In order better to look for a watering place which we hoped to find farther on, in the morning I sent the same exploring party with the orders appropriate for this purpose, and others which were of importance to our expedition. Raising our train, at two in the afternoon I set forth to the northeast for half a league,[1] on the trail of our explorers, and having traveled three and a half leagues we saw the party halted, which we thought was a favorable indication. At sunset we reached the party, and the corporal told me that, having discovered six heathen in the same place, he took them so by surprise that they were not able to escape. He asked them for water, making signs that he was suffering from lack of it, and they gave him part of what they were carrying for themselves, telling him that close by there was an abundance of it in wells, which they showed him, after which they begged of him as a reward that he should let them go free, because when they saw the approach of

to the plain, and pursuing Anza's trail northward, we essayed to cross Arroyo Pinto. We got stuck in the sand, and carried stones all night to make a road to enable us to back a hundred and forty feet out of the arroyo. Eldredge is completely lost here. He locates the wells at San Eusebio correctly, but calls them pot holes, whereas they were wells near a marsh. Although the diaries say that Santo Thomás was three leagues west-northwest and then two or three southwest from San Eusebio, he says it was in the Cocopah Mountains.

[1] This half league was traveled after leaving the canyon.

more people whom they had never seen before they became terrified. Therefore he granted their request after he had given them presents. Right here I halted for the night because there was an abundance of pasturage, since there was certain water for the next day.[1]

Tuesday, March 8.—At seven o'clock in the morning we took up the march over good country towards the northeast, and having gone about a league and a quarter we reached the wells mentioned, and when they were opened they poured forth an abundance of the finest water. We called them Santa Rosa de las Lajas.[2] Because there was some pasturage in this place and our riding animals had become badly worn out I decided to stop here for the day.

These wells are in such a location that in two convenient journeys we might have come to them from the Laguna de Santa Olaya. Indeed, the two places cannot be more than eighteen leagues apart, but traveling through unknown country inevitably involves these detours. Notwithstanding the one which we have made, we celebrated our arrival at this place, because from it the California Indian has

[1] Anza retraced his march down the canyon, reëntered the plain, crossed Arroyo Pinto (Pinto Wash) and passed Cerro Pinto on his left. Camp was made three or four miles southwest of Yuha Well, and about two miles north of the international boundary line.

[2] Santa Rosa of the Flat Rocks. These wells were near Yuha Well in the same wash, about four miles north of the boundary line, and about seven miles nearly due south of Plaster City. Anza's arrival here meant victory assured, for Sebastián now recognized his outgoing trail.

Photo by Bolton

Looking across Laguna Salada.

Looking west from Sierra de San Gerónimo (Cocopah Range).

Bogged down in the sand dunes, north of Santa Rosa de las Lajas.

Hills in front of Santo Thomás.

recognized that he is now near a place where he formerly was, and therefore we now promise ourselves that our expedition will not fail.—From Tubac to Santa Rosa de las Lajas, 197 leagues.

Wednesday, March 9.—At half past two in the afternoon we took up the march toward the north over good terrain, and having traveled about four leagues in this direction we halted to pass the night in a place where there was some pasturage.[1]

Thursday, March 10.—At daybreak we took the same direction, toward the north, and at seven o'clock we began to cross some little points of sand dunes which extend for about half a league. At the beginning of them most of the soldiers dismounted, agreeing among themselves to make most of the following journeys on foot, in order that they might not lack mounts on which to carry their saddles and other necessary things. Having traveled seven leagues, at one o'clock in the afternoon we reached the watering place. I named it San Sebastián, alias del Peregrino,[2] because the already mentioned native

[1] For three or four miles the way was over hills covered with black shale rocks (Las Lajas). D says that camp was made in a dry arroyo. This evidently was the south running arroyo to the east of Carrizo, a branch of Coyote Wash. Camp was north of Plaster City.

[2] "Alias del Peregrino" refers to the wanderings of Sebastián. San Sebastián was on San Felipe Creek near its junction with Carrizo Creek. The site is now marked by Harper's Well. In November, 1928, with V. E. Stanley and John Allen of Brawley, I drove from Yuha Well to Harper's Well, thence through Borrego Valley to Coyote Canyon. From Plaster City to Superstition Mountain the road was over a dry, hard, barren plain. Then for several miles followed very difficult sand flats, which forced us into the bottom of Carrizo Creek, to the left of Anza's trail.

of California had come out through here.—From
Tubac to the Ciénega de San Sebastián, 208 leagues.

This place is a very large marsh with many
waters and much pasturage, but both are very salty,
except one spring where we are, which is fair-sized
and running. Here we found a small village of
mountain Indians,[1] who took flight, abandoning all
their little possessions, which I did not permit anyone to touch. I had the native of California, our
guide from here forward, go to overtake someone.
He went after them and brought a woman to my
presence, and I gave her beads and tobacco, telling
her that she should call her friends, with assurance
that no harm would be done them and that it would
be good for them to accept our gifts. She did so,
and at three o'clock in the afternoon seven men
came, although with much perturbation, and I gave
them the usual presents. Among them was the chief
of this village, which the native Californian says
consists of more than four hundred persons when
they are all together, as he observed when he made
his journey through this place, where he was given
good hospitality by the ruler mentioned, whom we
shall call "Captain," and who celebrated seeing the
Californian with special demonstration.

After nightfall many more of these heathen
assembled, and I made them embrace two Yumas
who voluntarily have come with me. They have
been continually at war, but I gave them to understand that war was ceasing from this day, as the

[1] Serranos.

nations farther back had been informed. This news caused them great rejoicing, and they celebrated it by breaking the few arrows which they were carrying. At the same time they promised that they would comply with my precept, never more going to the Colorado River for war, but only to visit, since now the two Yumas were their friends. Before this, however, they informed me by signs, that solely on seeing tracks of the Yumas they were going to cut off their heads, although they were in our company. They were now so completely relieved of their terror that this night they camped with their rivals, and regaled each other with such miserable possessions as these people customarily have.

These mountain Indians are called by those of the Colorado River Jahueches and also Caguenches and Ajagueches. They say that they are as numerous as the Yumas. They live ordinarily in the mountains, subsisting on the mescal which abounds, and on seeds, supplemented by some deer hunting. They have no crops and no opportunity to plant them, for lack of water and lands. They are a naked people. They are of ordinary height, like those farther back, but less robust. With regard to the rest of their bodies they are like the people of the Colorado River. They are superior to these in the greater abundance of bows and arrows, although of the worst kind and construction, whereby they are seen to be equal. In spirit they appear to be more cowardly than the Yumas. They possess no horses, and they are so afraid of the Yumas that they are terrified even when they hear a horse whinny. They wear their hair short without adornment. In color they are very black and their features are very ugly.

Their language is related somewhat to the Yuma tongue; indeed, I noticed that they understand each other to some extent, although the language of these people of whom I am speaking is very rapid and extremely explosive. Their settlements extend from the mountains which begin at the place where the Colorado River empties into the Gulf of California and run from south to north beyond the place where we are. Their women wear, to cover themselves from the waist down, a skirt like that of the Yumas, with the difference that those which these wear are of thread, which they get from the leaves of mescal, like that which is called in the kingdom *de arria*. They have the ugliness which is usual with all the rest of the Indians.

OVER THE SIERRAS TO SAN GABRIEL

Friday, March 11.—At three in the afternoon we took up the march to the west, but because we had to cross some large marshes we lost much time, and it was not possible to advance more than a league and a half by nightfall,[1] so we made camp in the neighborhood of this marsh of San Sevastián, with no pasturage except the leaves of some mesquite trees. The pasturage of this marsh did so much damage to our weak saddle animals that two of them died on our hands from the purging which it caused them.

At the place where we spent the night there were five families of the tribe named. In reply to various questions which I asked them they told me that the sea must be distant three days' journey, and from the direction in which they pointed we inferred that it was the Philippine Ocean. They also gave me to understand that in a five or six days' journey some relatives of theirs who lived near them came to some people like ourselves. We were convinced that they must be those who live at the port of San Diego.

Saturday, March 12.—An hour before dawn we set forth west-northwest, toward a large valley formed by another sierra and the one which we

[1] Díaz and Garcés say two leagues west.

have had on our left since leaving Santo Thomás.
Having traveled over good terrain about six leagues,
we arrived at a little water which was running
slightly and of good quality, with better pasturage
than any which has been seen since we left the
Pimería. This place I named San Gregorio.[1]—From
Tubac to San Gregorio, 215 leagues.

When we arrived here we discovered more than
sixty heathen who were hunting. I made an effort
to have some of them come to where we were
encamped, sending the Californian to bring them,
but just as he arrived with them near to where I
was, our pack mules and relay saddle animals also
arrived. Scenting the water they began to bray
according to their custom, whereupon our much-
sought heathen made precipitate flight. While
among them the California Indian observed that
they spoke the language of San Diego. Our animals
reached this place in the most deplorable state that
can be imagined, because of the bad pasturage of
San Sevastián, as has been said, and for this reason
I decided not to travel tomorrow.

Sunday, March 13—We rested.

Monday, March 14.—A little before daybreak we
set forth toward the north, and having traveled
about six leagues through various valleys with reasonable footing, we arrived at a spring or fountain
of the finest water, which runs for about two

[1] San Gregorio was in Borrego Valley, on San Felipe Creek, just
west of Borrego or Red Mountain.

leagues, having many willows most of the way. At its head we halted for the night, and to the place I gave the name of Santa Catharina. Here was found much grass and other green plants, as well as wild vines and trees, which announce to us an improvement in the country from here forward.[1]—From Tubac to Santa Catarina, 221 leagues.

By means of the efforts which I have customarily made to communicate with the heathen whom I have encountered and to relieve them of the fear which they have for us, I was able to attract some of those who lived in this place but had abandoned it. I gave them the customary presents of glass beads and tobacco, which they reciprocated by corroborating the reports given us by those in the neighborhood of San Sevastián.

What tribe this may be I cannot say with certainty. Among them, says the California Indian, there are some who speak the languages of the missions of San Diego and San Gabriel. At any rate, whoever they may be they are very different from those farther back, for in stature and condition they are very degenerate, and are much more cowardly,

[1] Leaving Borrego Valley they ascended Coyote Canyon. Santa Catharina was on Coyote Creek. The springs are now known as the Lower Willows or Reed's Springs, and are just at the lower entrance to Collins Valley about four miles northwest of Beatty's Ranch. They are fine springs of fresh water and about them is a heavy growth of willow and other trees, including a few palms. The water of the Creek is now used for irrigating the lower end of the valley. In the summer of 1921, accompanied by Fred Clark and W. G. Paden, I rode on horseback down Coyote Canyon from Mr. Clark's Ranch and identified Anza's sites.

and without arms. Amongst all those seen today, who must have been more than a hundred, only one was seen with an arrow, but even he had no bow. Each one carried a crooked stick something like a sickle, which serves them to hunt hares and rabbits. They throw it from a long distance, and I am informed by the soldiers who saw them hunt, that not one of these animals at which the heathen threw these sticks was missed. These poor people remained with us until they heard a horse whinny, after which they stayed until after nightfall on the hills a long distance from our camp. In this place of Santa Catharina, judging from the humidity, in the land here some seasonal crops might be planted.

Tuesday, March 15.—Two hours before daybreak we set forth up the arroyo, which in general runs north-northwest, dividing the large mountain chain through which it flows.[1] The floor of the valley is very even and of considerable width for four

---

[1] Ascending Coyote Canyon Anza passed Middle Willows and Upper Willows (or the Fig Tree, so-called because of a fig tree growing there). At the head of the canyon they came to three forks, Horse Canyon at the right, Nance Canyon in the middle, and the main or Tule Canyon on the left. Anza climbed the ridge between Tule and Nance canyons. Following the ridge five or six miles, he dropped down into the upper valley of Nance Canyon, which swings around, and camped at the fine springs two hundred yards below Fred Clark's corral. Above them, leading through a low rocky ridge (right into Fred Clark's corral), was the Puerto Real de San Carlos, opening out into what is now Clark's field, at the southeast extremity of Cahuilla Valley. Eldredge, misled by the name "flat" on the map, had Anza turn off to the right up Horse Canyon ten or twelve miles to Vandeventer Flat. For this turn there is no authority in the diaries. Moreover, by going that way nothing fits the diaries, whereas by going through Clark's Pass, everything fits. Richman says he rode up Hemet Valley and verified Eldredge's findings. See p. 200.

leagues, where in various places running water is found. Two more leagues were traveled where the valley is narrower, and then, leaving it at the left, we climbed a ridge[1] which did not cause the animals the greatest fatigue, and at whose crest we camped for the night in a place with good pasturage and water.—From Tubac to the Puerto Real de San Carlos, 227 leagues.

Right here there is a pass which I named the Royal Pass of San Carlos. From it are seen most beautiful green and flower-strewn prairies, and snow-covered mountains with pines, oaks, and other trees which grow in cold countries. Likewise here the waters divide, some flowing this way toward the Gulf and others toward the Philippine Ocean. Moreover, it is now proved that the sierra in which we are traveling connects with the sierras of Lower California. In the course of the journey made today we have seen an improvement in the country in every way, and have concluded from its moisture that it may be suitable for seasonal crops and the planting of fruit trees, and that there are pastures sufficient for maintaining cattle.

In the same transit we met more than two hundred heathen, extremely timid, and similar in everything to those farther back except in their language, which we did not recognize. It was laughable to see them when they approached us, because before doing so they delivered a very long harangue in a tone as excited as were the movements of their feet

---

[1] Anza omits to say that it was two leagues over the ridge.

and hands. For this reason they were called the Dancers.[1] The few weapons which they use are not carried by the men themselves but by their women and children. The only thing of value which they were seen to have was a small net wound around the stomach or the head. They wear sandals made of mescal fiber, like all those from San Sevastián to here. The women cover themselves with the same fiber, or some of them use buckskin. Of all the tribes through which we have passed this is the one which has manifested the strongest desire to steal, at which they show as great dexterity with their feet as with their hands. For this reason they have not enjoyed our little gifts as have the others.

Wednesday, March 16.—Because it rained and snowed, like the night before, we were not able to take up the march during the forenoon. But at two in the afternoon we set forth, immediately climbing some small hills, where a fair-sized vein of silver ore was found.[2] From these hills we continued west for a distance of three leagues over good terrain,

[1] These people were seen at Upper Willows.

[2] They first climbed to the top of the rocky ridge through the pass. Continuing for some three miles northwestward up a gentle slope they reached the very summit of the divide, hardly perceptible, descended another gentle slope to the Valle del Príncipe, and camped on the banks of a good-sized lake. This was the one now called Dry Lake, at Contreras's Ranch in Terwilliger Valley (a part of the Cahuilla Valley), just east of the Hamilton School. Once it was large, but it has dwindled to small proportions and is even completely dry in summer. I have made three expeditions through Cahuilla Valley studying Anza's trail. Twice Mr. Paden accompanied me, and once the Hon. J. R. Knowland, on the occasion of the marking of San Carlos Pass by the Native Sons of the Golden West, on the basis of my identification.

halting for the night, because it threatened to rain, on the banks of a large and pretty lake, to which we gave the name of El Príncipe. It is surrounded by flower-strewn and pleasant valleys and by several snow-covered mountains, by which it is filled with water. In the hills nearby were found several springs of very agreeable water, independent of the lake.—From Tubac to the Laguna del Príncipe, 230 leagues.

Thursday, March 17.—Because it had rained and snowed during the night and part of this morning, we were not able to set forth until ten o'clock in the forenoon. We then started, marching northwest and north-northwest, through the valley which lies between two ranges.[1] We followed it until it narrowed between several other hills, at the foot of which we halted for the night, having traveled three leagues. From these hills there is seen a very pretty little valley which within itself contains water and trees in abundance. We called it San Patricio.[2]

In these hills another good vein of silver ore was found, and from it was taken a piece which shows this metal black and thick. We think that the same kind will not be lacking in all the hills between the Royal Pass of San Carlos and this place, for they seem to give indications of it.—From Tubac to the valley of San Patricio, 233 leagues.

[1] On the right was Thomas Mountain, and on the left Cahuilla Mountain. Because of my explorations a post office in Cahuilla Valley has been named Anza.

[2] The valley of San Patricio was Bautista Canyon, or perhaps Tripp Flat at the head of it. Anza appears to have crossed Cahuilla Valley diagonally and now was on the west side of it.

Friday, March 18.—Although morning dawned with very thick clouds, we thought because it had snowed and rained so hard during the night that we should free ourselves of these elements today. With this in mind, as soon as day dawned I sent a party of six men provided with axes, to clear out, if it was necessary, the road which we must follow down the canyon which we have close by. At eight o'clock in the morning, raising our train, we all set forth on the road, which we found favorable, for only for a league was it necessary to cut here and there a tree which impeded.[1] After this the canyon, which we followed to the north and north-northwest, kept getting wider and wider, until we reached a broad and most beautiful valley, six leagues distant from the place whence we had set out.

Through this beautiful valley, to which we gave the name of San José,[2] runs a good-sized river, on whose banks are large, shady groves. Likewise in

[1] He is descending Bautista Creek which, after flowing twelve or fifteen miles northwest, loses itself in the sands of San Jacinto Valley near Vallevista. I have wondered if it were not named for Juan Bautista de Anza, its discoverer. A horse trail and a rough wagon trail have long been in use up the canyon, and about five years ago an automobile road was opened from Hemet to Cahuilla Valley. Camp was some three miles above San Jacinto. I descended this canyon in 1924.

[2] San Jacinto Valley, through which runs the San Jacinto River. San Jacinto and Hemet may look upon themselves as the fulfillment of a prophesy. The Californian was the guide Sebastián. This passage is evidence that on his way east he went by San Jacinto Valley. Taken together with one farther back, telling of the emergence from Coyote Canyon, it leads to the query whether Sebastián crossed this mountain by way of Cahuilla Valley.

the mountains where the river forms there are seen pines, oaks, and various other trees. All its plain is full of flowers, fertile pastures, and other vegetation, useful for the raising of cattle, of which species as many as one might wish could be raised. And in the same way one could raise good crops, which I judge would be produced with great advantage, for although this is the cold season, from the verdure and the shadiness of the leaves there is no sign of any frost here, either now or earlier. In this place where we are today we saw some heathen women, but they did not wish to come near us, although they were coaxed in the same way that has been practiced at other times.—From Tubac to the valley of San José, 239 leagues.

Saturday, March 19.—At eight o'clock in the morning we took up the march down the valley toward the northwest. Its amenity and the beauty of its trees continued for three leagues, after which the trees came to an end but the amenity continued. We followed it for three more leagues, till we came to the banks of a large and pleasing lake,[1] several leagues in circumference and as full of white geese as of water, they being so numerous that it looked like a large, white grove.[2] I called this lake San

---

[1] This lake, named in honor of the viceroy, was San Jacinto Lake, or Mystic Lake. It was drained by the Winships of Arlington some years ago. Judging by the data I conclude that Anza descended the left side of San Jacinto River, and camped on the lake near its western end. I have been up and down San Jacinto Valley numerous times studying Anza's trail, the last time in August, 1929, with Herbert Bolton, Jr.

[2] B says they camped at the western end of the lake. See p. 202.

Antonio de Bucareli. Today several heathen came
to us here and along the road which we traveled,
talking with us now with greater freedom than those
farther back, but as soon as they were given presents they left us. There is nothing particularly
noteworthy about them, for in everything they are
similar to those last seen. In the crossing of the
sierra I have not seen very many of them, but it is
evident from their tracks and their dwellings that
it is thickly inhabited by them.—From Tubac to the
Laguna de San Antonio de Bucareli, 245 leagues.

Sunday, March 20.—At half past eight in the
morning we set forth, going northwest for five
leagues, keeping on our right a high, snow covered
mountain, which drains into the lake mentioned.
Having gone two more leagues to the west-northwest, we came to a valley similar to that of San
José, which likewise has a good river, to which was
given the name of Santa Anna.[1] At the end of
these two leagues another half league was traveled
in seeking a ford, but not having found one or having
any hope of finding one, I camped for the night near
a place where there was a village of heathen like
those mentioned before, and whose number would be
more than sixty persons.

At four in the afternoon, when we halted, we
began to make a little bridge, as a means of taking
over our train, and by nightfall it was completed.
The heathen mentioned came to our camp tonight,

[1] Swinging westward past the site of Moreno, Anza crossed Santa
Ana Valley past the site of Riverside.

some of them asking our native Californian, in the idiom of San Gabriel, if we came from the port of San Diego. They marveled greatly when they were answered in the negative, and were told that we were from the east, whence we had been traveling for three moons, and where there were more soldiers than they had ever heard of.—From Tubac to Santa Ana River, 253 leagues.

Monday, March 21.—Having taken over our train by the little bridge,[1] at half past eight in the morning we set forth west-northwest, over good country covered with pasturage, the Sierra Nevada continuing on our right. After going about seven leagues we halted for the night at a fertile arroyo which came from this sierra, and was thickly grown with cottonwoods, willows and sycamores. It was given the name of Los Osos,[2] because of several bears which were seen here and then ran away.—From Tubac to the Arroyo de Osos, 260 leagues.

Tuesday, March 22.—At seven o'clock today we continued our march and went three leagues northwest over country like the foregoing. Then we traveled five more to the west-northwest and also to the west, in order to free ourselves from many places miry with water that comes from the sierra on our right which we have mentioned. Having covered this distance we crossed the river that runs close to

[1] The river was crossed west of Rubidoux Mountain, near the Southern Pacific Railroad bridge.

[2] Camp on March 21 was on San Antonio Creek near Ontario. From here Anza swung past the site of San Dimas, thence westward to Mission San Gabriel.

the mission of San Gabriel, where I arrived at sunset and announced myself to the corporal of the guard of this new establishment.[1]—From Tubac to the mission of San Gabriel in Northern California, 268 leagues.

We found here four friars, its missionaries, from the College of San Fernando de Mexico, who welcomed us with unrestrained jubilation and demonstrations of joy, with solemn peal of bells and chanting of the *Te Deum,* in thanksgiving for our successful arrival. This was all the more pleasing to them because it was so unexpected, for they had not had any news, except very remote, of this expedition, which they had considered impracticable even for a hundred men. Even though the friars and the soldiers saw us, they could hardly believe that people could have come from Sonora, and they kept repeatedly asking me if it were true, tears springing to their eyes, caused by the joy and pleasure at seeing this expedition accomplished, and at knowing how close at hand Sonora was and how easy the transit from it.

I asked the friars if Don Fernando de Rivera y Moncada, the new commander of Monterey, was at this place. They replied that the only news they had regarding the matter was that he had been named for this post, a report brought only three days before from the commander of his Majesty's

[1] The mission was a league south of where it now stands, about eight miles from the center of the down-town business district of Los Angeles.

frigate, the *Nueva Galicia,* which had just arrived
at the mission and port of San Diego.

Wednesday, March 23.—As a further act of
thanksgiving to the Omnipotent God for the favor
which He had deigned to show the arms of his
Majesty in this expedition, these friars chanted a
solemn Mass, and preached a sermon in which with
propriety the piety of the king our master was
applauded because he desires to extend the Catholic
religion amongst the heathen of these regions; and
likewise the piety with which the most excellent
viceroy has coöperated to the same effect by deciding
upon this enterprise, from which no doubt will result
glory for both majesties.

The father who is occupying the position of superior[1] has had the grace to offer me his person and
whatever there is in his charge at this mission, notwithstanding the fact that with respect to provisions
these missions are in such straits, because of the
already mentioned misfortunes suffered by the vessels which sustain them; that the missionaries and
the soldiers of the guard have no other daily ration
than three tortillas of maize and the herbs of the
fields which each one seeks for himself; and that this
ration would last for less than a month. Yet he
offered it to me to remedy this same necessity in
which I arrived at this place, until I might supply
myself with such provisions as I might send to ask
for at San Diego, because of the arrival of the
frigate with a cargo of provisions, likewise offering

[1] This was Father Paterna.

me the few animals which he has at his disposition to enable me to get them. For this offer and the foregoing I gave the appropriate thanks to the father superior, and requested him, since we are compelled to take advantage of it, that he arrange to maintain us with this ration, to which we are reduced for all these days.

Because of this lack of provisions, and since the presidio of Monte Rey is still a hundred and twenty leagues away, we agreed, the two fathers and I, to send to ask for the necessary provisions at the port of San Diego, and also for some riding animals, so that if we obtained the one and the other we could continue our journey with all of our expedition to the presidio of Monte Rey, and from there go back by a direct route to one of the places from which we have come, to find out at once if it is possible to open a direct route from the presidio to the province of Sonora.[1]

Since the captain of engineers, Don Miguel Constanzó, and the captain of dragoons, Don Gaspar de Portolá, have already traveled the road which goes from here to Monte Rey,[2] I omit writing in detail concerning its settlements and the tribes which inhabit them, assuming that his Excellency will be already informed by those officials, and will set down only whatever occurs that is new and appears to me worthy of being noted.

Thursday, March 24.—We rested.

[1] Anza means that he will try to go from Monterey directly to Yuma or some other place east of the Sierras.

[2] In 1769–1770.

Friday, March 25.—Pursuant to the agreement made on the 23d, I sent four soldiers with seven mules to the port of San Diego, and for the purpose mentioned on that day I wrote to the commander of the frigate which is anchored there, and to the captain of the same port.

From Saturday the 26th to Thursday the 31st we remained in this mission, without any other happening than the continuation of the rains, whose season ends this month or the next.

From Friday the 1st to Monday the 4th of April we continued to be here.

Tuesday, April 5.—At noon today the men who went to San Diego returned. The commanders of the frigate and the port replied to me that the supplies which they are sending are all they can spare without injuring themselves, and that they can not spare any mounts. The provisions consist only of six fanegas [1] of maize, half spoiled, a tierce of jerked meat, unfit to eat, a tierce of flour and two fanegas of beans. Having made a calculation from the foregoing of the number of days which these things would maintain the men of my expedition, it was found that they would last scarcely sixteen days, even with the beans, which can be useful for my troop here only, because they do not use or carry pots in which to cook them.

In view of the foregoing, and because these supplies were not sufficient to make our journey to Monte Rey; and not being able to acquire for this

[1] The *fanega* is the Spanish bushel.

purpose the saddle animals which were asked for; and it not being possible without having both one and the other to undertake what we agreed to on the 23d just past; I therefore resolved anew, with one of the fathers who at present is with me,[1] the other having gone to San Diego, that when he returns he shall go back with this father and the rest of the troops to the Colorado River, to await my return from the presidio of Monte Rey, whither I decided to go in person in light order of marching, with six soldiers, to examine its situation, and in the light of this to decide upon the road which may be opened from Sonora at some other time, since for the present, for the reasons expressed, we are prevented from opening it.[2]

Because of this return to the Colorado River; having no information as to when the new commander will arrive at these establishments; and since the missionary fathers tell me of the delay suffered by letters in going to the port of Loreto and from there to San Blas or some other port, I considered it well that from the Colorado River two soldiers should escort as far as the presidio of Altar the extraordinary courier[3] who brought me the order of his Excellency the Viceroy to undertake this expedition, so that as soon as possible he may get the news that it has been accomplished in the main, for

[1] Garcés had gone to San Diego; Díaz went later.

[2] Anza had formerly planned to go direct to Sonora from Monterey.

[3] This courier was Juan Bautista Valdés.

this purpose sending to his Excellency the diaries
kept as far as this place, since he ordered me to
report to him from the port of Monte Rey in case
I should succeed in arriving there.

From Wednesday the 6th to Saturday the 9th
of April we remained at this mission without any
other happening than the continuation of the rains.

Sunday, April 10.—In view of the decision made
on the 5th of this month, I charged the Reverend
Father Fr. Juan Díaz that as soon as Father Fr.
Francisco Garcés, his companion, arrives at this mission, they shall set out on the return to the Colorado
River, with all of the soldiers remaining here, and
having arrived at the river they shall dispatch this
extraordinary courier, and I have requested likewise
that this journey shall be made in the same manner
as when we came, so that there may be no disturbance among the tribes living along the way.
With this caution, together with others, I separately
charged our soldiers.

TO MONTEREY AND BACK TO THE COLORADO

At nine o'clock today I set out from the mission of San Gabriel, and going to the west-northwest I traveled four leagues, as far as the Porciúncula River;[1] I followed this stream for two more leagues, and the remaining distance, up to fourteen leagues, I made to the west, traveling until vespers.—From Tubac to the vicinity of El Triunfo, 282 leagues.

Monday, April 11.—Shortly after sunrise I set out in the same direction, passing among many docile heathen. Toward the end of the afternoon, having journeyed sixteen leagues, I halted for the night on this side of the Rio de la Carpintería, and of the first village of the Channel of Santa Barbara.[2]— From Tubac to Rio de la Carpintería on the Canal de Santa Barbara, 298 leagues.

Tuesday, April 12.—At six o'clock I continued along this channel towards the west, until I arrived

[1] The Porciúncula River was the present Los Angeles River. The text is slightly ambiguous here: "el que segui" might refer either to the preceding direction or to the river. Anza evidently reached the Los Angeles River in the vicinity of the old Plaza, ascended the river to the vicinity of western Glendale, on the edge of San Fernando Valley, and then turned west, around the point of the mountain. His camp for the night was near Triunfo, still on the map, in Russell Valley, west of Calabasas.

[2] Camp was near Ventura. Anza's Rio de la Carpintería was Ventura River, then commonly called Rio de la Asunción.

at this side of the village of Mestletlitán,[1] having traveled sixteen leagues.

Wednesday, April 13.—Along the same channel and in the same westward direction I made fifteen leagues today, halting very close to the village of Los Pedernales.[2]

Thursday, April 14.—Going west, I traveled four leagues along the same channel, reaching the end of it, which is at Point Concepción, where likewise the river of Santa Rosa joins the point.[3] We could not cross the river because we arrived at high tide, and although it is true that the tide does not enter the river more than three-fourths of a league, farther up it does not offer a passage anywhere because of the gorge and the thick growth along the river, therefore it was necessary to wait until the tide receded, which I did, remaining here today.—From Tubac to the end of the Channel at Punta de la Concepción, and the vicinity of Santa Rosa River, 333 leagues.

All of this channel is thickly populated with heathen, who are more numerous than I have seen in any place between the Colorado River and here. Like most of the heathen they go naked. They are robust and tall, and are fairly well armed with bow and arrow, both of which are small, and they are

[1] On a lagoon a short distance west of Goleta. The island of Mescal still preserves the name.

[2] East of Rocky Point. By Punta de la Concepción Anza meant the whole triangle between Government Point and Santa Inez River.

[3] From Los Pedernales to Santa Rosa River was north rather than west. The Santa Rosa River was the one now called Santa Inez.

very timid. They live close together, for each town consists of forty houses or more, which they make round like a half orange. They are much given to trade and to industry, in which respect their equal will not be found in their class of heathen.

Many occupy themselves in building their launches and in making the necessary equipment for them. They make them with two prows, from thirty-six to forty palms long, and of corresponding width. All are made of more than twelve pieces, but so well joined, seamed, and calked that they do not leak. They make them so light that two persons carry them with little difficulty. The tools with which they build them are of flint, with which I saw them making them, and I even bought some. And I was forced to admire both their ingenuity and their patience. In each village they have fifteen or twenty canoes in use and in each one they were making not less than from seven to ten new ones.

Many other persons occupy themselves in working stones, from which they make vessels for cooking. They hollow them out with such perfection that it appears as if done with a wheel, and this not only with small pieces, but with large ones and of different forms, of which likewise I bought some from them, as well as others made of wood or of hard timber, like oak and madroño. Their women coöperate equally in these tasks, and especially in making what we call coritas, which they use for various purposes, and of which I had never seen finer specimens. All the Indians make them, since the materials of which they construct them are not found in other regions.

In their launches, with which the sea is covered nearly all day, engaged in fishing with hooks made of shell but as perfectly fashioned as those made of iron, these people go to the islands which are to the south of them, some of which I believe must be distant four or five leagues. I have seen in accounts the estimates which they made of these inhabitants of the channel, and they reach eight or ten thousand souls, and in these figures they do not include those who live on the islands or on the mainland at some distance. But of those recognized as Channel Indians it does not seem to me there are so many. All the lands which they occupy are as fertile and beautiful as the regions independent of this channel, and the sight of them is certainly a recreation, especially to one who has witnessed the extreme sterility along the Gulf of California, where there are neither trees nor even useless herbs to be seen, while here, on the contrary, fields as verdant as they are flower-covered touch the very waters of the sea.

Friday, April 15.—Having crossed the Santa Rosa River, at daybreak I continued west-northwest for twelve leagues, when I encountered more than two hundred extremely docile heathen, and some springs of asphalt which they have in abundance. After this I traveled four more leagues to the north in order to reach the mission of San Luís.[1] Here

[1] San Luís Obispo, on the same site, is now a good-sized city. The asphalt springs mentioned were north of Pismo, above Price Canyon, near Maxwellton.

there are four missionaries from San Fernando de Mexico, like the others mentioned, and a guard of eight soldiers, who gave me the same welcome that I received at San Gabriel.—From Tubac to the mission of San Luís, 345 leagues.

Saturday, April 16.—Continuing north-north-west thirteen leagues, I halted for the night at Nacimiento River.[1]

Sunday, April 17.—Continuing in the same direction for seven leagues, I arrived at the mission of San Antonio,[2] where there are the same number of friars and soldiers as in the foregoing mission. Taking up the march from here at two in the afternoon, and going north, I traveled six leagues, as far as the place of Los Ocitos,[3] where I halted for the night.—From Tubac to the mission of San Antonio, 365 leagues, and to the place of Los Ossitos on Rio de Monte Rey, 371 leagues.

Monday, April 18.—At daybreak I continued my march, going west-northwest and west for thirteen leagues. At the end of this distance I arrived at the presidio of Monte Rey, whose commander and troops welcomed us with the same joy and satisfaction as those noted hereinbefore. They were persuaded

[1] Anza went over the present highway northeast through Santa Margarita and Atascadero, and turned off to the left at Paso Robles to the Nacimiento River, still so-called.

[2] San Antonio mission at first was founded about a league southeast of the site of the present ruins.

[3] Los Ocitos, or Ossitos (the Bears), was on the Salinas River northwest of King City. From that point Anza descended the Salinas past the site of Spreckels, then turned westward to Monterey, practically along the present highway.

that with the opening of a road, recently effected, the stability of these missions and presidios would be assured, and that they would emerge in a short time from the infelicities and misery to which in all respects they are reduced because of the misfortunes suffered, as has been said, by the vessels in reaching this port, where all the inhabitants, our people, have told of their troubles, which at present are greater than those related of the mission San Gabriel. In view of these trials and of their long continuation, I cannot find words adequate to praise the merit of the friars, the commander, and the troops for remaining in these places.—From Tubac to the presidio of Monte Rey in California Septemptrional, 384 leagues. These 384 leagues comprise the entire distance traveled to this presidio.[1]

Tuesday, April 19.—I remained in this presidio.

Wednesday, April 20.—I went to the mission of San [Carlos del] Carmelo,[2] distant from the presidio a little more than a league, both to see this new establishment, the last in northern California, and to return the visit made me yesterday by the reverend father superior of its missionaries.

A few days before my arrival here the mast of a ship was stranded on the nearby beach, whose construction and the wood of which it is made are unknown to those of our people who live here, but

---

[1] To this number 25 leagues lost in the sand dunes are to be added, making the total 409 leagues.

[2] The present Carmel mission. The superior was Palóu, acting president.

they believe it was broken two-thirds off. It is entirely run through with very strong nails with long heads, and with two points which do not pass through to be clinched. Their iron has not rusted at all nor are the points blunt which projected where it was broken. From these last two circumstances the few persons who are experienced in the matter of vessels infer that it cannot be very long ago that the vessel from which this mast came was wrecked. At the first opportunity that offers it will be taken to the port of San Blas in order that it may be carefully examined.

Thursday, April 21.—After attending Mass, which was celebrated by the father superior of the missionaries, for the same purposes as were stated for the one at San Gabriel, I returned to the presidio of Monte Rey. Having suggested to its commander, Don Pedro Faxes, that it would be well for some of the soldiers in his command to become acquainted with the road or way out to the Colorado River (since for the road to Sonora there are plenty of guides), he agreed that this should be done, and for this purpose he detailed a squad of six soldiers.

Friday, April 22.—I set out from the presidio of Monte Rey to return to the one in my charge, by the marches and directions opposite to those by which I went, in the execution of which I made camp for the night at the place of Los Ossitos.[1]

Saturday, April 23.—By the road named I arrived at the mission of San Antonio.

[1] On Salinas River near King City.

Sunday, April 24.—I camped at the Nacimiento River.

Monday, April 25.—I arrived at the mission of San Luís.

Tuesday, April 26.—I camped for the night near the Santa Rosa River.

Wednesday, April 27.—At two in the afternoon I met Fray Junípero Serra, the father president of the establishments of this northern California, who was going to the last establishment mentioned, on his way from the City of Mexico.[1] He importuned me several times to stop with him so that he might learn about my journey. I yielded to his request, remaining with him for the rest of the day and for the night.

Thursday, April 28.—I came to camp for the night at the place which they call Dos Rancherías.[2]

Friday, April 29.—I camped at La Cuesta.[3]

Saturday, April 30.—I came to halt for the night at the Porciúncula River.

Sunday, May 1.—I again reached the mission of San Gabriel.—From Monte Rey to the mission of San Gabriel, 120 leagues.

Notwithstanding the fact that right here I rely on the reports which may have been given of the condition of the country from here to Monte Rey by Captains Don Gaspár de Portolá and Don Miguel

[1] The meeting was evidently somewhere on the Santa Barbara Channel.

[2] Evidently the same as Dos Pueblos, on Dos Pueblos Creek, near Naples.

[3] At the foot of Conejo Grade, east of Camarillo.

Constanzó, it has seemed proper for me to add a note on the present condition of these new establishments, subsequent to the departure of those officials, on the basis of what I have seen and have been told.

Among the heathen tribes there is no disturbance to alter the opinion which has been formed of their gentleness and docility, of which every day they give greater proofs, offering their children for baptism and some of them accepting it themselves. This boon has not been completely possible to them, because provisions have been so scarce that the missionaries have not had the wherewith to support them without living apart from them, which ought to cease as soon as they acquire the character of Christians. But here and at Carmelo there are more than five hundred who are now Christians, and I know that their missionaries maintain them with only a pint and a half of atole mixed with water, on which they live for the whole twenty-four hours.

The same fathers have told me that even if atole alone had been plentiful, they could have doubled or tripled the harvest, but that for this lack of it they have made their living outside of the missions. But they have hopes that in the future their labor will produce greater harvests, because this year there is promise of fair-sized crops of wheat, which have failed up to now, more through the lack of seed than because of the sterility of the soil. The fields of this crop which I have seen yield very abundantly, for with respect to rankness of growth, size of head and thickness of stalk I have not seen any so good in the provinces of Sonora. And the same is likewise true of barley, peas, beans,[1] and other vegetables. The barley, they say, depreciates greatly at the time of maturity, because of the continuous fogs, especially at Carmelo and Monte Rey, but this mission of San Gabriel is exempted from this drawback, for here all crops which they have planted with care have yielded well. And the missions below here without exception have good fields of this crop.

Monday, May 2.—After having dispatched his companion, Father Garcés, and our troops, to the Colorado River on the 13th of last month, the Reverend Father Fray Juan Dias, deciding himself to await me at this mission, by means of the astrolabe which he was able to obtain at the mission of San Diego, to which he took the trouble to go to be instructed, made an observation of the latitude and computed it as 33° 52′.[2]

Tuesday, May 3.—At two in the afternoon I set out from the mission of San Gabriel toward the east and east-southeast, straightening as much as I could the road which I followed when coming, an effort which will be made to save as many leagues as possible; and having traveled this afternoon five leagues we halted for the night at a creek which was named Arroyo de los Alisos.[3] It is the first one running to the neighborhood of San Gabriel from the

1 "Alberjón, aba, y otras verduras."

2 After Anza left San Gabriel, Father Díaz went to San Diego for the astrolabe and to receive instructions in its use.

3 Arroyo de San Antonio. Camp was near Ontario.

Sierra Nevada which we noted when we first came
to that mission.—From Monte Rey to the Arroyo
de los Alisos, 125 leagues.

Wednesday, May 4.—Going east I marched five
leagues and crossed the Santa Ana River, beyond
which five more leagues were traveled to the neighborhood of the Lake of San Antonio de Bucareli.
To the north of this lake in the snow-covered range
there is seen a good opening,[1] which I consider the
most suitable one by which to go directly to the mission of San Luís or the presidio of Monte Rey, when
coming from Sonora. In this connection I may say
that at the first place just mentioned I saw with
great distinctness the same snow-covered range, and
there is no other with which to confuse it.—From
Monte Rey to the Laguna de San Antonio Bucareli,
135 leagues.

Thursday, May 5.—Going generally to the east
and east-southeast, four leagues were traveled, as far
as the beautiful valley of San José,[2] whose latitude
was observed and proved to be 33° 46½′. After
making this observation we continued our march in
the same direction for five leagues, until we reached
the site of San Patricio.[3]—From Monte Rey to the
valley of San Patricio, 144 leagues.

Friday, May 6.—We set out from San Patricio,
and having traveled east-southeast about eight

[1] He evidently means Cajón Pass, through which he knew Fages
to have gone to San Luís, a point on which he is strangely silent.

[2] Near San Jacinto.

[3] He ascended the Bautista Canyon. Camp was near Tripp Flat,
in Cahuilla Valley.

leagues, we halted for the night at the site of Santa
Catharina.[1] We observed the latitude of the Royal
Pass of San Carlos and found it to be 33° 42'. As
we were going along today near some hills, some
arrows were surreptitiously shot at the saddle animals which were being driven behind, three of them
being slightly wounded. Efforts were made to ascertain who shot the arrows, and it was found that it
was four heathen. The chief culprit was given a
beating, and told that he deserved to be put to
death for what he had done, but that because of our
natural compassion we were sparing him. When
I arrived at this place of Santa Catharina I learned
by a note left me by Father Garcés, who is going
ahead, that the same thing happened to him.[2]

This occurrence apparently was due to the presence among these heathen of some Indians from the
neighborhood of San Diego, who were recognized
by the men who come from Monte Rey. They tell
me that they have always had this habit, and so I
infer that this is why the thing happened, for when
we came through the first time we saw more than
two hundred, but there was no other trouble than
the inclination which they manifested for stealing
a few of our belongings.—From Monte Rey to Santa
Catharina, 152 leagues.

Saturday, May 7.—With no other incident than
the one related, we left this place, going generally

---

[1] At Reed's, or Lower Willows, on Coyote Creek, at the lower end
of Collins Valley.

[2] Father Font tells us that this warning by Father Garcés was
carved on a willow tree.

toward the southeast, till we reached San Gregorio,[1] where we turned to the east-southeast; then, going in this direction, at the end of ten or eleven leagues we arrived at the marsh of San Sevastián.—From Monte Rey to the Siénega de San Sevastián, 163 leagues.

Sunday, May 8.—Shortly after sunrise we set forth on the trail of the troops who are going ahead, with the hope of finding some watering place between this marsh and the lake of Santa Olaya. We traveled as much as possible to the east-southeast, but also to the south, in order to go around the sand dunes which stretch across. I kept in this direction and on the trail mentioned for only seven leagues, after which I took a higher latitude than the one followed by the troops. In this direction I traveled ten more leagues, to the Pozo de las Angustias,[2] where I arrived after nightfall. Then, the men having refreshed themselves, because there was no pasturage in the vicinity we continued our journey for five more leagues to the east-southeast.

Monday, May 9.—Having covered the distance stated we arrived well toward morning at this lake of Santa Olaya. The march just described is the longest in all the new road which has been discovered. But by making it from the wells of El Carrizal to those of Santa Rosa de las Lajas, with all

[1] San Gregorio was on San Felipe Creek, at the lower end of Borrego Valley. San Sebastián was at Harper's Well on San Felipe Creek, near its junction with Carrizo Creek.

[2] This stop was evidently at El Carrizal. See Díaz's statement, p. 296.

convenience, and going from these by another march
to the marsh of San Sevastián, in this way any pack
train can accomplish it without very great trouble.
The latitude of this lake was observed and found
to be in 32° 34'.—From Monte Rey to the Laguna
de Santa Olaya on the Colorado River, 185 leagues.

This afternoon we proceeded up the meadows of
the Colorado River, going generally to the east, and
having traveled about four leagues we camped in
the territory of the Yumas.[1] The joy with which
they welcomed us was a matter for admiration,
for they all incessantly kept crying "Capitán,"
"Señor," "Soldados," "Compañeros," and in this
mood the many who assembled remained till morning. During the night they reported to me, with
extraordinary regret on their part, that the soldiers
whom I left to the care of Captain Palma had departed, contrary to the advice of the Captain himself and of many others, solely on account of the
vague report which had come from the sierra to
the effect that the heathen there had killed me and
all the soldiers. They told me also that these soldiers had left in charge of Palma some provisions,
which he had kept in his own house until the arrival
of Father Garcés, who was there now awaiting me,
but that there was no other occurrence.

Tuesday, May 10.—Traveling east-northeast[2]
and east for eight leagues, I arrived at noon at the
junction of the rivers and the site of San Dionicio.

[1] Camp was evidently at the place where Anza camped on February 11 of the same year.

[2] By a slip the MS, reads "east-northwest."

Shortly afterward Captain Palma arrived, rejoicing like all his tribe, many hundreds of whom I already had at my side. Treating me with as much assurance as if I were his own kind, he manifested his contentment at my return, and his great regret for the departure of the soldiers whom I had left in his care until the return of Father Garcés, to whom he told me he had delivered some packs of provisions and some cattle. He said that those who departed had gone without his approval. For all this and the fidelity which he has shown in this affair, I gave to this heathen captain the thanks and the praise which he merits.

At three in the afternoon of this same day the captain had ready for me a strong raft so that I might cross both rivers, accompanied by the hundreds of people, in order that they might guide it, and with whom I felt as secure as if they were my own people. The captain himself carried me and put me on the raft, together with Father Juan Díaz and a servant of mine. On it I crossed the rivers, whose waters must be six hundred yards wide, but I had such confidence that in all my life I have never crossed a river with greater assurance, since even though the craft had been wrecked I had close at hand more than five hundred persons ready to rescue me. The same security was felt by all those who accompanied me, and who were taken over by the Indians with all of our baggage this same afternoon.[1]

[1] The crossing was made above the Fort Yuma hill, and below the place where the rivers unite.

At five in the afternoon I arrived at the camp, where I was awaited by Father Garcés and the soldiers who had come ahead, and who corroborated the reports just related, saying that nothing else had occurred in their journey worthy of note.— From Monte Rey to the junction of the Gila and Colorado rivers, 197 leagues.

UP THE GILA AND HOME

Wednesday, May 11.—The latitude of this place, which is close to San Dionicio, was observed and found to be in 32° 44'. This does not agree with the observation made by the first discoverer, Father Francisco Eusevio Quino, as is related in the book of the *Afanes Apostólicos*[1] on folio 288, where it states that he found it to be in 35° 30'. This day was dedicated to rest for all. Since we have returned to the Colorado River from a much greater distance beyond it than any of our predecessors who have journeyed to it even thought of going, it will not be beside the point to say that we have tried to learn from these heathen and others, wherever we have gone, in what direction the famous Sierra Azul is situated, and the Laguna de Azogue, which is noted by Lieutenant Don Matheo Mange,[2] companion of this Father Quino, in a book which he dedicated to the most excellent Viceroy, Duke of Alburquerque, or the Rio Amarillo on the other side of the Colorado, but, even taking their existence for granted, we have not discovered any ground for concluding that these tales can be verified.

Thursday, May 12.—We still remained here, and since the Reverend Father Garcés had told me that

[1] José de Ortega, *Apostólicos Afanes* (Barcelona, 1754).
[2] Juan Matheo Mange, *Luz de Tierra Incógnita* (Mexico, 1926).

by the courier[1] who goes directly to his Excellency
he had requested the governor of the provinces to
send some provisions to this place, thinking that
with those which we have left we should not have
sufficient to go out to my presidio, I, knowing differently, decided to send today two soldiers to take
back any provisions which they might be bringing,
because I am not able to take the road by which they
ought to come.[2] This afternoon I had the party
which came from Monte Rey[3] recross the Colorado
River, in order that they might return to that post,
with knowledge of the directions and the routes
through which run the roads from there to Sonora,
and of the places where they can get guides if they
should wish to come to that province.

Friday, May 13.—Soon after sunrise we raised
our train to begin the march up the Jila River,
which most of them did. But I remained here until
Palma, the captain of the Yumas, finished taking
over to the other side of the Colorado River four
cattle which I gave to the party that was about to
return to Monte Rey. Having done this he came to
bid me goodbye. At the same time an old Yuma
came with the report that some individuals of the
Cojat tribe were waiting until I should leave, in
order to rob the party mentioned of some horses, because they were from the region where the Jahuen-

[1] Juan Bautista Valdés.

[2] Valdés went by way of Caborca and Horcasitas, the route by
which the supplies would come. Anza returned up the Gila River.

[3] These were the six soldiers of Monterey who accompanied Anza
to learn the road.

ches,[1] their enemies, lived, and whom therefore they did not recognize as their relatives, as they did me and my troops. The informant added that most of the same nation were opposed to this plan.

Since in such matters nothing ought to be depreciated, however simple and harmless it may appear, I decided immediately, in order to prevent any misfortune, fo send Captain Palma with the native of California to escort the party from that district, informing the corporal about the matter in writing, and sending him other orders pertinent to the affair, and bearing on all his journey, and likewise notifying the authors of the disturbance that I was waiting to see if they carried out their evil plan, in order to punish them. For effect I called back our train, which returned in the afternoon of this day, at the same time that a relative of Captain Palma reported to me that he was taking with him more than two hundred selected Yumas to go to conduct the party in safety.

Saturday, May 14.—Nothing particular occurred.

Sunday, May 15.—At twelve o'clock today Captain Palma returned with the native Californian, who brought me a report from the corporal of the party which is returning to Monte Rey, that he was about to continue his march from the place where they were leaving him. He said that thus far there had been no disturbance to cause him to worry, and that he did not expect any from that place forward;

---

[1] Cajuenches. Anza distinguished between the Cojats and the Cajuenches, whereas others generally consider them as identical.

that Captain Palma had delivered to him two mounts which, becoming lost the day before, had been stolen by two young heathen, from whose possession Palma took them, punishing the offenders; and that Palma at the same time recovered an ax which they had stolen from us.[1] Palma brought the ax and I gave it to him. In reply he informed me that the rumor mentioned was only the talk of some young men, whom he would have chided even without my presence; and that he will do this way as long as he lives, during which time neither he nor his tribe will cease their affection for us or their fidelity to the king.

I again told this heathen captain that he must maintain peace with the neighboring tribes, because it was the wish of both majesties, and that he should be sure to bring to our settlements any Spaniard who might come to his territory. This and other orders he agreed to carry out, and as a reward for the services which he has performed for the king I gave him my bastón, four beeves, and some articles of clothing; indeed, I should have been glad to be able to reward this heathen barbarian more liberally, for his equal is not to be found amongst his kind.

At three in the afternoon I said goodbye to this captain and set forth up the Gila River, which, from its source to its junction with the Colorado, runs in general from the northeast and east to the south and

<hr>

[1] Anza mentions this theft on his way to California. See p. 48.

west. I decided to ascend it in order to make my
return to my presidio more direct and convenient, as
well as to make peace among all the tribes which live
on its borders. Having gone three leagues I camped
for the night on the banks of the river at a place
where there is pasturage.[1]—From Monte Rey to the
Gila River, 197 leagues.[2]

Monday, May 16.—At daybreak I set out along
the river, whose abundance of water and good lands
for crops continue, although there is little or no pasturage, for in the distance of eight or nine leagues
only one small piece was encountered.[3]

Tuesday, May 17.—At daybreak I set out and
ascended the same river six leagues, at the end of
which we passed the point of the sierra from which
branches off the range of the Aguaje Empinado
mentioned in our coming, to which I gave the name
of San Pasqual.[4] To the distance mentioned we
added two more leagues, camping for the night at
a place where some pasturage was found.

Wednesday, May 18.—At the same time as yesterday we continued up the same river, striking a
trail of some heathen. Following it four leagues, it
led us to a village of about a hundred persons of
the Cocomaricopa tribe, most of whom were not
frightened, because there was a Pápago or Pima
among them. By means of him and of my interpreter in this language we all understood each other,

1 Up the river about half way from Yuma to the Gila Range.
2 This number is clearly an error. See p. 117.
3 Camp was near Laguna Salobre. Díaz says it was near a lake.
4 Mohawk Range. Camp was two leagues above.

and by the same means I exhorted them in the same way as the Yumas to maintain peace with this and other tribes, ordering everyone who might be injured by another to report to the presidios. I decided to remain the rest of this day amongst these heathen, who presented me with the few provisions which they had.

This tribe is known both to us and to the Pimas and Yumas by the name which I have given them. Their language is the same as that of the latter, and the same is true of their customs, stature, and robustness. They differ from the Yumas in that all go covered, especially their private parts, and better armed, customs which they have learned from the Pimas or Pápagos, to whom they are related. Some of them live on this river, but most of them dwell in the mountains between the Colorado and the Gila. Their number, I am informed by them and the Pápagos or Pimas, is not much less than that of the Yumas. At all times when our troops have passed through their country these Cocomaricopas have been friendly to them. The place where we are to-day I named San Bernardino.[1] The north latitude was observed today and it came out 33° 02'.—From Monte Rey to the first village of the Cocomaricopas and the site of San Bernardino on the Gila River, 221 leagues.

Thursday, May 19.—At daybreak I set out up the same river on the bank opposite the one which I followed yesterday, and at a distance of five leagues

[1] San Bernardino was near the present town of Palomas.

from San Bernardino we passed a good spring of hot water, from which it takes its name, Ojo Caliente.[1] The water is sufficient to irrigate a large piece of ground, which evidently was done in former times by the Cocomaricopas, but they have abandoned the place on account of the wars with the Yumas, as I am told by a Pima who is with me. In addition to these five leagues three more were traveled, until we stopped where there was pasturage and camped for the night.

Friday, May 20.—At sunrise we recrossed the Gila which here, as well as in all the stretch where we have followed it, is generally not less than four palms deep, although this is the time of the greatest drought. The natives tell me that when it is in flood, which is during the summer rains, it is not less than five hundred varas wide, and from the signs which it leaves this appears to be the case.

As soon as we had passed the river we climbed some good-sized hills which lasted for three leagues.[2] Then we descended to the river bottom, along which we continued for two more leagues, to the neighborhood of San Simón y Judas de Upasoitac, where I camped for the night. This place is well peopled by these Cocomaricopas, and others who really are the same, although they call them Opas, to which are added now some Pápagos or Pimas who have deserted their country on account of the great drought and the still greater famine which is experienced in it.

[1] Now called Agua Caliente.
[2] Painted Rock Range. Díaz gives added detail here.

Because of the first of these drawbacks mentioned, I cannot cut across from here to my presidio, which I ought to be able to do, for it is distant only forty leagues over good terrain with good pasturage. I therefore decided to make this journey by way of the settlements of the Pimas, for which purpose it is necessary to ascend the river still farther.

Saturday, May 21.—Having traveled a league I camped on the very site of San Simón y Judas de Upasoitac.[1] The latitude of this place was observed and was found to be in 33° 15'.—From Monte Rey to Opasoitac, last village of the Cocomaricopas on the same Gila River, 233 leagues.

Having been in this place on other occasions, the Reverend Father Garcés decided to remain here for the purpose of trying to find out whether, by means of the tribes who live between here and the province of Moqui, of which they tell, it is possible to send a letter to the province of New Mexico. A servant of mine voluntarily remained with him. At half past two in the afternoon I set out from here for the settlements of the Pimas, over good terrain, in order to cut off the bend which the river makes to the north, which is entirely uninhabited. Having gone seven leagues, by traveling into the night, camp was made to rest in a place where pasturage was found.[2]

Sunday, May 22.—At daybreak we continued the march, and having covered six leagues I halted at the Pima village of Sutaquison, which is maintained

[1] Upasoitac was at Gila Bend.

[2] About half way between Maricopa Range and Sierra Estrella. Díaz tells us they camped on an arroyo.

permanently on the river and has more than two thousand inhabitants. Its natives, as has already been said, are devoted to raising crops. One of the fields which I saw, and which they tell me is the smallest one they have, I estimate has planted in it from sixty to eighty fanegas of wheat, marvelously fine and about ready to harvest.—From Monte Rey to El Sutaquison[1] and the first Pimas on the Gila River, 246 leagues.

This village acknowledges as its juez or captain the person who is captain of my presidio. For this reason I appointed a governor here, as has always been the custom, which office, as well as that of the village which follows, was vacant because of the death of those who held them. Here there is seen very clearly, from the foundations and even parts of the walls, a palace[2] of the people who formed the nation which it is believed went to establish their empire in the City of Mexico. As far as the site of Upasoitac further back, and this one of which we are now speaking, reaches the infernal pest of the Apaches, who not long ago killed twelve natives of the former, and still more recently sixty of the latter settlement.

Monday, May 23.—Continuing along the bottom land, after traveling two leagues I halted for the night at the village of Juturitucan,[3] or San Juan Capistrano, which is larger in every way than the

[1] At Vah Ki, on the Gila, east of Sierra Estrella.
[2] The Casa Blanca (White House) at Vah Ki (Old House).
[3] Also called Uturituc.

foregoing village. Here I appointed as governor and alcalde two brothers, sons of the one who formerly held these offices. They have under their authority about three thousand persons, all of whom live closely united, having been harried by the last attacks of the Apaches. The fields of wheat which they now possess are so large that, standing in the middle of them, one cannot see the ends, because of their great length. They are very wide, too, embracing the whole width of the valley on both sides, and the maize fields are of similar proportions. Having observed the latitude of Sutaquison yesterday, it was computed to be in 33° 24'.—From Monte Rey to El Juturitucan, the last Pimas on the Gila River, 248 leagues.

Tuesday, May 24.—Raising our train at sunrise, and traveling two leagues along the same river, we halted on its banks at a place where there was pasturage.[1] At this distance up the river from where we are there is another palace which is known as the Palace of Moctezuma, and a town larger than the one mentioned farther back. The structure of this palace is a labyrinth, of which experts have made careful drawings. It is seen that it had several storeys, and even today the walls are so high that they can be seen for more than a league away. And it is at least a league from the river, which they introduced underneath the very palace and to the rest of the town, in order to have water at hand. The material of these buildings is purely of earth, but

[1] About at Comari, mentioned by Anza in his second expedition.

they also contain a mixture of small stones or coarse sand, which appears by its consistency like the finest mortar or cement, a better test of which is that it still endures after the many years which they estimate it has lasted.[1]

Leaving behind us the Gila River, at two in the afternoon we continued our march, now going south, in which direction we traveled until midnight, when a halt was made to rest for awhile.

Wednesday, May 25.—Before daylight we again took up the march in the same direction, traveling over level land the same as yesterday afternoon, and at eleven we halted at the point of the spring of the town of Tucsón, to recover from the heat of the sun. Continuing this afternoon, after going about a league and a half we arrived at the town named, which belongs to the jurisdiction of my presidio, and is now inhabited by Upper Pimas, of which it has eighty families.

This place is twenty-four leagues from the Gila, and, although I have traveled this distance without water, it is not because there is none in the middle of the stretch. Indeed, there is water at the site of Aquituni,[2] the residence of a village of Pápagos comprising sixty families, but I did not go that way because the land is broken, and because I feared some encounter with the Apaches, which are now

[1] This is the famous Casa Grande.

[2] In his diary of his second expedition Anza gives the name of El Aquituni to his camp just west of Picacho Peak, and I assume that the two are identical.

Presidio de Tubac que es el termino cargo

En el encargue all Reverendo Padre Frai Juan Diaz, que ha sido, quien a hecho las Observaciones, de nuestro transito, expresase, en un Mapa, el que hemos efectuado, pa darle una idea, al Exmo Sr Virrey, de los Rumbos, Ranchenias, y demas particularidades, que hemos Notado.

a 27   Dias doce de el. llego al mencionado Presidio, el resto   Del Monte Rey al
sen y   de la expedicion, que dese atras, en lo que se ha verificado, la   Presidio de Tubac
        totalo conclucion, de ella, con las felicidades, y ventajas que   290 legs
        quedan, expresadas, en lo descripto anterior, por lo que sea
        pug el Sr de los Exercitos, Vendito y Alavado.

Y trece de Noviembre de mil setecientos, setenta y quatro
años, saqué esta copia, pa entregar en el mismo dia, al
Exmo Sr Virrey, Governador, y capitan General, en esta Ciudad de Mexico, en cuias manos, quatrote tengo
entregado, el Mapa, que antecedente mte se cita ———

Juan Bapta de Anza

En 24 de Noviembre de
74 se saco la comunid
por principal Veste
Mano para dar cu-
enta à S. M.

Last Page of Anza's Complete Diary.

very frequent there, for I was not in condition to
bring our train through in safety, because all the
men with me are mounted on very crippled mules,
which even if they are not crippled are useless in
such cases.—From Monte Rey to the Pima pueblo
of El T[u]csón, 274 leagues.

Thursday, May 26.—Before daylight I received
through six soldiers of my company an order from
the adjutant inspector, Don Antonio Bonilla,[1] to
hasten my arrival at the presidio, he having been
told of my coming this way by the two soldiers mentioned on the 12th of the present month. In fulfillment of this order I set out from this pueblo a little
after sunrise toward the south, in which direction
my presidio lies, hoping to reach it today, although
it is twenty leagues away. I left appropriate orders
to the effect that all the soldiers who have accompanied me in the expedition and all our train shall
continue slowly, in order to arrive tomorrow morning.

In the company of the six soldiers mentioned and
of the Reverend Father Fray Juan Díaz, who wished
to come with me, I continued my journey, and at the
end of the first five leagues I passed through the
pueblo of San Xavier del Bac,[2] capital of the foregoing, having forty families of the same tribe; and
continuing for fifteen more leagues, at sunset I

[1] Bonilla later became a very able administrator in the viceroy's
corps at Mexico City.

[2] The mission is still in operation, now serving the Indians of the
Pápago Reservation.

arrived at the presidio of Tubac, which is the one in my charge. Here I requested Reverend Fray Juan Díaz, the one who has made the observations in our transit, to show on a map what we have done, in order to give an idea to his Excellency, the Viceroy, of the routes, villages, and other particulars which we have noted.

Friday, May 27.—At twelve o'clock today the rest of the caravan, which I left behind, arrived at this presidio. Herewith the expedition has come completely to an end, with the successes and advantages which are set forth in the foregoing document, wherefore may the Lord of Hosts be blessed and praised.—From Monte Rey to the presidio of Tubac, 294 leagues.

Today, the 13th of November, 1774, I made this copy to deliver on the same day to his Excellency, the Viceroy, Governor, and Captain-general in this City of Mexico, into whose hands likewise I have delivered the map which has been mentioned.

JUAN BAP.TA DE ANZA (Rubric).

On the 24th of December, 1774, a certified copy was made from the original of this diary, with which to make a report to his Majesty.

ANZA'S DIARY FROM TUBAC TO SAN GABRIEL

1774

DIARY OF THE MARCH AND OPERATIONS
WHICH I, THE UNDERSIGNED CAPTAIN OF
CAVALRY AND OF THE ROYAL PRESIDIO OF
TUBAC, IN THE PROVINCE OF SONORA, UNDER-
TAKE AND MAKE FOR THE PURPOSE OF OPEN-
ING A ROAD FROM THAT PROVINCE TO NORTH-
ERN CALIFORNIA BY WAY OF THE GILA AND
COLORADO RIVERS, ON WHICH EXPEDITION I
AM GOING BY COMMISSION OF THE MOST
EXCELLENT SENOR LIEUTENANT-GENERAL DON
ANTONIO MARIA BUCARELI Y URSUA, VICEROY,
GOVERNOR AND CAPTAIN-GENERAL OF NEW
SPAIN, AS IS SHOWN BY HIS ORDER OF THE
17TH OF SEPTEMBER OF THE PAST YEAR OF
1773.

PERSONS COMPRISED IN AND GOING ON THIS
EXPEDITION[1]

The commander of the expedition, Don Juan
    Baptista de Anza 1
The father preachers de propaganda fide of the
    College of the Cross of Querétaro
        Fray Juan Díaz.. 1
        Fray Francisco Garcés.................................. 1
Twenty volunteer soldiers of the same presidio,
    including a corporal... 20
A soldier sent from Mexico by order of his Ex-
    cellency, because he knows the roads from
    California to the ports of San Diego and
    Monte Rey[2] 1
A native of the same California, who, on the 26th
    of December of last year, came out to the Gila
    and Colorado rivers and from these rivers to
    the pueblos of the Pimería and the presidio of
    El Altar[3] 1
An interpreter of the Pima language, because
    most of the languages of the interior in the
    direction in which we are going are related
    to it 1

[1] Diario de la Ruta y Operaciones q.ᵉ io el Ynfrascripto Cap.ⁿ de
Cavallería y del R.¹ Pres.º de Tubac . . . Hago y practico en solicitud de Abrír camino de dha Provinz.ᵃ â la California Setemptrional.
A.G.P.M., Correspondencia de los Virreyes, Bucareli, 1774, Tomo
38/55. In Diario y Cartas de Anza.
[2] This soldier was Juan Bautista Valdés.   [3] Sebastián Tarabal.

A native of the presidio under my charge, to
serve as carpenter... 1

Five muleteers and two of my servants.................. 7

Total... 34

Item.—Thirty-five pack loads of provisions, munitions of war, tools, and other things useful for
roads or lands unknown.

Item.—Sixty-five beeves on foot.[1]

Item.—One hundred and forty mounts, including
those which it is proposed to obtain farther on
at the pueblo of Cavorca.[2]

January 8, 1774.—Having arranged for all the
foregoing, this morning Mass was sung with all the
ceremony which the country permits, to invoke the
divine aid in this expedition, and I named as its
protectors the Blessed Trinity and the Mystery of
the Immaculate Conception of Most Holy Mary.
This having been done the march was begun at
twelve o'clock, and having traveled for a league to
the north[3] from the presidio, a halt was made in
order to pass the night at the ford of San Xavier
del Bac.[4]

[1] These cattle were driven for food on the way.

[2] It is not certain just how many mounts were actually taken because Anza was unable to get his full quota at Caborca.

[3] The march was begun toward the north in order to get around
the end of Tumacácori Range, which lies west of Tubac.

[4] The ford of San Xavier del Bac was evidently a crossing from
the east to the west side of the Santa Cruz River.

January 9.—At eight o'clock in the morning we set forth south-southwest over the Camino Real [1] for the western pueblos of the Pima tribe and for the presidio of El Altar, which is situated among them and is the most advanced of the presidios of Sonora toward the head of the Gulf of California.

It was not necessary to go by way of this presidio and the pueblos in its neighborhood, since we ought to look for the port of Monte Rey toward the northwest and north-northwest of my presidio, in which directions it is certain there is a way out to the Gila and Colorado rivers; but I am obliged to depart from this plan, which I have always wished to adopt, for the following reasons:

The first reason is to go, as the safest way, by the road and country followed as far as my presidio by the above-mentioned native of California, who fled from the new mission of San Gabriel which, according to his report, is about half way between the ports of San Diego and Monte Rey, and came out after a long peregrination to the rivers named and from them to the presidio of El Altar. From these rivers, if it is possible, we shall turn straight to the port last named,[2] if it appears that by that route there is the same abundance of water, pasturage, and good land which this native says there is on the route by which he came.

[1] This tells us that Anza was on the regular highway to Saric and Altar.

[2] Anza started out with a very definite intention to go from the Yuma junction directly to Monterey.

The second reason is that a large number of Apaches attacked the horse herd of my presidio on the 2d of last month and carried off or stole from it about a hundred and thirty animals, including many of those set aside and destined for this enterprise. It was not possible to repair this loss in the neighborhood of my presidio; and to await there a reinforcement from other districts had the disadvantage that the animals which escaped such piracies were exposed to total loss. Besides, I should miss the season which I judged most favorable for this expedition. For these reasons and with the hope that in the vicinity of the presidio of El Altar the animals which we lack might be obtained, I decided to make my itinerary through it. And, by way of preparation, I requested the governor of the provinces to give appropriate orders to the effect that in it or its pueblos nearby they should furnish me any animals which they might have, in order to improve my equipment.

Finally, it was thought well to ascertain as soon as possible the road from the Pimería that runs near the Gulf of California, because that is the only region which without risk from the Apaches can supply the Peninsula,[1] which it is desired to sustain, with the provisions which it may need, for by the road which it is intended to open there will be complete security even as far as the City of Mexico, and this is not true of any other route.

[1] He probably refers to both Californias and not alone to what we now call the Peninsula.

Today's march was concluded at vespers, after we had traveled eight leagues, as far as the site of La Arivaca.[1] This place has an abundance of water and of the best pasturage. It was inhabited by Spaniards until the end of 1751, the year of the uprising of the Pima tribe, which massacred many of the inhabitants of the place and finally despoiled the ranch of all kinds of stock which they possessed. Experience shows that more than five thousand head of large stock might be supported here.

The site is memorable, too, for the battle which took place here a few months after this uprising of the Pimas. More than two thousand of these natives came under command of their captain-general to attack less than eighty soldiers of our presidios led by Captain Don Bernardo de Urrea, but they were cut to pieces with a loss of more than two hundred rebels who remained stretched out on the field, and from this punishment their pacification resulted.

This place has many good mines of silver, which were worked until the past year of '67, when they were abandoned by reason of increased raids of the Apaches, who on three occasions beat down those who were working the mines.[2] Small flakes of virgin silver have been found here and gold placers of medium-sized grains. These metals have been taken

[1] Arivaca is still on the map in the same general region. Three miles east of it is Arivaca Ranch. In his description Anza evidently included the whole valley, and from his directions I conclude that he camped on the upper waters of Arivaca Creek not far from Oro Blanco Mine.

[2] Numerous mines have been worked in the region in recent times, and some are operating now.

out in my time, and therefore I have seen them. There is also opportunity to plant here any kind of crop which may need irrigation.

January 10.—At nine o'clock in the morning we set forth to the south-southwest, passing on each side various mountain chains, and with a very strong south wind which threatened rain. Having traveled seven leagues we halted at Agua Escondida,[1] so-called because it is a quarter of a league off the highway to the right. The place has an abundance of good pasturage.

The 11th and 12th we remained in this place, because here and since the night of the 10th snow and rain have been falling freely.

January 13.—Because the day dawned clear and calm we set forth in the same direction, and after going seven leagues we reached the pueblo of El Saric.[2] This is a native pueblo of Pimas Altos,[3] is the farthest north of the western Pimas, and has forty families. It is administered in spiritual matters, like all those of this tribe and of this river downstream, by the apostolic fathers of the College of the Cross of Querétaro. The river which flows past the pueblo rises in the spring of El Búsani,[4] about a league and a half to the north. Because of its own abundance of water and its very fertile lands, both in its own meadow and in other places roundabout,

[1] On the southern slope of Sierra del Pajarito.
[2] Saric, called by the natives Sáriqui, is still on the map.
[3] Upper Pimas.
[4] The ruins of the old mission church of Búsanic stand by the roadside some four miles north of Saric.

it is capable of maintaining three thousand families
of Spaniards with any kind of grain which they
may wish to plant, and it would also maintain a thousand head of stock of all kinds. There is likewise
opportunity for cutting pine and other sorts of
timber.

Seven leagues to the northeast of this pueblo is
the site of La Arizona, or Las Volas, celebrated because of the nuggets of virgin silver which were
found there in the year 1736, some of them weighing
as much as a hundred and fifty arrobas.[1] This statement has been doubted, but it is well authenticated,
because there are still living many persons who possessed them. And I am able to furnish documents to
prove it, since my father sequestrated them, because
he thought that anything so marvelous and strange
ought to belong solely to his Majesty. And although
this procedure was not approved entirely by the
opinion of the Audiencia of Mexico, as a result of the
report which this Audiencia gave to the Council of
Castile, the decision of my father was sustained by
that body, which declared that he did right to seques-
trate the nuggets. In confirmation of this decision,
he was given a commission by his Majesty requiring
him to operate in that district on behalf of the royal
exchequer.

In the opinion of persons experienced in mining,
I have heard it said, they failed then and have still

[1] La Arizona, or Arizonac, was in Sonora some ten or fifteen miles
southwest of Nogales. An *arroba* is twenty-five pounds.

failed to discover the mother lode from which such
nuggets were produced. For they say that since
it has been learned that this was a natural deposit
of silver, and not buried treasure as some presumed,
there must be such a mother lode, whose value, if it
is found, will be beyond comparison with what has
been taken out, although even this is great. They
add also, apart from what has been said, that the
immense mines which are still in that district could
be worked by the quicksilver process, which is not
established in this province of Sonora, to the serious
injury of the royal exchequer and of its inhabitants.
The lack of this practice is the reason why this prodigious site and others that are in the province have
not checked with good establishments the inroads
of the barbarous Apaches, to whom the passage
which they now enjoy through these places would not
then be so easy. In this one of Las Volas they even
find good-sized pieces of the best kind of silver, such
as was found in the first year of its discovery.

January 14.—At seven o'clock in the morning
we set forth down the Rio del Saric toward the south-
southwest, and having traveled four leagues we
halted at La Cuesta, because there is no more pasturage for some leagues ahead.[1]

---

[1] La Cuesta (the Ridge or Grade), still on the map, is twelve miles
from Saric. Tubutama is seven miles from La Cuesta, on the left
bank of the Altar River. Santa Teresa is entirely abandoned, but the
ruins of the mission church are seen by the roadside four and one-
half miles below Tubutama. Atil is five or six miles below the ruins
of Santa Teresa church.

January 15.—About seven o'clock in the morning we continued the march to the southwest, down the same river, and having traveled two leagues we passed through the pueblo of Tubutama, which is a settlement of about thirty families of these Pimas. Judging by the circumstances of the site, it must be in every way about a third smaller than that of El Saric. After going another league and a half we passed through Santa Thereza, a pueblo with twenty families of the same tribe, the place being a little smaller in every way than the foregoing. Two leagues further on we came to the pueblo of San Francisco del Atí, of thirty families of the same tribe. This place enjoys most beautiful and abundant lands for irrigation, with which, if they were only well cultivated, the place could maintain six times as many people as now inhabit it. In this pueblo and the two preceding a fair amount of stock could be raised, notwithstanding that the river bottom is not very abundant in pasturage. Halfway between Santa Thereza and Tubutama placers of gold were found a short time ago, and still later others of better quality were found in the vicinity of this pueblo of El Atí, where we are remaining for the rest of the day.

January 16.—At seven o'clock in the morning we set forth on the march down the same river toward the west, and having traveled about six leagues we halted at the pueblo of Oquitoa,[1] which consists of thirty families of the same tribe, and twelve families

[1] Oquitoa is twelve miles below Atil. Anza's estimate of distance is a little too liberal here.

of Spaniards who have settled here because of the opportunities for agriculture. With all the crops which could be raised in this pueblo it would be possible to maintain five times the present number of inhabitants and to have sufficient stock. In its neighborhood upstream there is a most beautiful marsh, and right there silver mines to be worked by the quicksilver process, which in any other place, where this process is in use, would afford their laborers superior advantages.

January 17.—Going west we traveled two leagues and arrived at the presidio of El Altar,[1] where camp was made because it threatened to rain and did rain to some extent, and to effect the exchange of some horses which arrived in a very bad condition, which was accomplished through the good offices of its captain, Don Bernardo de Urrea. This presidio has the regular force of fifty men, like most of those of the jurisdiction of the province of Sonora, and is the one most advanced toward the Gulf of California. It does not suffer like the rest from the continuous plague of Apaches, for only a few of them reach here and this at infrequent intervals. The pueblos upstream as far as Tubutama suffer the pest, and in a lesser degree the other three from that place downstream. At this presidio there are not very

[1] Altar is seven miles below Oquitoa, on a barren flat. Pitic, now called Pitiquito, is fifteen miles below Altar. The old mission church is on the west side of the town, facing the west. The old mission church of Caborca is six miles from the Oquitoa church, on the right bank of the river, and on the edge of the town of Caborca. Vísani still stands on the same site, some eighteen miles below Caborca.

considerable crops, for lack of water. Indeed, the
river reaches this point very much decreased because
of the bad country through which it passes, and since
the same is true from here forward, the stream does
not reach the Gulf.

January 18.—Because it was rainy in the morning we did not set forth today.

January 19.—At the usual hour we began the
march, going west-northwest, somewhat apart from
the river named, and having traveled a little more
than five leagues we halted at the spring of the pueblo
of Pitic.

January 20.—Two leagues were traveled in the
same direction and along the same bottom lands, as
far as the pueblo of Cavorca, where a halt was made
because here we had to get some riding animals
necessary for the journey. In this pueblo, the preceding one of Pitic, and that of Vísani, six leagues
downstream, are found assembled the Pimas who remained after they surrendered, as a result of the
expedition made against them and their allies, the
Seris, in the past years from 1768 to 1770. Among
these natives now there is no indication of any new
uprising. Four leagues from Vísani and the same
distance from this pueblo of Cavorca there are fairly
good silver mines, but they are not esteemed here,
through lack of the quicksilver process, for, since the
ore is somewhat mixed with copper, in separating it
with fire the silver which it contains is lost. Twenty-
five leagues from Vísani, which is the distance to the

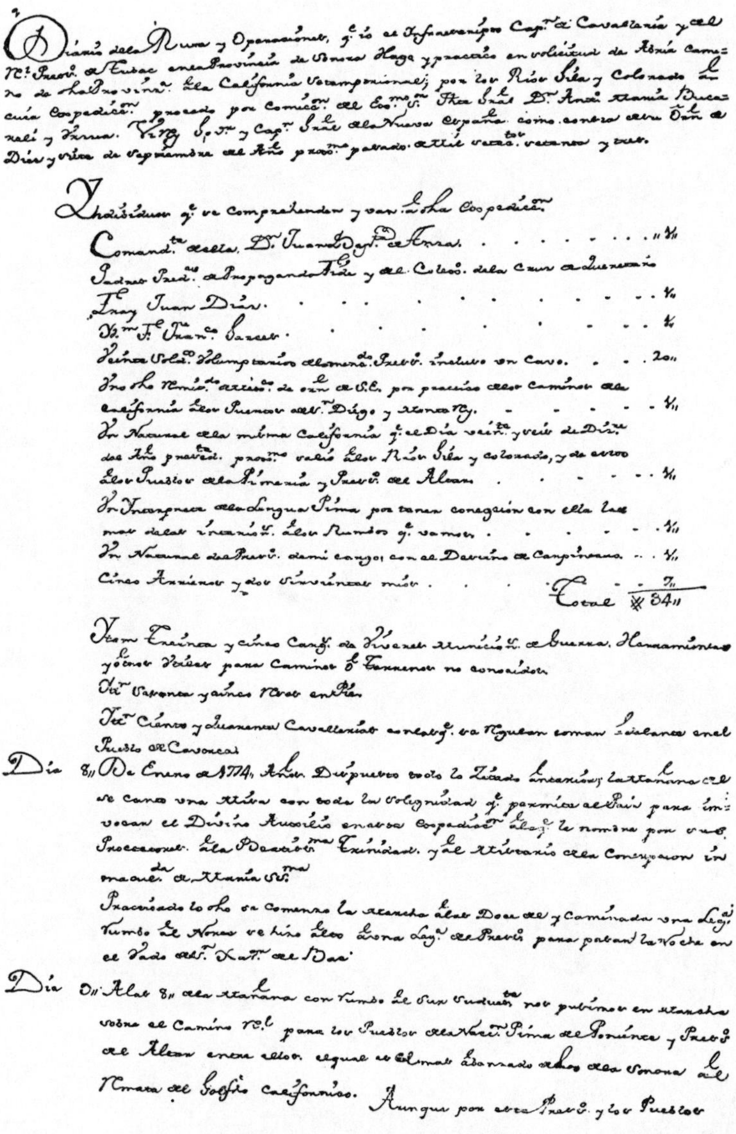

Diario de la Ruta y Operaciones, que yo el infrascripto Capitán de Cavallería y del Real Presidio de Tubac en esta Provincia de Sonora hago y practico en solicitud de abrir camino de dicha Provincia a la California Septentrional; por los Ríos Gila y Colorado, en cuya expedición procedo por comisión del Excelentísimo Señor Frey Don Antonio María Bucareli y Ursúa, Virrey, Gobernador y Capitán General de la Nueva España, como consta de su Orden de dos y veinte de Septiembre del Año próximo pasado de mil setecientos setenta y tres.

Individuos que se comprehenden y van en dicha Expedición

Comandante de ella Don Juan Bautista de Anza 1

Padres Predicadores de Propaganda Fide y del Colegio de la Cruz de Querétaro

Fray Juan Díaz 1

Ídem Fray Francisco Garcés 1

Veinte Soldados Voluntarios de mi mencionado Presidio inclusive un Cavo . . . 20

Otro de dicho Número agregado de orden de S.E. por práctico de los Caminos de la California a los Puertos de San Diego y Monterrey 1

Un Natural de la misma California que el Día veinte y seis de Diciembre del Año próximo pasado salió a los Ríos Gila y Colorado, y de estos a los Pueblos de la Pimería y Presidio del Altar 1

Un Intérprete de la Lengua Pima por tener conexión con ella las más de las Naciones a los Rumbos que vamos 1

Un Natural de este Presidio de mi cargo, con el destino de Carpintero . . . 1

Cinco Arrieros y dos sirvientes míos 7

Total 34

Item Treinta y cinco Cargas de Víveres, Municiones de Guerra, Herramientas y otros útiles para caminar por Terrenos no conocidos.

Ítem Sesenta y cinco Reses en pie.

Ítem Ciento y cuarenta Cavallerías con las que se regulan tomar [illegible] en el Pueblo de Caborca.

Día 8 De Enero de 1774 Años. Dispuesto todo lo dicho necesario, la mañana de este día se cantó una Misa con toda la solemnidad que permite el País para implorar el Divino Auxilio en esta expedición, a la que se nombra por sus Protectores a la Beatísima Trinidad, y al Misterio de la Concepción inmaculada de María Santísima.

Practicado lo dicho se comenzó la marcha a las Doce del día y caminada una Legua rumbo al Norte se hizo alto a una Legua del Presidio para pasar la Noche en el Vado [illegible] del Bac.

Día 9 A las 8 de la mañana con rumbo al Sudueste nos pusimos en marcha sobre el Camino Real para los Pueblos de la Nación Pima de Poniente y Presidio del Altar, [illegible] de la Sonora al Mar del Golfo Californico. Aunque por este Presidio y los Pueblos

First page of Anza's diary to San Gabriel.

sea, there are good beds of crystallized salt, which abounds or is scarce according to the amount of rain.

January 21.—By order of the governor of the provinces two droves of mules were brought to me that I might choose what I needed, but whereas I had dreamed of getting here some superior animals which I need for an enterprise of such importance, I saw only a few veritable skeletons of animals unfit for even light work. Notwithstanding that I had others shown me and that our necessity was so great, I was able to select only two which, although they were the best, were not considered able to make a march of even eight leagues. Therefore I was left in the same need as that in which I arrived at this pueblo.[1] Although I knew that this lack of equipment would be a considerable drawback for the continuation of my journey, I decided not to delay to make further efforts, for I ran the risk that even though I should make them, they might turn out to be as fruitless as those which I have made hitherto, on account of the bad state of this province with regard to saddle animals, and any further delay I judged to be still more prejudicial to the enterprise. No march was made today because our muleteer, who left us at the presidio of El Altar to go to the mining camp at La Sieneguilla[2] to bring shoes for his mules, did not arrive today as he promised to do.

January 22.—In order better to divide the journey, at noon we started northwest, leaving the river

---

[1] This failure to get mules was a serious handicap to Anza.

[2] Cieneguilla, now called Ciénega, is south of Altar.

of Cavorca almost at our backs, and having traveled about four leagues over good terrain, this continuing we came opposite the point of a fair-sized range which the Pimas call Piast and Buccomari at the right and smaller hills at the left, making plain the road which we have to travel. In addition to these four leagues two more were traveled, until we reached a flat with some pasturage, where camp was made for the night. I named the site San Yldephonso.[1]

January 23.—We set forth on the march at eight o'clock in the morning, continuing on the same road. Going northwest and north-northwest, we traveled eight or nine leagues, until we reached the wells of Baipia or Aribaipia, by both of which names they are known. The natives say these wells never fail to give forth the little water which they now afford. Some pasturage is also found here, although not much. In front of these wells, looking to the northeast, is the Sierra del Piast, which with another forms a pass leading to the center of the country inhabited by the Pápagos. Three leagues before reaching the wells, between some small hills at the foot of which the road runs, there is such a good opportunity to collect water that with a few hours' work enough could be gathered even to plant some crops.

[1] San Ildefonso was near Cerro Babura. Anza's route was close to the road used today, perhaps a little to the east of it. Sierra de Buccomari was clearly Sierra de Chupurate. Aribaipia, now called Arivaipa, is at the crossing of Arroyo El Coyote, on the Pápago trail. Sierra del Piast was the present Sierra de la Basura. The place where Anza said that Arroyo El Coyote could be dammed was evidently at Tajitos.

At these wells we found two families of the Pápago tribe. I do not know why they were given this name, for their language, their clothing, customs, and other characteristics are the same as those of the tribe we call Pimas. The only difference is that some are reduced to pueblos and others are not, although most of those who now enjoy such civilization were brought to it from the Papaguería, without which circumstance the pueblos of the Pimería would not exist today with even the few people which they now possess. These Pápagos are very little to be feared by us, as has been experienced on the few occasions when they have rebelled, in imitation or at the instigation of the Pimas, and for which these unfortunates have paid a heavy price.[1] Because of their proximity they commonly live most of the winter in our settlements, both of Spaniards and of Indians, being employed at some kind of labor by means of which they acquire a little clothing, at least enough for the requirements of modesty in either sex.

The country inhabited by these people, most of which I have traveled over before now, is deserted in the winter time for the reasons given above. It is one of the most sterile regions imaginable. The water which is to be found in a few places is very little in amount, and for lack of it they plant no crops. The only ones they raise are those which grow with little moisture, such as calabashes, watermelons and muskmelons, and the winter rains have

---

[1] The principal Pápago uprising was that of 1751, already mentioned by Anza.

to be unusually good in order that even these may not fail. Because of this lack of water there are no trees of any considerable size, and there is scarcely any game.[1] There are only two places where they have any running water and where they plant any maize or wheat. One of these is Sonóitac, toward which we are going, and the other is Quitovac. In spite of all this poverty, and of all the efforts which have been made, it has never been possible to take them out of their misery, which it is certain would result if they would go to the pueblos already established and having ministers.

Because of the scattered way in which these Pápagos live it has never been possible to determine their number, with respect to which there has been and still is great variety of opinion. Some have fixed it as high as six thousand souls and others less; but, judging from what I have seen and have been told, I estimate that they may reach two thousand five hundred, not including the heathen Pimas, their neighbors to the north, who live on the Gila River.

These people, among whom there are both Christians and heathen, occupy the space between our reduced pueblos and the Gila and Colorado rivers. This region, as has been said, is mostly sterile, although it would not be so bad if its inhabitants were industrious, for with a few dams, which could be easily made, they would be able to grow some crops.

---

[1] The most conspicuous game seen by us hereabout in January, 1928, were quails and white mule rabbits. Probably they are more numerous now than when the country was permanently inhabited by the Pápagos. Further on we saw a drove of jabalíes, or wild hogs.

I estimate that this district is sixty or seventy leagues from north to south, and thirty or forty from east to west.

January 24.—Having watered the animals at the wells which were opened yesterday, we set forth by an open road toward the northwest, with hills continuing on either side; and having traveled this afternoon about four leagues we halted to spend the night at a pond called by us San Juan de Mata,[1] which has plentiful and good pasturage, and likewise opportunity for gathering in it a large supply of water. Here we found four families of Pápagos, natives of the pueblo or village of Quitobac, through which we shall pass.

January 25.—At one o'clock in the afternoon we set out from San Juan de Mata, going northwest by an open road and over good terrain, the medium-sized hills continuing on both sides.[2] Having traveled six leagues camp was made for the night at a place where pasturage was found. From the road which we have followed two trails branch off to the left, both of which lead to and end at two different wells, which have very little and very bad water.

January 26.—At seven o'clock in the morning we set forth on the road to the northwest. Having

---

[1] San Juan de Matha was at or near Temporales (Temporal Llamarada). Here crops are now raised by seasonal rains, and shallow ponds have been formed by earthen dams.

[2] Sierra de la Campana was on the right, and Cerro del Cozón on the left. Just beyond Costa Rica Ranch the range on the left ends in a high isolated cerro. Anza's camp was in the flat some three miles nórth of this peak.

traveled for a league we came to some hills, to go around which one turns to the north for another league; then traveling three more leagues one comes to the village of Quitovac, which the Jesuit fathers in their journeys to the Colorado River called San Luís de Bacapa.[1] A little before I reached this place its justice or governor came out to meet me in a very friendly mood, and in the same way I saluted him and likewise all the inhabitants. Noting that the place had very few people, I asked him about the rest, and he replied that most of them were in our reduced pueblos, others being engaged in seeking the few herbs on which they live, a very usual food here being the abrojos. To prepare them they scald them in water, as a result of which the thorns fall off and they eat the meat which remains.

The place is surrounded on all sides by hills, except on the east and the north. It is one of the best sites of all the Papaguería, for with the water which is collected in a ditch from five small springs, although it is rather saline, they irrigate some small bits of very sandy land, in which they plant about half a fanega of maize and some calabashes. It has also fairly good pasturage which would keep five hundred head of cattle.

January 27.—At twelve o'clock we set forth on the march by the road which runs north from Quitobac to Sonóitac, between various hills that are higher

[1] Quitobac still exists on the same spot, a place of two hundred Mexicans and Pápagos, living at opposite ends of the town. From the springs a pretty lake has been formed.

than those of the preceding days. Having traveled about five leagues camp was made for the night on the skirts of a hill which has fairly good pasturage, and on the top of which toward the south was found a tank of good water which they told me had endured for a long time.[1]

January 28.—About eight o'clock in the morning we set out on the same road toward the north-north-west, going for a distance of three leagues along the skirts of the hills at the left, after which the road separates from them, and having gone a little more than two more leagues over some knolls one comes to San Marcelo de Sonóitac. This place is situated in a good plain surrounded on all sides by small knolls and low hills. It is open only to the north and north-northeast, and in these directions is the source of the water, which in some places is running, although it has not the best taste because it is marshy and somewhat salty. It runs a little more than a league and a half, in the course of which there are several little pieces of land where a little more than a fanega of maize might be planted and irrigated. It has a few willows, and in the marsh where the water begins, and farther up, there is plentiful pasturage for keeping as many as a thousand head of stock.

[1] Anza swung round the point of Sierra de Cubabi and camped near Piedra Parada, or Standing Rock. Next day he skirted the mountains for a distance and then swung northward over the hills to Sonóita. The trail followed by Anza is still used. The old Jesuit mission, of which nothing is left, was a mile and a half east of the new town of Sonóita.

This was the farthest northwest of all the missions of the Jesuit fathers. They established it in the same year of its destruction, which was the year 1751,[1] when with cruel and prolonged torture they killed its first missionary together with a Spaniard who kept him company. Notwithstanding that this is without dispute the best site in all the Papaguería, I did not find in it any more people than some six families, because the rest were engaged in the same occupations as those of Quitobac.

Today when we left the hills which we had kept on our left it was noticed that there were stones which they call *tepustete*, which is the best indication given by regions where gold placers are found. I therefore had some ore loaded, and on reaching the water I had it washed. None of this metal was found, but there was every indication that it might be found if greater efforts were made, and I shall not fail to do the same for the rest of the country which I have to pass through.

January 29.—At eight o'clock in the morning we proceeded down the Arroyo de Sonóitac, going mainly to the west, on the road to El Carrizal, which is on the same arroyo, and having traveled eight leagues camp was made for the night at a place where the water and pasturage are sufficient for travel, although of bad quality because it is salty. A league and a half after leaving Sonóitac, amongst

[1] First founded by Father Kino in the later 17th century, abandoned, then refounded in 1751. The missionary killed was Father Rhuen.

the hills on the right there is one that is very round
and in which there are veins of fine salt. I heard
of this a long time ago, and now the story is confirmed by the natives, who tell me that they use the
salt, and that on account of its hardness they are
able to take it out only by means of stakes and in
the rainy season, at which time it softens somewhat.[1]

January 30.—Having been told that the next
watering place is the most difficult one in which to
give the riding animals water, I decided to march to
it in two divisions. For this purpose I left here the
pack train and eight soldiers, and with the rest of
the soldiers, the extra horses, and the cattle, I set
out on the road for it at twelve o'clock today, going
north-northwest; and having traveled six leagues
camp was made just after going through a very good
pass.[2] There was no pasturage, and therefore the
animals ate only some leaves of the few trees which
were there.

January 31.—At half past seven we continued
our march along the same road which we had followed yesterday afternoon. Going northwest, and
having traveled over fairly good terrain for about
six leagues along the skirt of a sierra of bare rock,

[1] The road today runs essentially along Anza's route. Near Quitovaquita it forks, one branch crossing to the north side of the river.
Anza kept on the south side. His camp was evidently at Agua Salada.

[2] Anza's animals now went without water for forty-six hours. At
Agua Salada the trail turns sharply northwest. After going eighteen
miles in this direction Anza threaded a "white pass" (puerto blanco)
through O'Neill Hills, just north of boundary marker 179.

we came to a watering place very high up.[1] I
climbed up to it more with my hands than on my
feet. Having ascertained what water it had I found
it to be insufficient for the animals which we had
with us, and even if there had been enough it was
not possible to water all of them today, because of
its inaccessibility. I therefore decided to go forward to the next watering place, leaving all the
water which this one had for the pack train, which,
because it was coming loaded, could not go any
farther without refreshing itself here. In order that
it might the better do this, I left men to fix the trail
so that the animals might get to the water to drink,
using the tools which were brought for this purpose.
Setting out from this watering place, I took the
road for the next one, going west-northwest. In this
direction three more leagues were traveled; these
concluded, I camped among some small hills where
a little pasturage of bad quality was found.[2]

February 1.—At eight o'clock in the morning we
again took up the march, going northwest by an
open road which passes over some small hills; then,

[1] Aguaje Empinado. This was Heart Tank, in Sierra Pinta, about
eighteen miles from his last camp. Sierra Pinta is so-called because
the southern end is of dark rocks and the northern of light rocks.
The tank is high up in the mountains, and is reached by a canyon a
short distance north of the line between the light and the dark parts
of Sierra Pinta. See Kirk Bryan, *Routes to Desert Watering Places*,
404.

[2] Anza's three leagues west-northwest took him nearly west across
the plain into the gap between Tule Range and Cabeza Prieta Range.
Camp was in an arroyo northeast of Tule Well. The hills are quite
open here.

having passed these hills, which last for a league, two more leagues were traveled in order to reach the watering place, which was given the name of La Purificación.[1] This supply is of rain water collected in six tanks of very hard rock. The animals can go and drink at the foot of the first tank, for by forcing out or emptying the water in the last one by its natural passage, the first one is filled with the overflow of the others, and in this way it is possible to water a thousand animals which might come in a short time, as we did ours. Hereabout there is some pasturage, although it is bad, and I decided that here I would have the pack train which is coming behind rejoin me. At this watering place, at the foregoing, and at another of the same kind which they tell me is ahead, a few Pápagos camp during the dry season, through interest in the only animal which inhabits this country and the highest peaks of the hills. These are wild sheep, which in their skin and their shape are the same as deer, differing from them only in their horns, which they wear backward, and which are thicker than the largest horns of an ox.

February 2.—I heard that the pack train arrived at Aguaje Empinado yesterday with most of the animals tired out, for which reason it could not reach here today.

[1] Anza now swung northwest into the Cabeza Prieta Range, evidently striking the trail that runs from Tule Well. Aguaje de la Purificación was Cabeza Prieta Tanks, seven miles northwest of Tule Well. Anza's description of them is excellent.

February 3.—At noon the pack train arrived completely out of commission, and for this reason I decided not to march today.

February 4.—At half past eight in the morning, going west-northwest, we set forth on an open road which runs between hills on either side, and having traveled five leagues over good terrain we halted to pass the night at some wells which were called Pozos de en Medio.[1] They have good water, sufficient in quantity for travelers, and near them there is some pasturage of bad quality like the foregoing.

February 5.—At half past seven we set forth on a made road to the west-northwest, and having traveled seven or eight leagues we arrived at a watering place which, because it is so far from the trail, I infer must be the one which the Jesuit fathers called Agua Escondida.[2] Because of its inaccessibility most of the riding animals could not be watered today.

At this place we found a Pápago Indian, native of Sonóitac, toward which he was going with his family, having come from the Gila and Colorado

[1] Pozos de en Medio (Half-way Wells) were Coyote Water, or wells close by in the same arroyo, four or five miles northeast of Tinajas Altas. Lumholtz's map places Cabeza Prieta too far north and thus distorts the directions here.

[2] Anza's entry would be inconclusive here if it were not for the supplementary statements of Garcés and Díaz, who tell us that they went through Tinajas Pass in the Gila Range. Agua Escondida was in Arroyo San Albino, near Albino Tank. Anza was mistaken about the Agua Escondida of the Jesuits. Kino, at least, always went up the east side of the Gila Range. His Agua Escondida was Tinajas Altas, below Tinajas Pass.

rivers. He told me that, having heard that I was coming by another route, the inhabitants of both rivers above the junction had decided to prevent my passage, and likewise to kill me and everybody who was with me, in order to get possession of our riding animals and whatever else we were bringing. He said that they could not be dissuaded from this purpose by the captain of the Yumas who, because he comes annually to our presidios is known to us and called by us Salvador Palma, and whom I had already seen and regaled last month at the presidio of El Altar and told of my coming through his country.

He said that two others, subordinates of this captain, shared his good intentions, and that these three had declared to those who wished to attack me that they would defend me with their Yuma tribe and others, their allies from downstream; that these three told the rebels that if they provoked us they would feel the fury of our anger and our arms, whereas if they did not wish to be lost they would profit by our good treatment, just as they experienced it, especially Captain Palma, when they came to our presidios and other settlements; and that if they comported themselves well, as he wished to deal with everybody, they would receive our presents and gifts. He said that in spite of all these exhortations Captain Palma had accomplished nothing, and that therefore he, the bearer of this news, had come to communicate it to me, in order that I might

arrive at the rivers forewarned, for he was certain
that they would receive me with immediate warfare.
I therefore gave this informant due thanks for his
fidelity and regaled him and his family, and when
I talked with him again concerning the matter he
confirmed what he had said.

Although the foregoing tale did not cause me the
greatest anxiety, I did not wish to depreciate it, so
that in case it should prove to be true there might
not be lacking timely measures adapted to prevent
all restlessness at the beginning of such a heathendom as the one on those rivers, since their example,
good or bad, naturally would be followed by others.
I therefore proposed to adopt a plan calculated to
effect my transit with the greatest tranquillity, keeping in mind what the most excellent viceroy and the
council of war and royal exchequer were pleased to
command me regarding the matter.

I therefore consulted concerning the affair with
the two friars who are with me, and as their opinion
agreed with mine, I decided to send the same informant to the rivers to request Captain Palma to
come out to meet me before our arrival there, for
if he were faithful to us, as we were told, presumably
he would not excuse himself from coming, and in
that case he would tell us what was best, and through
him we could dispel the disturbance or in his presence adopt other means for the same purpose.

I proposed to the Pápago that he should return
this very afternoon, offering him a horse on which
to go, as well as to make him a good present.   He

very willingly agreed to go, asking me only that he
might wait until the following day, since he was now
very tired, and since, because I was not to start till
the next afternoon, he had time to come with Captain Palma on the morning of the 7th and meet me
just before my arrival at the Gila River. I agreed to
this proposal, and had this person remain to sleep
or pass the night amongst us, having him watched
without his knowing it.

February 6.—At eight o'clock in the morning I
sent the emissary on a good horse carrying a present for the captain, whom he again promised to
bring. An hour before his departure a beginning
was made of watering the stock, because the water
flowed slowly, and since it was necessary to set out
from here today because what little pasturage there
was had been consumed the night before by the riding animals. At two o'clock in the afternoon we
set forth over a made road, going south for about
a league and a quarter in order to double the sierra
of Agua Escondida at the right, after which five
more leagues were traveled to the northwest[1] in
order to camp, as we did, at a place where pasturage
was found.

On the march today and yesterday we have
skirted the sand dunes by way of which the Jesuit

[1] Anza back-tracked about four miles south to get around the
Sierra de Agua Escondida, or San Albino Point. Doubling this point
he advanced five leagues northwest and camped in the plain, then
went next day six or seven leagues across the plain to the Gila River
near Yuma junction. By a slip Anza here wrote *sudueste* for
norueste.

fathers made their journeys to the Colorado River.[1] That country cost them such fatigues as they relate, and the failure of their plans, which doubtless they would have brought to success if they had come by the route which I am following, and especially would they have been able to cross to the other side of the Colorado River.

February 7.—Shortly after sunrise we set forth on the road and in the direction stated, continuing to skirt the sand dunes, although for a distance of about two leagues a few short stretches of them were crossed.

At eleven o'clock today our emissary came out on the road with one of the chiefs or headmen of the Yumas, because Captain Palma was absent from his house. This chief came without any weapons, on foot, accompanied by eight others mounted on good mares. He saluted me most pleasantly and I responded in the same way. Immediately he told me that he came in place of Palma, his captain, whom he had already sent for, and that while waiting for him he wished me to know that the reports of disturbances of which I had heard had been entirely dispelled by his captain, himself, and another; that in faith of this and that all the Yuma people were anxiously waiting to see me, I must hasten my march, in order to arrive quickly and have time to eat what they had provided for me. These and other expressions, and the friendly attitude manifested

[1] Kino and Salvatierra tried to reach the head of the Gulf by way of Sierra del Pinacate and the sand dunes.

by this headman and his companions, attested the truth of what they were telling me. This impression was confirmed by the Pápago, our emissary, for today he talked to me without the melancholy of the preceding day. And especially were we reassured when we saw troops of men entirely unarmed coming to salute us, giving proof of their pleasure with yells, throwing themselves on the ground, and other festive demonstrations.

About three in the afternoon we descended to the Gila River with a following of more than two hundred persons, and halted at the first pasturage, after having traveled today six or seven leagues.[1] At five o'clock in the afternoon, by which time the number of people of both sexes who had come down to the Gila with us had doubled, Captain Palma arrived at our encampment, accompanied by about sixty persons, most of them unarmed like the captain, who asked me to embrace him. I did so with the greatest manifestations of affection, causing much surprise as well as satisfaction to his people, and immediately he made me a present of some food.

I requested him to be seated and he took some refreshments, after which he began to talk, asking me to pardon him for not having come out to meet me, because he had just come from a long distance. He said that he had reprimanded his people because they had not taken me to his house, which was nearby; and he was sorry for the report which they had

1 Camp was a short distance above the Gila-Colorado junction.

given me of a rebellion against us, adding a statement of the facts of the case. He said that they were simply that certain people living upstream, who had come down to his residence, had started the talk, thinking that we were people who would do them injury, and whom it would be easy to rob of our riding animals, which was their principal object. He said that, although they were not to be feared, because of their lack of spirit, he had expelled these people from his jurisdiction, and that in all of it his people and his allies down the river did not wish any other thing than to serve us and entertain us, in addition to seeing us; that I must not be offended if they should come to touch me, and all such things; and that he had already warned his people that they must steal nothing from us or commit any other wrong. On this point he assured us, and added other expressions of affection for us which left us convinced.

The captain observed that our troops kept their horses ready for any event, and that the soldiers went about with swords in their belts, others being posted as sentinels among the horses which were feeding; and immediately he told me that I must put them all at rest, for in this country there was no risk and nothing to fear, especially amongst his people, who had already assured me of their good faith. To this proposal I replied that I was convinced of his friendship, but that the disposition of men which he saw was indispensable to my profession, even though there might be no risk, as he had seen within the presidios, where guards were placed daily. With this explanation he was satisfied.

In view of the friendship which this Indian has always manifested for the Spanish nation, of which he has given many proofs, and of the great importance it might have for us at all times to win him and hold his affection, I decided to make some demonstration with him which he might consider as a reward for his good conduct, and so that his people might get an idea of how much we esteemed him, and therefore might render him greater obedience. All being assembled I asked them if they recognized Captain Palma as their superior. They all replied in the affirmative, and then I told them that in the name of the king who had sent me through these parts and was lord of all the inhabitants of this kingdom, I was confirming him in his command, in order that he might rule legally and with greater authority, and be respected by them. Then I hung about his neck, suspended by a red ribbon, a coin of the realm bearing his Majesty's portrait. He appreciated it beyond measure and the same was true of all those assembled, who now looked upon their captain almost with awe.

Having finished this ceremony, which was a celebrated event for the Yuma tribe and their captain, I decided to give Palma to understand who the king was and the obligations of the chief in the midst of his heathendom. I called him to my tent with two of his subordinates, and by means of a good interpreter I told him that God was creator of man, of the heavens, and of all things; that He had given to the king these and even greater lands in which we lived, and that therefore an infinite number of Spaniards as well as Indians obeyed him; that the king did not require of his vassals anything except observance of the law of the God who created us; that we should live in peace, profiting by the fruits of the earth and of our personal labors, by means of which we acquired clothing, horses and other things which we use and for which we are thankful; and that in order that we might not have to go to seek it outside of the place where we lived, the king had taken care to provide all his realms with all the things which we needed; that the king greatly loved all of us, but with greater pity and charity he loved the Indians, and especially those who lacked knowledge of him and of the law of God; and that in order to make known to them one and the other, he was sending me with such toil to see them and give them peace in his name.

I told them that in virtue of this, from this day forward an end must be put to the continuous wars which they waged amongst themselves, for this was the express order of God and the king; that since all were his children the king did not wish them to be killed; that to prove that the Spaniards were such we were calling them brothers, for the king had ordered it thus; that they must wait until with the passage of time we might send them greater knowledge of his royal person, in order that they might learn many things of which they were ignor-

ant, and from which they would receive many bene-
fits; that this which I had told them, Captain Palma
and his subordinates must make known to their
people, in order that a knowledge of who his Majesty
was might come to the notice of all. I told them at
the same time that they must come to see me, with
entire confidence and freely; that they would receive
from me no injury, but on the contrary every good
and hospitality; and that in proof of this and that
the king had ordered me so to do, on my passage
through their villages I would give them presents
in his name.

Having been instructed in these and other particulars, Captain Palma and the other two, who had
listened with the closest attention, thanked me in
their fashion, telling me that they had never heard
more pleasing talk, and since Palma did not wish to
delay repeating it to his people, he asked me for
my bastón and permission to go and tell them. I
granted his request, and immediately he began to
shout to his people, who were there in hundreds.
We saw that every little while they covered their
mouths, a sign of surprise amongst such people.
Having concluded his harangue he told them in
closing that since it was now night they must go to
their villages to sleep, but very few of them did so.

Coming to me, he told me that his subjects had
been informed in the matter, and that those who
were not present he would inform likewise; that he
with all the rest acknowledged and would obey the
king, and that in view of this I should command him,

just as we commanded the governors of our reduced pueblos, and that for this purpose he would not leave me while we were going through his tribe; and that to others, his allies, he would transmit the talk which I had made to him, in order that amongst them all wars might cease.

February 8.—At eight o'clock we set forth down the Gila River, and having traveled about half a league we reached the ford, to which we were guided by Captain Palma and hundreds of his people, there being many more on the other side. I gave orders to unload right there, that the Indians might take over the packs on their heads, being invited to do so with much urgency by their captain and his people, to which I consented since there was no reason for distrust. Nevertheless, I told him to guide me to the ford, and following him I crossed over with half of the soldiers to the other side, and immediately the horses and cattle followed me. Then the cargo was taken over, the Indians carrying it through water breast high. This finished, the rest of our men crossed over, and I decided to remain in this very place for the rest of the day, since there was not time to cross over to the other side of the Colorado.

At the place where we have crossed the Gila it has already been joined by an arm of the Colorado, thus making an island, which I named La Trinidad. Here Captain Palma ordinarily lives, for he only leaves this place at the time of the great floods which occur in the beginning of summer, according

to what they say. He made a second and still larger
present of his own comestibles, and there came to
see me more than six hundred persons, so lacking
the fear of us which they had yesterday that today
he asked me to bear with them. For, during the
whole day they did not give us time to prepare any
food, although I afterward took advantage of the
distribution which I made them of beads and tobacco
to give them two beeves. Nevertheless, well after
nightfall Captain Palma made me go to his house,
but I quickly returned, and thus we were able to
have a little quiet.

I have inquired here what tribes inhabit both
rivers and they tell me that up the Colorado the
first is the Soyopa tribe, and that on the Gila there
are the Cocomaricopas and others, but I am not writing them down individually now, in order to do so
with greater certainty and foundation on my return,
when I must perforce ascend the Gila, where it will
be possible to get information of a better quality
than I can get here.

One thing in which it appears there can not be
much doubt is that the province of El Moqui in New
Mexico can not be very far away, for there are seen
here many mantas or blankets, and other fabrics
peculiar to that province and brought by the Soyopa
tribe. According to what they tell me, this tribe
must be situated about thirty or forty leagues from
the junction of these rivers. These things are sold
to the Soyopas by the tribes near them, and to the
latter by the natives of El Moqui themselves. This

information has been given me by one of the Soyopa tribe as well as by other natives. And apart from this report, from what I have learned from my travels in the Apache country and ascertained there about the location of these provinces, I infer that they can not be very far distant from this region.

February 9.—Today, observing the method of yesterday, at nine o'clock in the morning we began to cross the Colorado River by a special ford[1] which was shown us by Captain Palma. The crossing was effected with all success in the presence of more than six hundred persons, most of whom, even the women and children, assisted in order that we might not stray from the best part of the passage, and they did the same with the loose animals. To celebrate this crossing, because it was the first time that it had been accomplished by the troops of his Majesty, I had a salute fired and some rockets discharged. The Yumas enjoyed this hugely, although the noise frightened them so much that when they heard it they threw themselves on the ground.

After we had crossed I measured the Colorado River at its average width, and found it to be a little more than ninety-five regular fathoms wide and five palms deep in most of its current, the branch which enters the Gila being one-fourth less. I did not measure the Gila, but, considering it alone, I estimate that it must be on the average a half less than the Colorado, to which it contributes some saltiness.

[1] The crossing was just above the junction.

Soon after we had effected our crossing I halted with all our train at the very place where the rivers unite.[1] The Jesuit fathers called this place San Dionicio and observed its latitude from the other side, saying that it was in thirty-five and a half degrees. Right where we halted there are two small hills between which both rivers pass. They must be a hundred and twenty yards apart. The site is suitable and safe for a settlement, and we named it the Pass of La Concepción. From it one can see clearly the junction of the rivers and the immense grove of cottonwoods, willows useful for thatching, and other trees, both upstream and down. One sees also to the north-northwest, in a medium-sized sierra not very far distant, a great peak which we named the Giant's Head,[2] near which is the opening where the Colorado River comes through the range. To the east-northeast there is another sierra which likewise has an opening where it is cut by the Gila, in which there is a peak smaller than the other, which because of its form or figure we called the Bonnet.[3] The Indians told me that downstream below these hills there is never a ford, it being always necessary to swim a considerable distance, although the river is divided into parts.

An Indian of the Soyopa tribe told me here that three days' journey up the Colorado River, where he lives, this stream divides when it is in flood. The

[1] Just above the hills at the Southern Pacific Railroad bridge across the Colorado at Yuma.

[2] Cabeza del Gigante. Now called Castle Dome.

[3] El Bonete. Now called Chimney Peak.

larger branch, he says, is this one, and the other
branch turns to the north to join another river
larger than this Colorado, which they understand
turns toward the west.   Likewise, an Indian of one
of the tribes downstream told me that about thirty
leagues or less from this place there were natives
who were saying that five days' journey from them
there ran a road used by Spaniards, which I presume may be the one going from San Diego to one
California or the other.   I have tried to learn
whether this river has any fall, and they assure me
there is none downstream, nor for many leagues up
either of the rivers.

February 10.—A little after eight o'clock we set
forth downstream, going west-northwest, with a
following of more than six hundred persons, who
went showing us the best trails and clearing them
even of little brush.   In this direction we traveled
about four leagues to the skirts of a peak which they
call San Pablo, and then, turning west for another
league, camp was made for the night in some large
fields of maize and bean stubble.[1]

February 11.—At eight o'clock in the morning we
set forth downstream with the same following,
which continued with us until a league before we
finished the day's march, which we did after traveling six leagues to the west,[2] to the last district in-

[1] Camp was at the village of San Pablo, near Pilot Knob, and
just south of the present international boundary line.

[2] Camp was at a small lake near the river, at the border of Palma's
territory. The place was a little above the west end of the line between Arizona and Sonora. All the diaries give the day's march as
six leagues west, but the direction was undoubtedly southwest.

habited by the Yumas. For this reason only about sixty persons, including the residents of the place, came this far.

Hitherto I have not spoken in detail of the Yuma tribe and of their country, because, since I had still to travel over this district described, I wished to observe these things better, in order to speak of them with more foundation. They are a heathen and barbarous people, but of this class they are the best that I have seen in their attitude toward the Spaniards, for in their affection and liberality they exceed all the tribes whom we have reduced. In robustness and height they are superior to these, being in general more than nine palms high. In intellect they are by no means dull. They are not as dark-skinned as other tribes, nor do they go so much striped. They are not naturally ugly, but they make themselves so in a superlative degree with many and diverse paintings with which they cover the entire body.

The men go entirely naked, but without any shame, and to cover their private parts they consider a womanish custom, as they themselves have told me. They have good heads of hair, with which they arrange exquisite coiffures, being aided in this by the very fine mud over which they sprinkle a powder which in its whiteness and lustre looks like silver. In order not to discommode this adornment they take care not to lie down, and so for three or four days they sleep sitting up. The women do not observe this practice, but they do paint themselves.

The men have their ears pierced, most of them with five holes, and they also have a hole in the cartilage of the nose, in which they wear as a decoration many colored feathers, or a little stick a palm long and thicker than the largest bird's quill.

To arms they appear little inclined. Only a third of them carry weapons, and this with little liking. Their arms consist of bow and arrows, both one and the other of poor quality, besides being few, for amongst all whom I have seen only two carried quivers containing as many as six arrows. The other two-thirds carry a long club or lance, which is used for a game, but both this and their weapons they lay down when it becomes a little cold, employing the hands then with a great firebrand which they pass all over the body in order to get warm. Their language appears to be easy to pronounce and to write. Castilian is not difficult for them, for whatever we say to them in it they repeat quickly and clearly.

The women in robustness, height, and appearance correspond in every way to the men. From the time of their birth they wear little skirts divided in two pieces, made of the interior and soft bark of willows, cottonwood, and mesquite, with which they cover themselves from the waist to the knees. The rest of the body they cover only when it is cold, with fabrics of the same kinds of bark and as rough as the cloth which in the kingdom we call *guangoches,* or with some garments of twisted skins of hares and

beaver, which they afterward sew together, and anyone who enjoys this treasure may be called rich.

The population of this tribe, according to what
I have seen, and have learned from them and from
Father Garcés, who before this has observed them
better, I judge will reach three thousand five hundred persons. All live without any civilization.
Nevertheless, according to reports, it seems that this
Yuma tribe and the Pimas who live on the Gila
River are the only heathen who show any subordination to the one who is made captain. With the
present captain of the Yumas, if we know how to
manage him, I think it will be possible to subdue
the nearby tribes. The Yumas, of whom we are
speaking, have no other habitations than some
simple huts of branches or grass, according to the
number of persons in the family, all of whom, few
or many, live within them.

The country which I have seen, from the place
where I came down to the rivers, as far as here,
is under cultivation. That which naturally is without trees is planted with wheat and barley, and
withal it is better than many of the fields of other
countries which have abundant irrigation. In the
same way one can see and learn where they plant
their maize, beans, calabashes, watermelons, and
cantaloupes, in such abundance that we have wished
that our reduced Indians, who have the advantage of
oxen, harrows, and other necessary implements of

agriculture, would dedicate themselves to it half as well as these heathen.

The fertility of the land they tell me is the same upstream, both rivers being understood and each one separately, and much better downstream below the junction. And from there to this place where I am much aid is given by the annual inundation which is received each spring by all the bottom lands, as a result of the melting of the interior snows, with the added circumstances that it does not destroy the trees or any of the crops, because the water comes with force only in the very channel, although it extends as a rule for half a league on each side, and in some places twice this distance. In view of the foregoing circumstances and of the little frost which they tell me they have here, it has seemed to me that this climate, in which we have scarcely felt any cold at night, would be most advantageous for the planting of vines and many other fruit trees and plants.

At the hills of the Pass of La Concepción, in my poor opinion, two secure dams can be made, on one side and the other, to carry the water and irrigate as much land as might be desired. This river is lacking only in pasturage, although there is sufficient for relay stock; and of carrizo, to which they are accustomed, there is an abundance through all the bottom lands. And in the time of the summer rains, which are the only ones in this region, although they are small in amount, many herbs useful for pasturage grow and last until the beginning of winter.

The horses kept by the Yumas, however it may be, are seen to be fat in the extreme. Perhaps this may be due to the little work which they do, for naturally this would not be much, in view of the fact that these people go naked; and riding on the horses in this same way, for they always ride bare-back, it follows that the heat which is communicated to the body of the riders prevents them from making long journeys.

Because at this point the territory of the Yumas ends, and because some persons of the Cogat tribe,[1] which follows, had come to meet me, I asked one and another who the natives are who inhabit the river as far as the place where it empties into the Gulf, and how many leagues it is to that point. And they all answer that this last point must be thirty or forty leagues distant; that the other bank from almost opposite this point, as far as the very mouth, is possessed by the Quiquima tribe, of a language different from the Yumas. They say that the region from the mouth on this side, including the adjacent sierras as far as here, is inhabited by the Cogat tribe, whose language differs from that of the Yumas only in its velocity; that these Cogats are much more numerous than the Yumas; and that for a long time these three tribes have been at war with each other, but are now at peace, since there have been many intertribal marriages in order the better to bring this about.

[1] More commonly called Cajuenches.

February 12.—At half past eight in the morning we set forth on the march, still going down the river, leaving it now at some distance, going southwest and at times to the south. Having traveled in these directions about four leagues, camp was made at a lake with plentiful pasturage, one of many which remain full of water when the river departs from its channel. To this lake I gave the name of Santa Olaya.[1] Here assembled a great many people of this Cogat tribe, who are more humble and timid than the Yumas. I made them a present of glass beads and tobacco, and tried to learn from them if they had any captain to rule them. They said "No," that they were governed by themselves alone, each person managing his own family. This tribe is different from the Yumas in only a few respects, such as their being smaller in stature and darker in color. They understand each other very well in spite of the rapidity with which they speak. In customs, clothing, nakedness, and lack of weapons they are equal. They confirm the statement that the lands which these people plant are better than the foregoing, but since they are more distant from our pueblos they possess no horses.

February 13.—At nine o'clock today we set out from Santa Olaya toward the west-northwest by an open trail, guided by some of the Coxas to a good-sized watering place, which we reached at the end of the afternoon, the pack mules being very much worn out because of their bad condition, and since the

[1] This lake was some distance apart from the river. See p. 54.

road, although level, was very soft. On the way there are two wells of bad water, and in less degree this is true of the water of this place, although it is more abundant. It is distant from the foregoing camp seven leagues. Its pasturage consists only of a little carrizo.[1]

When I said goodbye this morning to Palma, captain of the Yumas, he was not able to restrain the sorrow caused him by our departure, which he manifested with tender and copious tears, an action notable in a heathen Indian, whose kind ordinarily are not moved as much by death or the loss of those possessions which naturally they most ought to love. A little before this occurrence he said to me, "When you return from your journey the river will be at its highest flood. But do not worry about your crossing, because I am going to occupy myself from right now in gathering logs to make large and safe rafts, on which I myself will take you and your men across."

February 14.—At nine o'clock we set forth from this place, which we called El Carrizal. After going a league the guides took us down to the same arroyo, saying that this was the best water for making camp, to enable us to reach another watering place to which led an open road. But to it the guides, who were two, could not go, because it was in the land of

[1] At El Carrizal. Díaz and Garcés give the distance as nine leagues instead of seven. Two-thirds of the way to El Carrizal they reached the well of El Rosario, which Father Garcés recognized. Here he pointed out San Xacome, near Cerro Prieto, "to the west-southwest by west." This gives us a definite clue to the location of El Rosario, and makes Eldredge's map untenable at this point.

their enemies, for fear of whom early in the morning their relatives and companions already had gone back. Since these guides felt the same fear, we had no little trouble to detain them today, in order that they might tell us more about the next watering place and the road to it. At these wells, which we called Pozos de en Medio[1] (their real name amongst the natives who live near them), I decided to remain today, partly because the pack mules arrived very much worn-out, in spite of the shortness of the journey, and partly because to reach the watering place which follows there is no opportunity to apportion the march between the two days.

February 15.—At seven o'clock we set forth west-northwest on the trail by which the guides told us we should reach today a watering place near a sierra which they showed us.[2] Following these directions we came to a pool of water and a little spring of bad quality. At an equal distance we came to a deep well with little water, but not so bad as the foregoing. Having examined it, we went forward over the same trail, which continued until we reached some sand dunes, where it was blotted out by the natural movement which is given them by the winds.

[1] Half-way Wells. A gives the distance as a short league, and D as two leagues.

[2] The sierra which the guides pointed out to them was Signal Mountain. Díaz says the deep well where the packs were left (Pozo de las Angustias) was three leagues (Garcés says two) from El Carrizal and on the same Arroyo as El Carrizal and El Rosario. All three were evidently on Rio Paredones. Eldredge shows the route on Rio Alamo, but this is too far north to fit the specifications of the diaries.

Because the pack train had arrived at the last well in such bad condition, in order that the march planned for today might be concluded it was necessary to leave there half the load with eight soldiers to guard it. In making these arrangements I suggested to the two fathers who are with me that it would be better to send back the half load from here to the Colorado River, on the most crippled animals, with half of the soldiers, because I thought that in this way only should we be able to succeed in our efforts to go forward, for to attempt it with the whole train would be idle, and perhaps would cause the total failure of the expedition. I said that this plan would have better effect if one of the two fathers should care to remain, as I requested them to do, for with their presence the soldiers and the other persons would be more contented until my return; and that if I could take some subaltern with me I would adopt this plan immediately, for I felt certain that either here or farther on it would be necessary to do this, in order to reach our destination, for, as has been said, with all the train this is impossible.

My proposal did not find support with the fathers, especially with Father Garcés, who did not consider wise the division of the forces or his separation from my company. In view of this I did not wish to insist, in order that this plan might not be attributed solely to me, lest it might come out badly at a time when in the opinion of these fathers it was not necessary to adopt it.

So we continued our march straight for the watering place which we were seeking. Having traveled it must have been about five leagues,[1] at times amongst sand dunes, with great weariness to our riding animals, at the end of this distance there rose before us another and larger one, which we felt sure these worn-out beasts would not be able to conquer in the whole day, and on the other side of which was seen the peak of the watering place, farther away than we had inferred from the report of it.

While meditating whether or not to attempt to cross it, Father Garcés said that at another peak, which was seen toward the south and must have been less than four leagues away,[2] there was a habitation of heathen, with water and pasturage. This place he called San Jacome, and said that it was the last one which he saw in the journey made by him through these parts. Assured of this, and that from there we should find the road free from sand dunes, he urged that we should go there, saying that he would guide us. Considering this plan advantageous, I decided to adopt it, and that the pack train, horse herd, and cattle, which were coming somewhat behind, should go straight to that site, for which I sent the corresponding order.

Having directed our march toward San Jacome, at sunset we had reached and even passed the place

[1] Anza means five leagues in all to the turning back place. Díaz gives it as six and Garcés as five. It was southwest of Sesbania.

[2] Garcés gives the direction to San Xacome as south-southeast. The Cerro de San Xacome was Cerro Prieto. Its identity is fixed by his exploration of 1771.

where it was thought to be, but I did not see any
signs of a habitation. In view of this, and of the
fact that to travel at night would be useless, and
since most of the soldiers were now traveling on foot,
I decided to halt there and have some of them seek
the place. In this undertaking Father Garcés made
more strenuous efforts than anyone else. Accompanied by two soldiers he traveled until nightfall,
but at this hour he returned without finding San
Jacome or any indications that it was in the vicinity.

Under these circumstances, and in view of the
fact that it was necessary to find some place suitable
for resting our animals for several days, since it is
entirely impossible to go forward with them to the
place where it was thought we might emerge from
the sterility of this region, I decided to go straight to
a known place in order not to travel with uncertain-
ties, for however well they may come out they involve
great delays, as has been seen in the search for the
two foregoing water holes, notwithstanding that
there were good reasons for thinking that the last
one might be found.

February 16.—The pack train, the horse herd,
and the cattle not having appeared throughout the
previous night, I decided to go back by the road over
which it might come, in order to send it to the wells
which we have passed on the road, and from them to
the lake of Santa Olaya, which of all places seen in
this vicinity is the best in which to give our animals
the necessary rest. A short time after starting back
and a little after sunrise I met what I was looking

for, in such a terrible state that all the soldiers of the horse herd, pack train, and the cattle herd were traveling on foot.[1] The corporal told me that in order that they might not become more completely worn-out he had decided to halt for the previous night, but that in spite of this he already had left behind six riding animals and three cattle incapacitated for continuing the march. So I ordered him to follow my trail to the well where the half load remained. As to the animals which he had left behind, I told him that he must send someone to bring them to that place even though it might not be accomplished until night, and in fact they arrived after nightfall and with only four animals because it was impossible to move the rest.

At two o'clock in the afternoon we all reached the Well of Little Water, and I immediately sent the loose riding animals to the wells which were called Pozos de en Medio, since these were the ones of the best quality and there was some carrizo there which they might eat.

February 17.—After twelve o'clock today, when the necessary mules and horses arrived from the wells, we returned to them with a half load, over the same road already traveled, arriving there at four o'clock in the afternoon. This method of transporting the load in halves will be followed from here to the Lake of Santa Olaya, because the weakness of

[1] Anza did not go straight to the place where the half-load was left. He first swung north to meet the pack train and then northeast to Las Angustias.

the mules makes it impossible to carry more; and for this purpose the necessary guard of troops will remain. Today, as a result of their leanness and illness, seven of our riding animals died, there contributing finally to this result the fact that for lack of grass they have eaten an herb which abounds in this region and causes them a black and evil-scented slobbering.

Because most of the soldiers were on foot and those here had arrived on foot, I spoke a few words to cheer them in their trials. They replied that no loss and no hardship would be so grievous to them as the failure of this enterprise, to which they offered themselves with entire devotion, saying that even if all the riding animals should fail they were ready to attempt to accomplish it on foot. This willingness I recompensed with the thanks due them under such circumstances.

In this retrogression and delay one might see misconduct or lack of reflection, through not having undertaken our journey over the road by which the native of California,[1] who as was mentioned at the beginning of this diary, came out to the rivers, if one did not know the circumstances making it impossible to make use of him. The fact is that this Indian came out to those rivers lost, through the sand dunes which we have kept on our right. In this predicament he went four days without finding any water, which caused the death of his wife. For this reason

[1] Sebastián Tarabal.

he decided not to guide us, but he promised to do so from a lake forward, and this lake is the one which we are now seeking, and the best way out to it is the one which we have followed.

February 18.—At seven o'clock in the morning I sent the pack train to the well which we left behind, in order that everybody might reach this one so that we might go forward, as has been said, and in order that all the animals might not experience the scarcity of pasturage which is felt here, where there is none. With all the animals remaining free I arranged to set out for the mentioned lake of Santa Olaya, and did so, going by the same road which I followed in coming. Having traveled over it a little more than five leagues by vespers, we made camp at a place without pasturage, because some of the loose animals had become tired out.

February 19.—At sunrise we continued our journey, and at half past eight arrived at Santa Olaya. A short time afterward arrived a Yuma, whom I hired and charged to go to his village and from there send a message from me to Captain Palma, asking him to come and see me. A short time after he set out many Indians of this tribe and of the Coxas assembled and celebrated our return.

February 20.—At sunset a Yuma came from upstream saying that he had crossed the trail of two of our riding animals. There volunteered to go and get them an under-chief of this tribe,[1] who a few hours earlier had come to offer to serve me in place

1 Captain Pablo.

of Captain Palma until the latter should come, which he said would not be very soon because he was absent from his house, to which he had sent for him. At eleven o'clock at night the pack train arrived with the half load, so worn-out that I thought it wise to permit them to rest all the next day.

February 21.—At four o'clock in the afternoon the under-chief of the Yumas returned with one mule and the shoes of another, both of which had fled from the place where the pack train had remained. He reported that the mule to which the shoes belonged had been killed by an Indian of the Quiquima tribe, who live on the other bank of the Colorado, and into whose hands both mules had fallen. Not being able to punish the thief for the theft which he had committed against us, because he escaped from him, he had killed his wife with an arrow, which he showed me. He even wished me to take it in my hand, but I immediately chided the barbarian for the deed; but they are so unscrupulous and thoughtless in this matter that he said that he was more sorry for my disapproval than for the murder which he had committed.

February 22.—At five o'clock in the afternoon I sent back the pack train to bring the half load which is lacking.

February 23.—At ten o'clock at night the pack train arrived with the half load which had not been brought to this place.

February 24.—At three o'clock in the afternoon Father Garcés went down the river voluntarily to

visit several villages which he says he visited during
his last journey through this region, for the purpose
of seeing if he could obtain among them any information which would be useful to our enterprise.[1] Two
hours later Captain Palma arrived, manifesting the
greatest joy for my return, and at the same time
sorrow for my setbacks. But the thing which caused
him the acme of grief was the death of our riding
animals, of which he had already heard, for he
thought that our loss of these left us poor for the
rest of our lives.

Since the only means by which we can accomplish our journey to Northern California, to learn
where we ought to go in the future, is to go with the
least possible baggage, and since not all our riding
animals are useful for making this journey, as has
been seen, unless they should be allowed to rest for
a couple of months, I have been obliged ever since
I decided to return to this lake to consider whether
there is any objection to the plan of leaving at this
river the impedimenta which prevent me from having now accomplished, or being near to accomplish,
the enterprise to which I am commissioned.

Before deciding upon this plan I sounded out
Captain Palma. Finding him with the same good
intentions as always, I told him of it, with the ar-
rangement that I would leave in his care a part of
my pack animals and mounts for a month, when I
would return with more men from the place toward

[1] The journey of Father Garcés is narrated in his own diary.

which I was going. I told him that from the place whence I had come[1] they might come to seek me, in which case he must tell them when I would be back, in order that they might await me at his house. He agreed to do this, and also to give me a good account of whatever I might leave in his care, just as he had done with Father Garcés, and with the native of California, at the times when they have been alone in his country.

In view of all the foregoing, I made my plan known to most of the persons of the expedition, saying that if they could think of a better one by which to succeed with the enterprise they should tell me of it. All agreed that there was no better plan than this one, and that it ought to be followed, as the one best suited to bring success to the expedition. As to leaving at the Colorado River in the care of Captain Palma everything that would be an embarrassment to us, there was no risk, they said, for before now he had given many proofs of fidelity; and even if there should be some risk, all were willing to undertake it in order to succeed in the enterprise. Indeed, in order that this might not fail, they all pledged themselves, if all the riding animals should play out, to undertake the journey on foot, and to risk even greater losses and hardships, urging that with this understanding I should put my plan into practice. I therefore promised to do so.

February 25 to 28.—These days were devoted like the foregoing to resting and recuperating the

---

[1] He means Tubac.

riding animals, and during this time nothing important occurred.

March 1.—Today was devoted to the same object.
In the afternoon Father Garcés returned, with only
the satisfaction of having visited many people downstream, but without being able to obtain or acquire
from them any information favorable to our journey. Having told him of the plan by which we wished
to undertake it again, he said that it had his approval, and that he very gladly agreed to it.

March 2.—According to what has already been
stated, I decided to leave in care of Captain Palma
three trustworthy soldiers of good conduct, three
muleteers, most of our cargo, and all the cattle and
the saddle animals which are unable to go forward.
I gave the soldiers the necessary instructions for
any emergency that might occur until my return.
Three Pimas who are very much attached to us also
remained in our pay in order that they might aid
the soldiers in taking care of the things that are left.

At two in the afternoon of this same day we
set forth on the march with ten light loads and provisions for a month or a little less, which is the time
estimated that we shall spend in coming out to one
of the new establishments of Northern California on
the best and most recuperated mules. We went down
the river toward the west,[1] passing through various
villages of the Cogat tribe, whose country appears

[1] D gives the direction as west, A says west-southwest, F says
west with some declination to the southwest. The camp was called
Laguna de la Merced, or Laguna del Predicador.

to be richer than that farther up. At vespers, after having traveled four leagues, a halt was made near one of these villages in a good field of maize stubble, and because many of the tribe mentioned had come to see me and some of the Yumas were accompanying me, I caused them to ratify the peace, with which all were very well pleased.

March 3.—At half past seven I continued in the same direction along the river bottom. We traveled about a league and a half,[1] at the end of which we halted at a site as good as the preceding, in order to make a part of the next journey in the afternoon, so that with greater ease we might reach the next watering place. From this one where I am, to the Lake of Santa Olaya, there is an abundance of pasturage, and they tell me that the same is true below this place. Likewise, I have noted that there are larger fields here than in the country of the Yumas.

March 4.—At one o'clock in the afternoon we set forth west-northwest, accompanied by an Indian who voluntarily offered to guide me to the sierra toward which I am going, because the people who live there are his relatives. We traveled about seven leagues, until well after nightfall, when the guide said we were half way on the road, a statement which he affirmed on three occasions. For this reason we halted to take some rest, although without pasturage.[2]

---

[1] A, D, and F give the distance as three leagues. Camp was near Volcano Lake, a little more than four leagues from San Xacome, and therefore some five or six leagues from Cerro Prieto.

[2] Camp was a short distance northwest of Cerro Prieto.

March 5.—Before dawn we again took up the march to the west-northwest, having on our left a fair-sized sierra and on the right the sand dune which confronted us on the 15th of last month. In this direction we traveled about six leagues and, contrary to what our guide had said, three more to the northwest, in order to enter a good pass in the sierra which we were keeping on our left, and three more to the northwest after having passed through it. Then, at nightfall, we came to a well whose surface water was good, and where some pasturage was found. To reach this place, which I named San Eusevio, we crossed a large estuary. We do not know when it may have been formed, but it is plain that it is or has been one, although according to appearances the sea must be far away, because on the banks there are stranded an infinite number of fish of the kind and size appropriate to the sea, the like of which never grow in lakes, however large they may be. A short time after our animals drank, the water became bad and dried up, the little which flowed out being salty and therefore very harmful to the animals.[1]

March 6.—In the morning we learned that our guide had fled, leaving the poor weapons which he carried at the place where he slept with two other Yumas who have come with me voluntarily. This flight is regrettable only because we are in unknown country. Nevertheless, as soon as I learned of it I

[1] This day's march took Anza through the Lower Pass of Cocopah Mountains, and across the head of Laguna Salada (Lake Maquata, or Maqueque).

sent a corporal with six soldiers to go this very
morning toward the place in the sierra of which he
told us, to see if there was water, with the understanding that if he did not find any he should tell me
promptly, returning with all his party, who would
find me on his own trail.

After having unsatisfactorily watered our animals at the well of San Eusevio, at two o'clock in the
afternoon I set out on his trail. Traveling west-
northwest over good terrain for about three leagues
to the end of some hills, there I was met by two
soldiers whom the corporal had sent to tell me that
he had found running water and a heathen near it.
From these hills we went down to a valley which
ran out from the center of the sierra, to whose upper
end we traveled a little more than two leagues until
we reached the watering place, two hours after nightfall. On my arrival the corporal told me that shortly
after he sent me the report mentioned another heathen came to the place where he was and gave him
to understand that he was the father of the first one,
and that although he gave them presents and urged
them both to await me, he did not succeed, since in
obedience to my orders he did not wish to use force
to detain them.

In this place, which I named Santo Thomás, there
is some pasturage, for it is damp because of the
water which runs.[1] Not all the water is good, for of

[1] Santo Thomás was in the main California Sierra, in Pinto Canyon,
some ten miles south of the boundary line. Anza entered it right
along the present highway and ascended it southwest for some two
leagues. See p. 78.

five rivulets only one is fresh and clear, the others being extremely salty. Near them we remained to pass the night. We conclude that the sierra in which this watering place is found may belong to those which form the chain of California. In it there is an abundance of mescal.

March 7.—In order better to seek water in the direction in which we are going, in the middle of the forenoon today I sent an advance party of six soldiers with the instructions necessary for the purpose. In the afternoon at two o'clock I set out from Santo Thomás with all our train, going northeast for half a league in order to free ourselves somewhat from the bad footing of the sierra which continues on our left.[1] After going this distance and turning north we traveled about three and a half leagues over good terrain until we reached a place with some pasturage where our advance party was halted.[2] They told me that a league and a half from here there was an abundance of water of good quality which had been shown them by six heathen whom they met in this very place. They remained here until they saw me approach, but on seeing me they became afraid and asked permission to go, which was granted them in view of my orders; for I have not thought it well to obtain anything by means of violence or force from people who see us for the first time. With this favorable report I halted to pass the night at the very place where I received it.

[1] This half league was traveled after emerging from the canyon.

[2] Camp was three or four miles southwest of Yuha Well, a little above the boundary line.

March 8.—At seven o'clock we set forth over good terrain toward the northeast, in which direction we traveled about a league and a quarter, in order to reach some wells of the best and most abundant water which could be desired, and to which I gave the name of Santa Rosa de las Laxas.[1] They also have some pasturage, although bad in quality and somewhat distant. This place is situated in a large plain. It offers such an opportunity to go out to the Colorado River that from it without any inconvenience one can reach the Lake of Santa Olaya in two days, for it can not be more than twenty or twenty-two leagues from here, and from the Pozos del Carrizal it is only twelve or thirteen, for to such detours and contingencies anyone who is ignorant of a country is exposed, since it is necessary for him to trust to Indians, who for any personal reason when acting as guides think nothing of making any detours which may suit their whims.

Notwithstanding the detours which we have suffered, we have celebrated our arrival in this district, because from here the native of California has recognized that not far distant is another watering place from which he came out, and from now forward he will guide us with all confidence. In this place I decided to rest our riding animals today and a part of tomorrow, for with the bad water of San Eusevio they have become very much weakened, for which reason most of the soldiers have traveled from here forward on foot.

[1] Santa Rosa of the Flat Rocks, at or near Yuha Well, some four miles north of the boundary.

March 9.—At half past two in the afternoon we set forth on the march over good terrain, going north and leaving the great mountain chain some distance at the left. Having traveled four leagues we halted for the night at a place where there was some pasturage, because it was known to become more scarce from here forward.[1]

March 10.—At daybreak we set forth in the same northern direction, going over good terrain until we entered some sand dunes which lasted for a league, but which might be circumvented. Having passed these we again had firm footing, which continued until we reached the watering place mentioned hereinbefore, which must be about six or seven leagues from the place where we spent the night. To this site I gave the name of Ziénega de San Sevastián, alias del Peregrino.[2] In the place where we halted there is a good spring of very potable water, and there are many others to the west which are saline. From them is formed a marsh more than a league long with plentiful pasturage, although it is likewise salty. To this in time stock becomes accustomed, especially cattle, but to ours it caused great injury, so much indeed that two of the riding animals will not be able to go forward.

Here we found a village of heathen. At first sight of us they deserted the place, but I having been able to talk with a woman and give her a present, she

[1] D says camp was in a dry arroyo, evidently a north branch of Coyote Wash. The place was four or five miles north of Plaster City.

[2] San Sebastián was at Harper's Well on San Felipe Creek near its junction with Carrizo Creek.

went to spread the news, and half an hour later
several men came, among them being the one who
was ruling. I gave them food, glass beads, and
tobacco, and then they completely lost their fear. I
exhorted them to peace and quietude, and as a demonstration of it I had them embrace two Yumas who
are with me and of whose tribe they are enemies.
They were mutually pleased with the proceeding,
and together they spent the night in the village,
where they regaled each other.

The Yumas call this tribe, like all those who live
in the sierra, the Acaguechis, Gaguenchis, and Aca-
guechi. They are as little warlike as their rivals
and their arms are even of worse quality. I judge
that the language is the same, with slight variation,
for they understand each other very well. The men
go naked like the rest. In height they are inferior
to the Yumas and they are darker in color. They
appear to be less intelligent and more timid in spirit,
although this may be due to the fact that they have
heard less of us. Their women wear the same kind
of clothing as the Yumas, with only the difference
that in place of the strips of the inner bark of the
willow and the cottonwood, these make their skirts
of threads which they get from the fiber of mescal,
while some cover themselves with deer skin. This is
usually the case from here forward, the native Californian tells me, since for the lack of these fibers
both sexes make their moccasins of deer skin and
therefore do not have to go barefoot. They wear
their hair very short, and do not stripe or paint

themselves very much, although this may be due to
a lack of materials for one or the other purpose. I
cannot estimate their numbers, but according to
what I have learned from them and from the Yumas,
I am assured that the mountain range in which they
generally live is very thickly settled by them. And
this is indicated likewise by the trails which we have
seen, as well as by the reports concerning this matter which have been given me by the native Californian, who by reason of his peregrination through
these parts noted the many people who inhabit them,
and whom he through necessity sought, in order that
they might give him food, without which he would
not have been able to go out to our country.

March 11.—After three o'clock in the afternoon
we set forth west, going toward an opening or pass
in the sierras which we have on our left and which,
as has been said, we assume to be the range which
comes from California. Until vespers we labored
hard to emerge from some mires which must have
lasted for half a league, after which another league
was traveled,[1] when camp was made for the night,
although without pasturage. During the night several
heathen who were living here assembled. After we
had given them presents, through the Yumas we
asked them various questions, among them how far
it was to the sea, to which they replied that it was
three days, pointing about south and across the great
range. I also asked them how long it took to go to

[1] Díaz and Garcés say two leagues west.

the place where our people were, and they replied six days, pointing in the same direction, where the sea was. From this we inferred that it must be San Diego, and this being the case that port is very near the mouth of the Colorado River where it empties into the Gulf of California.

March 12.—About an hour before daybreak we set forth over good terrain on an open road toward the west-northwest, and having traveled along it about six leagues we came to a watering place with some current and a considerable amount of good pasturage. To this place we gave the name of San Gregorio.[1] Near it there must have been more than sixty heathen. They were so timid that although they came when I sent for them, yet, notwithstanding that they approached quite near to our camp, they would not come clear to it because our riding animals caused them great terror. The native Californian who brought them says that among them there were some who were speaking the San Diego idiom, which seems to confirm the opinion which has been formed that this port is not very far away. Because of the bad conditions in which our riding animals have come, resulting from the injury done them by the salty pasturage of San Sebastián, I decided to devote today and tomorrow to rest, in order that they might recuperate to some extent.

The 13th was devoted to rest, as has been said.

[1] They went over a low ridge and swung to the right of Borrego Mountain. San Gregorio was on San Felipe Creek, just west of Red or Borrego Mountain.

March 14.—At break of dawn we set forth on the
march, going north four leagues and entering the
sierra by a valley which comes out of it and has hills
on either side. Besides this distance two more leagues
were traveled, during which we saw running water
and at the end of which we came to an abundant
spring, where we halted for the night. To this place
we gave the name of Santa Catharina.[1] It is well
grown with plants and some willows; it has plentiful
pasturage, and with some labor it would be possible
to use the water to irrigate some small pieces of
land. Here there was a goodly number of heathen
who at first sight fled, but after the accustomed procedure about twenty came.

They are less warlike people than those farther
back, much smaller, and more unhappy in every
way. Most of them employ their hands solely with
a stick shaped like a sickle, which serves them to kill
jack rabbits by throwing at them when they are on
the run, because the weapon flies so. These miserable people were given presents, and they stayed
with us until a mule brayed, when they precipitately
fled, terrorized, to a nearby hill, where they remained
until nightfall. The language of these people was
not understood, and for this reason we do not know
of what tribe they may be or what they are called.

March 15.—Two hours before dawn we set forth
up the arroyo, which in general comes from the north

[1] Ascending San Felipe Creek through Borrego Valley, they entered Coyote Canyon and camped on Coyote Creek at the lower end
of Collins Valley. Santa Catharina was at Reed's Springs or Lower
Willows. See p. 87.

or north-northwest, dividing the great range, and along which we traveled about three leagues with good footing. The stream dried up only in the middle of this stretch, there being running water the rest of the way. After traveling another league along the same arroyo where it is dry, it is seen to run again where the valley narrows. From here one goes along the narrow part an equal distance and then, leaving it, begins to climb the sierra, without the greatest difficulty for the loaded animals. Having traveled two more leagues we came to a very beautiful site with good pasturage and with several abundant springs. From this place various snow-covered mountains are seen, with much rock, and flower-covered meadows which indicate great fertility. Looking toward the South Sea and toward our new establishments on its coasts, all the view is most beautiful.

To this place I gave the name of Puerto Real de San Carlos.[1] It has advantages for a good settlement, especially for the raising of many cattle, vines, and other fruits. All the trees seen from it are those natural to a cold country, such as pines, live oaks, and others. From our observation of the plants it seems that it does not frost here out of season. In our journey today we have seen more than two hundred heathen, who in every way look like those farther

---

[1] They ascended Coyote Canyon. This canyon forks into Tule, Nance, and Horse canyons. Anza climbed the ridge between Tule and Nance canyons. Camp was made at the fine springs in the *bajío* or flat east of Fred Clark's corral, just before they emerged through the rocky pass—the Puerto Real de San Carlos.

back, except that the women have a greater abundance of deer skins for skirts than those of San Sevastián, but in all other matters they are the same as those of Santa Catharina.

March 16.—At daybreak it was raining and snowing in the mountains, the storm having begun yesterday, and it was not possible to march until two o'clock today, when the weather cleared. After leaving San Carlos we traveled through a valley of very fertile lands, and having gone three leagues along it we halted for the night at a lagoon formed by several arroyos and other rivulets that come from the sierras which we have on both sides, and run toward the coast of the South Sea. This lake was given the name of El Príncipe.[1] It has near at hand some hills which dominate it toward the north, and several very good springs. Because of its fertility this site would be suitable for whatever might be desired.

March 17.—Day dawned the same as yesterday, and last night was the same. But it cleared somewhat, and at ten o'clock we set forth on the road between the sierras mentioned.[2] Having traveled

---

[1] Climbing to the top of a rocky pass—a matter of a few hundred yards—they emerged into Cahuilla Valley, ascended a gentle slope, and descended another equally gentle to Laguna del Príncipe (now Dry Lake, but not always dry) at Contreras's ranch. Here Eldredge disregarded the readings of the diary and went astray. Misled by a modern map showing Vandeventer Flat at the head of Horse Canyon and Hemet Lake in Hemet Valley, an artificial lake made in recent times, and ten miles out of position, he routed Anza by Horse Canyon, Hemet Valley and Kean Camp, locating the pass of San Carlos in Red Hill. Manifestly he had never explored the route. See p. 88.

[2] Thomas Mountain on the right and Cahuilla Mountain on the left.

for about two and a half leagues along an arroyo which begins to be formed in the neighborhood of the Laguna del Príncipe, we halted because it threatened to rain, because the valley is narrowing here, and because the animals were in bad shape, as a result of the many mires encountered. Half a league from this place the arroyo which we have followed is joined by another with a great abundance of water coming from the sierra which we have had on the left, and toward which we have seen large groves appropriate to rivers, and a very good valley to which was given the name of San Patricio.[1] In this valley a good vein was found from which pieces of silver ore were taken or dug. At the Puerto de San Carlos another like it was seen, and from there to this place the hills give many indications of minerals.

March 18.—It was very cloudy at daybreak, but preparatory to beginning the march I sent a party with axes and other tools to make this valley passable, because it is very thickly grown with trees and seemed to be very narrow. The trees and narrowness lasted only a league, after which it began to widen out, and therefore we passed through it without any difficulty.[2] This valley runs generally north and north-northwest, in which directions we traveled six leagues, when we reached another and very beautiful valley into which a large river flows from the

[1] Camp was near Tripp Flat. San Patricio Canyon is now called Bautista Canyon.

[2] Down Bautista Canyon to San Jacinto River (Rio de San Joseph) just above the town of San Jacinto. See p. 92.

sierra on the right. I say it is large, for the native
Californian who crossed it higher up, and in the dry
season, says it carried the same amount of water
then as now. We called this valley San Joseph. It
is suitable even for a city because of its beauty,
abundance of timber of various kinds, lands for crops
with irrigation and without it, pasturage, and other
things which might be desired. We remained here
to pass this day, and five heathen women were seen,
but, although they talked with some of our men, they
could not be persuaded to come to camp.

March 19.—At eight o'clock we continued our
march northwest down the valley of San Joseph for
about three leagues from the place where we spent
the night. It appears to be converted into a great
marsh in whose spacious circumference are seen
several brooks, some of which run to the south and
others to the northwest. These brooks join several
arroyos which come from the same sierra on the
right, and altogether they form, three leagues beyond this marsh, a most beautiful lake several leagues
in circumference.[1] To its natural beauty is added
another object of diversion, namely the numberless
birds which live on it, especially white geese, in such
a multitude that they look like great sand beaches.

I called this lake San Antonio Bucareli, and
almost at the end of it, which must be about six
leagues from the last camp, I halted for the night in

[1] San Jacintó Lake (or Mystic Lake) northeast of Lakeview. It
was drained some years ago.

good pasturage on the skirts of some hills where, before reaching them, we thought there must be some drainage. But this assumption turned out to be quite erroneous, for both from these hills and from others that are larger the water runs to this lake. On the banks of the lake we have seen a number of deer of various kinds which for months past and since we set out from the neighborhood of my presidio we have not encountered. Today we have seen also some heathen, who look the same as those noted formerly and who, having accompanied us for a short distance, returned to their houses or habitations.

March 20.—At eight o'clock in the morning we set out on the road to the northwest. Going five leagues, leaving on our right various sierras, all snow-covered, and having traveled two more leagues to the west-northwest, we came to a valley almost in every way equal to that of San Joseph already described.[1] It has a good river which the native Californian tells me empties into the sea, and which they called Santa Anna when they passed it on the first expedition to Monte Rey. We traveled a league and a half to it to discover a ford, but none was found because it runs in a narrow gorge, so I decided to halt for the night and make a little bridge, in order to take the packs safely across, since the riding animals

[1] Swinging across Moreno Valley, Anza descended through the site of Riverside to Santa Ana River and camped some distance below Mt. Rubidoux.

have to swim for a short distance and even the loose ones mire on emerging. This work was begun immediately after we halted.

Right here and a little farther back there were several villages of heathen. They were not disturbed on seeing us, but they were excited when they asked the native Californian, whom they recognized, if he came from the same Peninsula, for when he said, "No," and pointed in the direction from which we had come, they marveled greatly. This native understood their language, which he says is the same as that spoken in the new mission of San Gabriel. Only in this have I distinguished these people from those farther back, for in their nakedness, their harmlessness, their lack of robustness, and other circumstances they are the same.

March 21.—A little after daybreak the bridge was finished, and at eight o'clock, when the packs were carried over, we immediately set forth on the march. Going northwest five leagues, having on the right various snow-covered mountains, we came to a good arroyo grown with trees; and having traveled two more leagues we came to a better one, with a greater abundance of water and trees, where we halted for the night.[1] Today many deer of different species were seen pasturing in the fields, and on the skirts of the sierra to the right many sites which would be useful for good settlements.

[1] Camp on March 21 was on San Antonio Creek, near Ontario. Continuing northwest to the vicinity of San Dimas, Anza then swung west.

March 22.—At seven o'clock today we continued
the march over good terrain. We went northwest
for about three leagues and five more west and west-
northwest, in order to avoid many wet places where
it was miry, because of the drainage from the sierra
which we have had on our right. Having with some
difficulty effected the crossing of the river of the
mission of San Gabriel, which is established in
Northern California, I reached the mission just at
sunset, and immediately made my arrival known to
the corporal and the eight soldiers who constitute
its guard.[1]

In the mission there were four friars *de propaganda fide* of the College of San Fernando de Mexico.
They welcomed us with great jubilation and demonstrations of joy, with solemn peal of the bells and
the chanting of the *Te Deum*, as an act of thanksgiving for our successful arrival in this country.
This was all the more pleasing to them because it
was unexpected, since they had no more than a vague
rumor of this expedition, which they even considered
to be impracticable. Even after these friars and
soldiers saw us they could not quite persuade themselves that we were from the province of Sonora,
nor that so few men would undertake such a journey,
nor that Sonora, and especially the Colorado River,
could be so near by. I asked these fathers if the new
commander, Don Fernando Rivera y Moncada, was
in Monte Rey, and they replied that three days ago

[1] The mission was then about three miles south of its present
location.

the news of his appointment was made known in the port of San Diego by the frigate *Santiago* or *Nueva Galicia* which was anchored there, but that they did not know where he might be at the present time.

March 23.—As a more solemn act of thanksgiving to the Omnipotent God for the good fortune which he has been pleased to give this expedition, these friars chanted a Mass, and preached a sermon in which was applauded the piety of the king and of the most excellent señor viceroy in wishing to extend the true religion among so many heathen, sole object of the attention of both. After this had been done, with a view to continuing my route I asked various questions of the missionary fathers here.

I asked the minister himself[1] if he could aid me with some provisions and mounts with which to make the journey, since I lacked both the one and the other. But, although he was generous in the matter, he made plain to me his inability, for with respect to provisions he was so hard up that he himself, his three companions, and the guard, had no other ration than three tortillas of maize and some herbs from the fields; and as for mounts, he needed the few animals which the mission possesses to send to the port of San Diego for some provisions for all these friars and their reduced Indians who are in such straightened circumstances, because the frigate mentioned is anchored there. And since the establishments from here forward, as far as the presidio of Monte Rey, which this frigate has not been able to

[1] Father Paterna.

reach, although it has attempted it, are in worse circumstances, I was not disposed to demand more than what this friar offered me, and this meant that for fifteen days I must maintain myself with all my men on the rations mentioned, which I accepted with thanks until I might find recourse elsewhere.

In consequence of this I consulted with the two fathers who are with me as to what means we should take for continuing our journey, and we agreed to send to the port of San Diego to get supplies and mounts; that the supplies should be brought on the few animals which with some sacrifice to himself the father missionary had offered us; and that if we obtained both of these kinds of aid we should go on with all of the expedition to Monte Rey in order from there to go out directly to one of the places which we have passed through, notwithstanding that from the reports which they give us of the location of that presidio we judge that the best route will be from Sonora to the mission of San Luís, which is distant from this one seventy leagues.

Since engineer Don Miguel Constanzó and Captain Don Gaspar de Portolá have traveled over the road which runs from here to Monte Rey, I omit setting down the details regarding the sites and the tribes which inhabit them, in view of the fact that through these officers the superior authorities will be better informed in these matters, because of their natural ability, and to whose power of expression my poor talents cannot attain.

March 24.—This day like the foregoing was devoted to rest.

March 25.—I sent four soldiers with seven pack mules to seek provisions at the port of San Diego, for which purpose I wrote to the commander of the port and the commander of the frigate *Nueva Galicia,* which is anchored there.

From the 26th to the 31st we remained in this mission.

From the 1st to the 4th of April we continued to be here.

April 5.—At twelve o'clock today the men sent to the port of San Diego returned with replies from the commanders hereinbefore named, who tell me that, try as hard as they may, they can not provide more supplies than those which they are sending, these consisting of six fanegas[1] of maize half spoiled, a tierce of jerked beef almost unfit to eat, a tierce of flour, and two fanegas of beans.

Having made a calculation from the foregoing of the time that the men of my expedition can be maintained, it is found to be scarcely sixteen days, even making use of all the beans. But these can be used here only on condition that they lend the soldiers ollas in which to cook them; for after setting out on the march, for lack of these ollas this grain can not serve as food. And the same is true of the maize, since it is not of the kind that can be reduced to pinole, which is the regular ration of the soldiers.

---

[1] The *fanega* is a Spanish bushel.

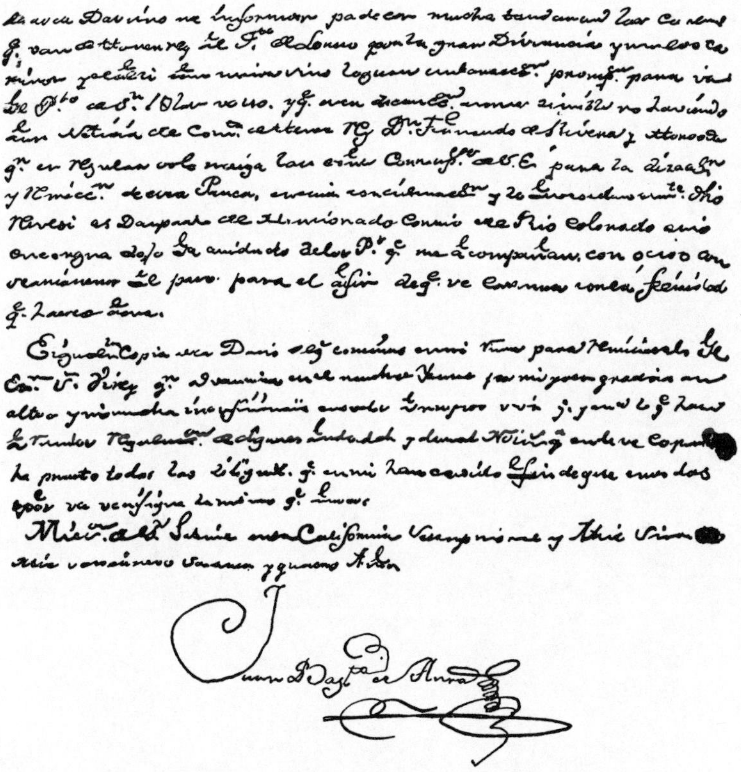

Last page of Anza's diary to San Gabriel.

In view of the foregoing, the provisions are not sufficient for making our journey to Monte Rey, for we shall not be able to accomplish it in two weeks, not having reserved any extra riding animals, and ours being in such a bad condition as has been stated before. And this would be worse if we should go on to that presidio, for those experienced in the road consider it very difficult because of the many mires, and because of the continuance of the heavy rains which are being experienced the same as here, where they do not cease. I have therefore decided, in conference with one of the fathers who are with me, because the other has gone to San Diego[1] and has not returned with the provisions, as I have said, that the present father shall return to the Colorado River with most of the troops, to await me there till I return from the presidio of Monte Rey. And to Monte Rey I shall go with six soldiers in light order of marching, to examine its situation, and in the light of this information to form a more exact opinion regarding the road which may be opened to it from Sonora, since the plan which I desired to follow and was set down on the 23d of last month is now impossible. And I shall set out for that presidio on the 10th of this present month.

In view of this return to the Colorado River we also agreed that when our troops reach it the soldiers shall conduct to the presidio of El Altar the extraordinary courier who by command of his Excel-

[1] Garcés had gone to San Diego. Díaz went later.

lency brought me my orders for the present expedition, and that he shall take the diaries which have been kept on the journey.[1] His Excellency commands me to send them from the presidio of Monte Rey, but I assume that he will approve this plan, which aims only at letting him know as soon as possible that the greater part of the expedition is finished, which would not result as quickly in that way as I promise myself it will be accomplished by the method indicated.

The missionary fathers located here inform me that much delay is experienced by the letters which go from Monte Rey to the port of Loreto, because of the great distance and the bad roads, and from there even greater delay if they do not find a vessel ready to go to the port of San Blas or to another port. And this delay is more to be feared because there is no word of the commander of Monte Rey, Don Fernando Rivera y Moncada, who doubtless only bears orders from his Excellency for the direction and dispatching of mails from this place. In view of this and of what has been said before, I have decided to dispatch the courier mentioned from the Colorado River, leaving his orders to the care of the fathers who are with him, with other instructions concerning the march, to the end that it may be effected with the same success as up to now.

I likewise have copied this diary of what has taken place on my journey, in order to send it to

[1] The courier was Juan Bautista Valdés. The diary was transmitted with a letter of April 10. See Volume V of this work.

his Excellency the Viceroy. He will note in it many errors due to my lack of practice in keeping diaries and to my great shortcomings in all things; although with respect to directions, estimate of leagues traveled, and other things which are set forth in it, I have taken all the pains of which I have been capable, to the end that at all times whatever I have set down may be verified.

Mission of San Gabriel in Northern California, April 5, 1774.

JUAN BAP.TA DE ANZA (Rubric).

ANZA'S RETURN DIARY

1774

(C)

CONTINUATION OF THE DIARY OF THE CAP-
TAIN OF THE PRESIDIO OF TUBAC, DON JUAN
BAUTISTA DE ANZA, COMMANDER OF THE EX-
PEDITION SENT TO EXPLORE A ROAD BY LAND
FROM SONORA TO MONTE REY, BEGINNING ON
THE 6TH OF APRIL, 1774, WHEN HE WAS AT THE
MISSION OF SAN GABRIEL, FIRST OF THE NEW
ESTABLISHMENTS, AND INCLUDING HIS RETURN
TO THE PRESIDIO OF TUBAC, ALREADY MEN-
TIONED.[1]

From Wednesday to Saturday, April 6 to April
9, we remained at this mission,[2] without any other
occurrence than the continuation of the rains.

Sunday, April 10.—In virtue of what was decided on the 5th of last month I charged the Reverend Father Fray Juan Díaz that as soon as his
companion, Father Fray Francisco Garcés, should
reach this mission,[3] they should set out upon the
return to the Colorado River with all the soldiers
remaining here, and having arrived there dispatch

[1] Continuacion del Diario del Capitan del Presidio de Tubac D.ⁿ
Juan Bautista de Anza. A. G. I., 104–6–15. Certified copy. Mexico,
November 26, 1774.

[2] San Gabriel.

[3] Father Garcés had gone to San Diego.

the extraordinary courier mentioned.[1] I have also requested him to make the journey in the same manner as when we came, in order that there may be no alteration among the tribes who inhabit it, and this admonition, together with others, I have made separately to our soldiers. At nine o'clock today I set out from the mission of San Gabriel, and going west-northwest I traveled four leagues to the Porciúncula River. I followed this stream for two more leagues, and for the rest of the fourteen leagues I traveled west, continuing till vespers.[2]—From Tubac to the vicinity of El Triunfo, 282 leagues.

Monday, April 11.—Shortly after sunrise I set out in the same direction, passing among many docile heathen. At the end of the afternoon, having traveled sixteen leagues, I halted for the night on this side of the Rio de la Carpintería and the first village of the Channel of Santa Barbara.[3]—From Tubac to the Rio de la Carpintería on the Channel of Santa Barbara, 298 leagues.

Tuesday, April 12.—At six o'clock this morning I continued along the same channel and in the same western direction until I came to this side of the

[1] This was Valdés.

[2] The Porciúncula River was the present Los Angeles River. Anza ascended the Los Angeles River to the edge of San Fernando Valley, and turned west, around the point of the mountain. His camp for the night was near Triunfo, still on the map, in Russell Valley, west of Calabasas.

[3] Camp was near Ventura. Anza's Rio de la Carpintería was Ventura River, then commonly called Rio de la Asunción.

village of Mestletlitán, after having traveled sixteen leagues.[1]

Wednesday, April 13.—Along the same channel and in the same western direction I made fifteen leagues today and halted very close to the village of Los Pedernales.[2]

Thursday, April 14.—Going west I traveled four leagues along the same channel to the place where it ends, which is the point of La Concepción, where also the Santa Rosa River joins the same point.[3] We could not cross the river because we arrived at high tide, and although it is true that this does not enter the river more than about three-quarters of a league, yet above this point, because of the high, steep banks and the thick growth along the river, it does not afford a crossing anywhere else, and therefore it was necessary to wait for the tide to go down, which I did, remaining here today.—From Tubac to the end of the channel at Point Concepción and near the Santa Rosa River, 333 leagues.

All this channel is thickly settled with heathen, so thickly indeed that they are the most numerous that I have seen from the Colorado River to here. They go naked like most all of the heathen. They are robust, tall, and fairly well armed with bow and arrows, both of which are small, and are very

[1] On a lagoon west of Santa Barbara near Goleta. Mescal Island still preserves the name.

[2] East of Rocky Point. See p. 103.

[3] From Los Pedernales to Santa Rosa River was north rather than west. The Santa Rosa River is now the Santa Inez.

timid. They live close together, for each town is composed of forty houses or more, which they make round like a half orange. They are very much given to commerce and to labor, in which respect their equal will not be found among their class of heathen.

Many devote themselves to making their launches and the things necessary for their equipment. These launches they make with two prows and from thirty-six to forty palms long, with corresponding width. All are made of more than twelve pieces, but they are so well joined, seamed, and caulked that they do not leak at all, and they make them so light that two men carry them with very little trouble. The tools with which they make them are of flint. With these I saw them working, and I even bought some, and I had to admire both their skill and their patience. In each village there are fifteen or twenty launches in use, and in each one they were making not less than from seven to ten new ones.

Many others occupy themselves in working stones from which they make little vessels which they use in cooking, with such perfection that they look as if made by a wheel, and this is true not only of small pieces but of large ones and of many modes of construction. I also bought some of these, as well as others of hard wood or timber, such as live oak and madroño. Their women also take a part in these labors and especially in the making of what they call coritas, which serve them for various purposes and are finer than any of the kind which I had seen hitherto. The reason why all the Indians make them, indeed, is that the materials of which they are made are not found in other regions. In their launches, with which the sea is covered most of the day, engaged in fishing with hooks made of shells which are as perfect as those fashioned of iron, these people go to the islands to the south of them, some of which I think must be four or five leagues distant.

I have seen in accounts the estimates which they make of the population of the channel and it reaches to eight or ten thousand persons, but unless we include those who live on these islands and those who live on the mainland apart from that which is strictly known as the channel, I do not think they will reach that number. All the country which they occupy is as fertile and beautiful as the regions independent of this channel, where it is certainly a re-creation to the sight, especially to one who has observed the extreme sterility of the Gulf of California, where neither trees nor even useless shrubs are seen, while here, on the contrary, fields as green as they are flower-strewn reach to the very waters of the sea.

Friday, April 15.—Crossing the Santa Rosa River at daybreak, I went west-northwest for twelve leagues, at the end of which I encountered more than two hundred excessively docile heathen, and some springs having an abundance of asphalt. After this I traveled four more leagues to the north to reach the mission of San Luís,[1] where there are four missionaries from San Fernando de Mexico, the same as those already mentioned, and eight soldier guards, who gave me the same sort of welcome as the one described at San Gabriel.—From Tubac to the mission of San Luís, 345 leagues.

Saturday, April 16.—Going north-northwest and having made thirteen leagues, I halted for the night at the Nacimiento River.[2]

Sunday, April 17.—Continuing in the same direction, and having traveled seven leagues, I arrived at the mission of San Antonio,[3] where there are the same number of friars and soldiers as in the former mission. Continuing my march from here at two o'clock in the afternoon, going north, I traveled six leagues to the place of Los Ossitos, where I camped for the night.[4]—From Tubac to the mission of San Antonio, 365 leagues. And to Los Ossitos on the River of Monte Rey, 371 leagues.

Monday, April 18.—Starting at daybreak, I traveled west-northwest and west for thirteen leagues, at the end of which I arrived at the presidio of

[1] San Luís Obispo, on the same site, is now a good-sized city. The asphalt springs mentioned were near Maxwellton.

[2] Anza went over the present highway northeast through Santa Margarita and Atascadero, and turned off to the left at Paso Robles to the Nacimiento River, still so-called.

[3] San Antonio Mission at first was founded about a league southeast of the site of the present ruins.

[4] Los Ocitos or Ossitos (the Bears) was on the Salinas River northwest of King City. From that point Anza descended the Salinas River past the site of Spreckels, then turned westward to Monterey practically along the present highway.

Monte Rey. Its commander and troops received us with the same jubilation and satisfaction as those mentioned farther back. And they were convinced that the opening of a road recently effected would assure the stability of these missions and presidios, and that in a short time they would emerge from the infelicities and misery to which in all things they are now reduced because of the misfortune suffered, as has been said, by the vessels in their efforts to reach this port. All of our people living here have told me of their troubles, which today are greater than those related of the mission of San Gabriel, and in view of them and of their long duration I can not find words to praise the merit which the friars, the commanders, and the troops have demonstrated by remaining in these posts. The total distance that has been traveled to this presidio is 384 leagues.—From Tubac to the presidio of Monte Rey in this Northern California, 384 leagues.

Tuesday, April 19.—I remained in this presidio.

Wednesday, April 20.—I went to the mission of San [Carlos del] Carmelo,[1] distant from the presidio a little more than a league, both to see this new establishment, the last of Northern California, and to repay the visit made me yesterday by the reverend father superior of its missionaries.[2] A few days before my arrival here the mast of a vessel, the construction and the wood of which are not known by our people who live here, was stranded on the beach which is very close by. They conclude that it broke

1 The present Carmel Mission.   2 This was Father Palóu.

two-thirds off. It is pierced clear through with very strong nails, with large heads and with two points which are not clinched, and the iron of these nails has not rusted, nor are the points which stuck out blunt. For these last two reasons such experts in the matter of vessels as are here infer that the one to which this piece belonged was wrecked not very long ago. On the first occasion that arises it will be taken to the port of San Blas, in order that it may be carefully examined.

Thursday, April 21.—After having attended Mass, celebrated by the father superior of the missions for the same purposes as at San Gabriel, I returned to the presidio of Monte Rey. Having suggested to its commander, Don Pedro Faxes, that it would be well if some of the soldiers in his command should be made acquainted with the road or way out to the Colorado River (for as to that for Sonora there are plenty of guides) he agreed that this should be done, and for this purpose he detailed a party of six men.

Friday, April 22.—I set out to return from the presidio of Monte Rey to the one in my charge by marches and directions opposite to those by which I came, in the execution of which I halted for the night at the place of Los Ossitos.[1]

Saturday, April 23.—By the road mentioned I reached the mission of San Antonio.

Sunday, April 24.—I halted for the night at the Nacimiento River.

[1] On Salinas River near King City.

Monday, April 25.—I reached the mission of San Luís.

Tuesday, April 26.—I halted for the night near the Santa Rosa River.

Wednesday, April 27.—At two o'clock in the afternoon I met the father president of the establishments of this Northern California, Fray Junípero Serra, who is going to the last establishments mentioned, on his way from the City of Mexico.[1] He requested me with repeated urging that I should stop with him that he might learn of my journey, and I consented, remaining with him the rest of the day and night.

Thursday, April 28.—I came to camp for the night to the place which they call Dos Rancherías.[2]

Friday, April 29.—I halted at La Cuesta.[3]

Saturday, April 30.—I reached Porciúncula River and halted for the night.

Sunday, May 1.—I again reached the mission of San Gabriel.—From Monte Rey to the mission of San Gabriel, 120 leagues.

Notwithstanding that right here I rely on the report which Captains Don Gaspar de Portolá and Don Miguel Constansó may have given of the circumstances of the country from here to Monte Rey, it has seemed to me well to add a statement of the present condition of these new establishments sub-

[1] The meeting was evidently somewhere on the Santa Barbara Channel.

[2] Evidently the same as Dos Pueblos, on Dos Pueblos Creek, near Naples.

[3] East of Camarillo, at the foot of Conejo Grade.

sequent to the departure of these officials, according
to what I have seen and have been told. Amongst
the heathen tribes nothing has happened to alter the
opinion which has been entertained of their gentleness and docility, of which each day they give
greater proofs, offering their children for baptism
and some of them even offering themselves. This
has not been completely possible, for, since provisions have been so scarce, the missionaries have
not been able to support them without allowing them
to live outside, which should cease just as soon as
they acquire the character of Christians. But I
know that the missionaries support more than five
hundred, which there already are between here and
Carmelo, with only a pint and a half of atole mixed
with water, on which they live through the whole
twenty-four hours.

The fathers themselves have told me that if even
this atole had been abundant there would be twice
or three times as much harvest, but for lack of this
food they have supported themselves, as they say,
"outside of the house." They have hopes that in
the future their labor will be better rewarded, since
this year there is probability that they will reap a
reasonable harvest of wheat, which has failed up
to now more for lack of seed grain than because of
the sterility of the soil. The fields of this grain
which I have seen yield very abundantly. With
respect to rankness of growth, the size of the head,
and the thickness of stalk, I have not seen any so
good in the provinces of Sonora; and the same is

Copia

Continuacion del Diario del Capitan del Presidio de Tubac Dn.
Juan Bautista de Anza Commandante dela expedicion destinada à descubrir Camino por tierra desde Sonora à Monte Rey que empieza en el dia
6. de Abril de 1774. que se hallaba en la Mision de Sn. Gabriel primera
delos Nuevos establecimientos, y comprehende su Regreso hasta el expresado Presidio de Tubac.

Dia 6. à 9   Nos mantubimos en esta Mision sin mas novedad que
de Abril
Mirst à ese la continuacion de Lluvias.

Dia 10. Domo   En virtud delo resuelto, el dia 5. ultimo, antecedente on-   De Tubac
cargué al R. P. Fr. Juan Diaz que luego que llegue à esta   à la Inmes
Mision, su compañero el P. Fr. Francisco Garces, pongan on   del Triunfo
practica su Regreso al Rio Colorado con el todo dela Tropa, que   282.
queda aqui, y arrivados à el el despacho, al enunciado Correo,
estrahordinario cuio transito igualmente le hè Suplicado ve
haga en la misma conformidad que quando hemos venido pa.
que no haiga Alteracion, en las Naciones que lo Pueblan.
cuia adwertencia con otras hize separadamente à nra. Tropa.

            Alas nueve de este dia, salì dela Mision de San
Gabriel, y con rumbo, al Oest - Noxueste Camine quatro
leguas hasta el Rio de Porciuncula, el que segui por otras
dos, y las restantes hasta catorce, yve al Oest hasta las
oraciones dela noche.

Dia 11   A poco que salió el Sol, tomé el proprio rumbo-   De Tubac
Lunes   pasando por entre mucha, y docil Gentilidad, al fin dela   al Rio dela
          tarde, y caminadas diez y seis leguas, paré para pasar la mas Carpinteria
          noche, de esta parte del Rio dela Carpinteria, y primera 298 en la Ca
          Rancheria, dela Canal de Santa Barbara.   nal de Santa
                                                    Barbara

Dia 12   Mas 6. de él continué por la mencionada Canal, y-
Martes   Rumbo al Oest, hasta llegan à este lado dela Rancheria

First page of Anza's return diary.

true of barley, peas, beans, and other vegetables, but they say that the barley deteriorates greatly at the time of heading, because of the continuous fogs, especially at Carmelo and Monte Rey. But from this damage this mission of San Gabriel is exempted, where all the crops which they have sown with care have yielded well. And the missions below this one without exception have good-sized fields of this crop.

Monday, May 2.—By means of the astrolabe which he was able to obtain at the mission of San Diego,[1] to which he took the trouble to go to be instructed for his intelligence, the Reverend Father Fray Juan Díaz, after he had dispatched his companion Father Fray Garcés and our soldiers to the Colorado River on the 13th of last month, he having decided to await me in this mission, made an observation of its latitude and found it to be in thirty-three degrees and fifty-two minutes.[2]

Tuesday, May 3.—At two o'clock in the afternoon I set out from the mission of San Gabriel toward the east and east-southeast, straightening out as much as possible the road which I followed on coming, as I shall continue to do in order to shorten the distances. Having traveled this afternoon five leagues we halted for the night at a stream called Arroyo de los Alisos, the first one which we mentioned on our first arrival at San Gabriel as

[1] After Anza left San Gabriel, Father Díaz went to San Diego for the astrolabe and to receive instructions in its use.

[2] The correct latitude is nearly 34° 6'.

running out to the neighborhood of that mission from the Sierra Nevada.[1]

Wednesday, May 4.—Going east I traveled five leagues, at the end of which I crossed the Santa Ana River, and afterward I went five more leagues to the neighborhood of the lake of San Antonio Bucareli.[2] To the north of this lake, in the snow-covered range, a good opening is to be seen. This I judge to be the most suitable way to go straight to the mission of San Luís or the presidio of Monte Rey when coming from Sonora, since from the first of these two places named I descried very distinctly the same snow-covered range, there being no other to confuse with it.[3]—From Monte Rey to the lake of San Antonio Bucareli, 135 leagues.

Thursday, May 5.—Going generally east and east-southeast, four leagues were traveled, as far as the beautiful valley of San Josef, whose latitude was observed and found to be in thirty-three degrees and forty-six and a half minutes. After having made this observation we continued our march in the same direction for five leagues, when we reached the site of San Patricio.[4]—From Monte Rey to the valley of San Patricio, 144 leagues.

[1] Arroyo de San Antonio. Camp was near Ontario.

[2] After crossing the Santa Ana River Anza evidently reached San Antonio Lake by a route more direct than his former trail.

[3] He evidently means Cajón Pass, through which he knew Fages to have gone to San Luís, a point on which he is strangely silent.

[4] He ascended Bautista Canyon. Camp was near Tripp Flat, in Cahuilla Valley.

Friday, May 6.—We set out from San Patricio, and having traveled east-southeast about eight leagues we halted at Santa Catharina[1] to pass the night. Having observed in passing the latitude of the Puerto Real de San Carlos, it was found to be in thirty-three degrees and forty-two minutes. On the march which we made today, in the neighborhood of some hills some arrows were surreptitiously shot at the riding animals which were being driven loose, and three of them were slightly wounded. An effort was made to see who had shot the arrows and they were found to be four heathen. The most guilty one was given a beating and made to understand that for his deed he deserved to be put to death, but that this was not done on account of our natural compassion. On arriving at this place of Santa Catharina I learned by a writing left me by Father Garcés, who is going ahead, that the same thing happened to him.[2] This occurrence seems to have come from the fact that among these heathen there are some from the neighborhood of San Diego, who were recognized by the party which comes from Monte Rey. They inform me that these have always had this custom, and I infer that this explains why the affair happened, for when we passed through the first time we met more than two hundred, and they did nothing more than manifest an inclination for

[1] At Reed's, or Lower Willows, on Coyote Creek, at the lower end of Collins Valley.

[2] Father Font tells us that this warning by Father Garcés was carved on a willow tree.

stealing a few of our belongings.—From Monte Rey to Santa Catharina, 152 leagues.

Saturday, May 7.—With no other occurrence than the one just related we set out from this place, going in general to the southeast until we came to San Gregorio. Here we turned to the east-southeast, by which route we arrived, after having gone ten or eleven leagues, at the Ciénega de San Sebastián.[1]—From Monte Rey to the Ciénega de San Sebastián, 163 leagues.

Sunday, May 8.—A little before sunrise we set forth on the trail of the soldiers who were going ahead, with the hope of finding some watering-place midway between this marsh and the lake of Santa Olaya. We traveled as far as possible to the east-southeast and also to the south, to go round the sand dunes which stretch across. But I went in this direction and on the trail mentioned for only seven leagues, at the end of which I took a higher latitude than that followed by those soldiers. By this route I traveled ten more leagues to the Pozo de las Angustias,[2] where I arrived after nightfall; and, the men having rested, because there was no pasturage in that neighborhood we continued our route for five more leagues to the east-southeast.

Monday, May 9.—At the end of the distance just mentioned we arrived late in the morning at this

[1] San Gregorio was on San Felipe Creek, Borrego Valley. San Sebastián was at Harper's Well on San Felipe Creek, near its junction with Carrizo Creek.

[2] This stop was evidently at El Carrizal. See Díaz's statement, p. 296.

lake of Santa Olaya.—From Monte Rey to the lake
of Santa Olaya on the Colorado River, 185 leagues.

The foregoing journey is the longest on the new
road which has been discovered, but by going from
the wells of El Carrizal to those of Santa Rosa de
las Laxas it can be made with all ease; then going
from the last named wells by another day's march
to the Ciénega de San Sebastián, in this way any
pack train will accomplish the marches without any
great difficulty. The latitude was observed at this
lake and found to be in thirty-two degrees and thirty-
four minutes.

This afternoon we continued eastward along the
meadows, up the Colorado River, and having traveled about four leagues we halted in the territory
of the Llumas.[1] The rejoicing with which they welcomed us was a matter to admire, for all incessantly
went about shouting "Capitán," "Señor," "Soldados," "Compañeros." This was kept up all night
by the large crowd which assembled and remained
with us. During the night they told me with great
grief on their part that the soldiers whom I left in
care of Captain Palma had departed, contrary to
the advice of the captain himself and of many of
these people, solely because of the vague rumor
which had come from the sierra that the heathen
living there had killed me and all the soldiers. They
said that these soldiers had left some provisions in
the care of Palma, who had kept them in his house

[1] Camp was evidently at the place where Anza camped on February 11 of the same year.

until the arrival of Father Garcés, who was there now awaiting me, nothing else having happened.

Tuesday, May 10.—Traveling east-northeast[1] and east eight leagues, at noon I reached the junction of the rivers and the site of San Dionisio, where Captain Palma soon arrived, rejoicing like all his tribe, many hundreds of whom I already had at my side. Treating me with as much confidence as if I were one of his own kind, he made known his pleasure at my return, and how inconsolable he was for the departure of the soldiers whom I had left in his care until the return of Father Garcés, to whom he told me he had delivered some pack-loads of provisions and some beeves left him by those who had gone without his consent. For all this, and for the fidelity which he has shown in this occurrence, I gave this heathen captain the thanks and the praise which he deserves.—From Monte Rey to the junction of the Gila and Colorado rivers, 197 leagues.

At three in the afternoon of this same day this captain had a strong raft ready, in order that I might cross both rivers accompanied by the hundreds of natives mentioned, that they might guide it, and with whom I felt as much at home as if they had been my own people. The captain himself carried me and put me on the raft, together with Father Juan Díaz and a servant of mine. On it I crossed the rivers, which must be six hundred varas wide, but I felt so secure that in all my life I have never crossed another river with greater confidence, since even

[1] By a slip the MS. reads "east-northwest."

though the craft might have capsized I had close by me more than five hundred persons ready to rescue me. The same security was felt by the others who accompanied me, all of whom they got over with all our baggage this same afternoon. At five o'clock in the afternoon I reached the camp, where Father Garcés and the soldiers who had come ahead were awaiting me, and they confirmed the reports already related, saying that nothing else worthy of note had happened during their journey.

Wednesday, May 11.—The latitude of this place was observed, very close to the site of San Dionisio, and found to be in thirty-two degrees and forty-four minutes, which does not agree with the observation made by the first discoverer, Father Francisco Eusebio Quino, as is related in the book of *Afanes Apostólicos*,[1] folio 288, where it is said that he found it to be in thirty-five and a half degrees. This day was dedicated to rest for all. Since we have returned to the Colorado River from a much longer distance than our predecessors who came to it ever imagined going beyond it, it will not be out of place to say that although we have tried to learn from these heathen and from others where we have traveled, in what direction are situated the famous Sierra Azul and the Laguna de Azogue, which are told of by Lieutenant Don Matheo Mange,[2] companion of Father Quino just mentioned, in a book which he dedicated to the most excellent señor viceroy, Duque de Alburquerque, as well as the Rio Amarillo on the

---

[1] José de Ortega, *Apostólicos Afanes* (Barcelona, 1754).

[2] Juan Matheo Mange, *Luz de Tierra Incógnita* (Mexico, 1926).

other side of the Colorado, we have not discovered, even taking their existence for granted, any foundation to lead us to think that these reports may be verified.

Thursday, May 12.—We still remained in this place, and since the Reverend Father Garcés has told me that through the messenger who goes directed to his Excellency he asked the governor of the provinces to send me some provisions to this place, thinking that we would not have enough, together with those which are here, to enable me to reach my presidio, I, knowing the contrary to be the case, decided to send two soldiers this very day to turn back those who might be bringing them, because I am not able to go by the route over which they must come.[1] This afternoon I sent back across the Colorado River the party who came from Monte Rey,[2] in order that they might return to it posted as to the routes and directions of the roads which go from here to Sonora, and of the places in which they can get guides if they should need to go there.

Friday, May 13.—Shortly after sunrise we raised our train to march up the Gila River, which most of them did. But I remained in this place until Palma, the captain of the Yumas, should finish taking to the other side of the Colorado River four beeves which I gave to the party that is returning to Monte Rey. Having done so, he came to tell me goodbye. At the

[1] Valdés went by way of Caborca and Horcasitas, the route by which the supplies would come. Anza returned up the Gila River.

[2] These were the six soldiers of Monterey who accompanied Anza to learn the road.

same time an old Yuma arrived with the report that some members of the Cojat tribe were waiting till we should leave in order to steal some horses from that party, because they had come from the country where their enemies, the Jahuenches,[1] live, and whom therefore they do not consider their relatives, as they consider me and my soldiers. But the informant added that most of the members of the tribe were opposed to this plan.

Since in such cases nothing ought to be despised, notwithstanding the simplicity and the artlessness which the deed displays, I decided, in order to obviate any unfortunate occurrence, immediately to send Captain Palma with the native Californian to conduct the party from that district, and to tell the corporal about this report, together with other instructions which I sent him in writing pertinent to the matter throughout his journey. And likewise I sent a notice to the authors of the disturbance that I was waiting to see whether or not they were carrying out their evil plan, in order to crush it; and for greater effect I sent word to our train to return, which it did this afternoon, just at the time when the relative of Captain Palma told me that the latter had taken with him more than two hundred chosen Yumas to go to conduct our party mentioned in safety.

Saturday, May 14.—Nothing in particular happened.

---

[1] Cajuenches. Anza distinguished between the Cojats and the Cajuenches, whereas others generally consider them as identical.

Sunday, May 15.—At twelve o'clock today Captain Palma returned with the native of California, by whom I received word from the corporal of the party which is returning to Monte Rey, that he was about to continue his march from the place where they were leaving him, that thus far nothing had occurred to cause him anxiety, and that from that place forward he did not expect any trouble. He added that this Captain Palma had delivered to him two riding animals which he had lost the day before, they having been stolen by two young heathen, from whose possession the same Captain Palma took them, punishing the offenders. At the same time Palma recovered an· ax which had been stolen from us;[1] he brought it and I gave it to him. Both told me in the same terms that this occurrence was only the talk of some young fellows. Palma said he would have punished it even without my presence, and that he would do likewise so long as he lived, during which time he and all his tribe would never lose their affection for and fidelity to the king.

I again admonished this heathen captain to maintain peace with the neighboring tribes, because it is the wish of both majesties, and to escort and bring to our settlements any Spaniard who may arrive in his territory. He agreed to carry out these and other instructions, and I gave him as a recompense for the services which he has performed for the king my bastón, four beeves, and some articles of clothing, and I should have been glad to be able still

[1] Anza mentions this theft on his way to California.

further to reward this heathen barbarian, whose equal perhaps is not to be found among people of his kind.

At three o'clock in the afternoon I said goodbye to this captain and set forth up the Gila River, which from its source to its junction with the Colorado runs generally from northeast and east to south and west. I decided to ascend this stream in order to make my return to my presidio more direct and easy, as well as to establish peace among the tribes which live on its banks. Having traveled three leagues I halted for the night on the banks of the river at a place where there was pasturage.[1]

Monday, May 16.—At daybreak I set forth along the river, which continues with an abundance of water and good lands for crops, although with very little or no pasturage, for in the distance of eight or nine leagues only one small patch was found.[2]

Tuesday, May 17.—At daylight I continued up the same river six leagues, at the end of which we passed the point of the range where ends the sierra of the Aguaje Empinado mentioned in our going and which I called San Pasqual.[3] To this distance we added two more leagues, going to a place where some pasturage was found and where we camped for the night.

Wednesday, May 18.—At the same hour as yesterday we continued along the same river, where we

[1] Up the river about half way from Yuma to the Gila Range.
[2] Camp was near Laguna Salobre, west of Wellton.
[3] Mohawk Range. Camp was two leagues above.

found a trail of heathen. Following it for four leagues, it led to a village of about a hundred persons of the Cocomaricopa tribe, most of whom were not afraid of us because there was a Pápago or Pima among them, by means of whom and of my interpreter in this idiom we were able to understand everybody. And through the same persons I exhorted them, in the same way that I have described among the Yumas, to peace with these and other tribes, instructing them that any one who might be injured by another must report it to the presidios. I decided to stop for the rest of the day among these heathen, who presented me with the few provisions which they had.

This tribe is known both to us and to the Pimas and Yumas by the name which we here give them. Their language is the same as that of the last-named, and also their customs, stature, and robustness. They differ from those in that all these Cocomaricopas go covered, at least as much as decency requires, and are better armed, a custom which they have received from the Pimas or Pápagos, with whom they are related. Some of them live on this river but most of them among the sierras which are between the Colorado and the Gila. Their number, as I was informed by them and by the Pápagos, is slightly less than that of the Yumas. These Cocomaricopas, whenever our soldiers have passed through their country, have been friendly to them. The place where we are today I named San Bernar-

dino.[1] Its north latitude was observed and found
to be in thirty-three degrees and two minutes.—
From Monte Rey to the first village of the Cocomaricopas and the site of San Bernardino on the
Gila River, 221 leagues.

Thursday, May 19.—At daybreak I ascended the
same river on the bank opposite the one I followed
yesterday, and at a distance of five leagues from
San Bernardino we passed by a good spring of hot
water, known as Agua Caliente.[2] It is sufficient to
irrigate a large piece of land, which it is seen
that in other times the Cocomaricopas did irrigate.
But they have abandoned it on account of the wars
with the Yumas, as I am told by a Pima who is with
me. Besides these five leagues, three more were
traveled until we halted for the night at a place
where pasturage was found.

Friday, May 20.—At sunrise we recrossed the
Gila. Both here and in the part which we have
already followed, its general depth is not less than
four palms, notwithstanding that this is the time
of the greatest drought. The season when it is in
flood, the natives tell me, is during the summer
rains, and they say that then its width is not less
than five hundred varas, which is corroborated by
the signs which it leaves. As soon as we recrossed
the river we ascended some good hills[3] which lasted

---

[1] San Bernardino was near the present town of Palomas.

[2] Still called Agua Caliente. Camp was at El Aritoac. See p. 301.

[3] Painted Rock Range.

for three leagues, after which we descended to the
bottom lands of the river, along which we traveled
two more leagues to the vicinity of San Simón y
Judas de Upasoitac,[1] where I halted for the night.
This place is well populated by these Cocomaricopas, and others who are really the same although
they call them Opas, to whom are added now some
Pápagos or Pimas who have abandoned their country because of the great drought and the even
greater famine which is experienced in it. For the
first of these reasons I can not make the transit
from here direct to my presidio, as I ought, for it
is distant only about forty leagues over good lands
and pasturage. But even without these I decided
to make it from the settlements of the Pimas, for
which reason it is necessary to ascend this river still
farther.

Saturday, May 21.—Having traveled a league I
halted at the very site of San Simón y Judas de
Upasoitac. The latitude of this place was observed
and found to be in thirty-three degrees and fifteen
minutes.—From Monte Rey to Opasoitac, the last
village of the Cocomaricopas on the same Gila
River, 233 leagues.

The Reverend Father Garcés, who has been here
on other occasions, decided to remain for the purpose of trying to find out whether by means of the
tribes who live between here and the province of
Moqui, of which they give report, it is possible to
send a letter to the province of New Mexico, a

---

[1] Upasoitac was at Gila Bend. Camp was a league west of there.

servant of mine voluntarily remaining with him. At half past two in the afternoon I set out from this place to the habitations of the Pimas, over good terrain, to cut off the bend which the river makes to the north, uninhabited by people, and having traveled seven leagues by continuing into the night, camp was made to rest in a place where pasturage was found.[1]

Sunday, May 22.—At daybreak we continued the march, and at the end of six leagues I halted at the Pima village of El Sutaquison,[2] which is permanent, has more than two thousand souls, and whose natives, as has already been said, are devoted to agriculture. One of the fields which I saw, and they say that it is the smallest one which they have, I judge has planted from sixty to eighty fanegas of wheat of marvelous quality and ready to be harvested.

This village acknowledges as its justice or captain the person who is captain of my presidio, and I therefore appointed here a governor, which it has customarily had, this office and the governorship of the village which follows being vacant because of the death of those who occupied them. Here are very plainly seen the foundations and even a part of the walls of a palace of the people who formed the tribe which it is believed went to establish its empire at the City of Mexico. To the foregoing site

1 About half way between Maricopa Range and Sierra Estrella.
2 Sutaquison was at Vah Ki (Old House). The ruins are now called Casa Blanca.

of Upasoitac and to this one of which we are speaking reaches the infernal pest of the Apaches, who
not long ago killed twelve natives of the former
place and more recently sixty of the latter.—From
Monte Rey to Sutaquison and the first Pimas on the
Gila River, 246 leagues.

Monday, May 23.—We continued two leagues
along this river bottom and camped in order to
spend the night at the village of Juturitucan,[1] alias
San Juan Capistrano, which is larger in every way
than the foregoing village. Here I appointed as
governor and alcalde two brothers, sons of the one
who had held these offices. They have under their
rule about three thousand persons, all of whom live
in close union, being frightened by the last attacks
which the Apaches have made on them. The fields
of wheat which they have at present are so large
that, standing in the middle of them, one can not
see the ends, because they are so long. Their width
is also great, embracing the whole width of the
valley on either side, and their fields of maize are
of corresponding size. Having yesterday observed
the latitude of Sutaquison it was found to be in
thirty-three degrees and twenty-four minutes.—
From Monte Rey to Juturitucan, the last Pimas on
the Gila River, 248 leagues.

Tuesday, May 24.—Raising our train at sunrise
and traveling two leagues along the same river, we
halted on its bank at a place where pasturage was
found. At this distance farther up, above where we

1 Also called Uturituc.

are, there is another palace which is known as the
Palace of Moctezuma,[1] and a settlement larger than
the one mentioned before. The construction of this
one is a labyrinth of which experts have made careful drawings. It is seen to have had storeys, and
today the walls are still so high that they can be seen
more than a league away. It is at least that distance
from the river, which they introduced under the same
palace and the rest of the settlement, in order to
have water at hand. The material of these works is
purely of earth, but is also mixed with small stone
or coarse sand which appear by their consistency
like the finest mortar or cement, the best test of
which is its permanency during so many years
which it is thought to have existed. At two o'clock
in the afternoon, leaving the Gila River at our backs,
we again took up our march, going south, in which
direction we traveled until midnight, when a halt
was made to rest for a while.

Wednesday, May 25.—Before daybreak we again
took up the march in the same direction, going over
level country the same as yesterday afternoon, and
at eleven o'clock we halted at the point of the spring
of the pueblo of Tucson to take shelter from the
heat of the sun. Traveling this afternoon about a
league and a half, we arrived at the pueblo named,
which belongs to the jurisdiction of my presidio and
of the Pimas Altos,[2] of whom it has eighty families.
It is distant from the Gila twenty-four leagues, and
although I have traveled this distance without water,

---

[1] This is the famous Casa Grande.   [2] Upper Pimas.

this is not because it is lacking on the way, for there is water at the place of La Aquituni,[1] where there is a village of sixty families of Pápagos. But I did not go that way because it is rough country and because apart from this I feared some encounter with the Apaches, now very frequent in that region, and I was not in good shape to come out safely with our train, because all who are with me are mounted on very badly crippled mules, which even though they are not crippled are useless in such cases.— From Monte Rey to the Pima pueblo of T[u]cson, 274 leagues.

Thursday, May 26.—Before daylight I received through six soldiers of my company an order from the adjutant inspector, Don Antonio Bonilla,[2] that I should hasten my arrival there, he having learned of my coming this way from the two soldiers who are mentioned on the 12th of this month. In obedience to this order I set out from this pueblo shortly after daylight, going south, in which direction my presidio lies, hoping to reach it today, notwithstanding it is twenty leagues away. I gave the appropriate orders to the effect that all the soldiers who have accompanied me on the expedition and all our train shall follow slowly to arrive tomorrow. In company with the six soldiers mentioned and the Reverend Father Fray Juan Díaz, who wished to come with me, I continued my journey, and at the end of the first five leagues I passed through the

[1] Just west of Pichaco Peak.

[2] Bonilla later became a very able administrator in the viceroy's corps at Mexico City.

pueblo of San Xavier del Bac, which has forty families of the same tribe, and is head of the foregoing pueblo; then continuing for fifteen more leagues, at sunset I arrived at the presidio of Tubac, which is the one in my charge. Here I requested the Reverend Father Fray Juan Díaz, who has made the observations in our transit, to represent on a map what we have accomplished, to give the most excellent señor viceroy an idea of the directions, villages, and other particulars which we have noted.

Friday, May 27.—At twelve o'clock today the rest of the train, which I left behind, arrived at this presidio. And thus the expedition is fully accomplished, with the success and the advantages which are set forth in what is written hereinbefore, for which may the Lord of Hosts be blessed and praised. —From Monte Rey to the presidio of Tubac, 294 leagues.

Today, November 13, 1774, I made this copy in order to deliver it this same day to the most excellent señor viceroy, governor, and captain general, in this City of Mexico, into whose hands likewise I have delivered the map which hereinbefore is mentioned.   JUAN BAUPTISTA DE ANZA.

Compared with the diary of his expedition which was presented by Don Juan Baptista de Ansa to the most excellent señor viceroy, and which remains in the Secretaría de Cámara del Virreynato in my charge, to which I certify. Mexico, November 26, 1774.   MELCHOR DE PERAMÁS (Rubric).

DIAZ'S DIARY FROM TUBAC TO SAN GABRIEL

1774

(D)

DIARY KEPT BY FATHER FRAY JUAN DIAZ, APOSTOLIC MISSIONARY OF THE COLLEGE OF SANTA CRUZ DE QUERETARO, DURING THE JOURNEY WHICH HE IS MAKING IN COMPANY WITH THE REVEREND FATHER FRAY FRANCISCO GARCES, TO OPEN A ROAD FROM THE PROVINCE OF SONORA TO NORTHERN CALIFORNIA AND THE PORT OF MONTERREY BY WAY OF THE GILA AND COLORADO RIVERS, UNDER ORDERS OF THE MOST EXCELLENT SENOR LIEUTENANT-GENERAL DON ANTONIO MARIA BUCARELI Y URSUA, VICEROY, GOVERNOR AND CAPTAIN-GENERAL OF THIS NEW SPAIN, BY HIS DECREE OF SEPTEMBER 17 OF THE YEAR 1773 JUST PAST.[1]

The persons named for this expedition are thirty-four, to-wit:

Don Juan Bapta. de Ansa, its commander, and captain of the royal presidio of San Ignacio de Tubac.

The reverend fathers Fray Francisco Garcés and Fray Juan Díaz, apostolic missionaries.

Twenty soldiers of the presidio of Tubac.

[1] Diario, que forma el Padre Fr. Juan Díaz . . . en el Viage, que hace . . . a la California Septentrional. A.G.P.M., Historia, Tomo 396.

A soldier who knows the roads from the port of San Diego to the port of Monterrey.[1]

An interpreter of the Pima language.

An Indian native of California who on the 26th of December of the year mentioned came out by land to the royal presidio of Santa Gertrudis del Altar.[2]

An Indian carpenter, five muleteers, and two servants of the commander.

For the expedition there are taken thirty-five pack-loads of provisions and baggage, sixty-five cattle on foot,[3] and one hundred and forty saddle animals.

It is to be noted that the computation of leagues made in the course of this diary is based solely on my estimate of the distances, from my experience in traveling over long roads already inspected and measured by experts. The directions assigned are the principal ones followed in each day's march, leaving out some minor variations, which are of no value in giving an idea of the route, and may only serve to confuse. For lack of the necessary instrument, observation cannot be made of the latitude in which each place is found, and therefore the orders of his Excellency the Viceroy cannot be fulfilled in this particular.

Because the Apaches attacked the horse herd of this royal presidio of Tubac on the 2d of January of this present year of '74, carrying off some of the

---

[1] This was Valdés.   [2] Sebastián Tarabal.

[3] The cattle were for food on the way.

saddle animals which were destined for this expedition, the commander, in conference with the fathers,
decided to go by way of the missions of the Pimería
which are to the west of this royal presidio, in order
to replace the animals lost and to protect the rest
from a new assault. We were moved to this decision
also by the desire to inspect the road that runs near
the coast from the mission of Caborca to the Gila
River, because if it should prove to be passable it
would be very useful for the desired communication
with the port of Monterrey, through freedom from
all perils and hostilities.

On the 8th of January of this present year, 1774,
in the presence of all the persons named, Mass was
chanted in the church of this presidio with all possible solemnity, the Most Blessed Trinity and the
Immaculate Conception of Most Holy Mary being
proclaimed as patrons of this expedition. A vigorous
volley and repeated "Vivas" well manifested the
joy at the auspicious beginning of a journey which
may yield such glory to God, happiness to souls, and
honor, merit, and luster to our Catholic monarch.

After midday the march was begun, and it continued with apportioned journeys until we arrived
on the 20th of the same month at the mission of
La Purísima Concepción de Caborca, having passed
through the intervening pueblos, whose particulars
I do not relate because I have already given such
copious notices and extensive reports of them.[1] In

[1] Father Díaz was a missionary among the Pimas, hence had
written about the missions.

this mission of Caborca which, together with its two *visitas,* has been for six years in my charge, live all the rebels commonly called Los Piatos, who in the years '70 and '71 surrendered to the rule of our sovereign.[1] At present they are very quiet and devoted to such labor and commerce as their poverty permits them, although some of them, because of their restless spirits, do not maintain perfect subordination to their superiors. In this pueblo two Masses were chanted with great solemnity for the happy outcome of our expedition, on the occasion of our having stopped here until the 22d to equip ourselves with the horses and mules which were lacking.

January 22.—At one o'clock in the afternoon we set out from this pueblo, and, having traveled seven leagues to the northwest and north-northwest, we halted in a plain which we called San Yldefonso, in whose vicinity there is some pasturage, enabling travelers to divide this march,[2] which is difficult for lack of water.

January 23.—Having celebrated the holy sacrifice of the Mass we set out from this place, and, keeping on the right a sierra of considerable height[3] and on the left one of less elevation, we traveled seven leagues in the same direction, in order to reach a place called San Eduardo de la Aribaicpia,[4] where

[1] These Indians were reduced during the Elizondo campaign, in which Anza took part. The *visitas* were Pitic and Bísani.

[2] He means enabling travelers to divide the march between Caborca and Arivaipa, the next watering place.

[3] The high range on the right was Sierra de la Basura. The one on the left was the Sierra de los Placeres, or Sierra del Cozón.

[4] Now called Arivaipa.

we halted.   Here there is very little water, but it is permanent all the year in an arroyo in whose sands some wells are made from which to water the animals.   There is also a scarcity of pasturage, although it is sufficient for travelers.

January 24.—At noon we began the journey along the middle of the valley formed by the sierras mentioned, and having traveled four leagues to the northwest we halted in a plain with abundant and good pasturage, where there is a large pond with some rain water, which has the name of San Juan de Matha[1] and in which sufficient water for the use of travelers might easily be gathered.

January 25.—In order to divide the march, which is long because of lack of water, we set out at noon, and taking the same direction we camped in a flat without water and with very little pasturage, distant from the foregoing pool five leagues.[2] Before reaching this place the sierra which we have had at our left comes to an end, the other one continuing its course to a point opposite the village or pueblo of Quitobac, where it terminates.[3]

January 26.—At eight o'clock in the morning the march was continued in the same direction. Having traveled two leagues we swung to the west-northwest and part of the way to the west, in order to

---

[1] This camp was near Temporales.

[2] Five or six miles northwest of Costa Rica Ranch.

[3] The sierra on the right coming to an end at Quitovac is Sierra de la Espuma, and is not the same as Sierra de la Basura which Father Díaz mentions farther back. Two ranges, Sierra de la Campana and Cerro El Durasno, lie between.

reach the pueblo of San Luís de Quitobac,[1] which is distant six leagues from the last camping place. In it there live a few families of Pápagos under the rule of a governor, for whom they observe some respect and subordination. It is not easy to estimate the population because of its continual shifting and its entire lack of stability. This place has five springs of water nearby, but from all of them it flows in such limited quantity that it would scarcely be enough to irrigate a fanega of maize, the greatest amount which could be planted in the small area which could enjoy the benefit of irrigation. In the vicinity there is also some pasturage with which some cattle and a few range horses could be supported. Of the qualities of these natives I will speak later on, in the light of experience.

January 27.—At noon we set out from this pueblo, going north in order to pass the point of a rocky range. Then, turning west-northwest and continuing our course, we halted near the range,[2] having traveled five leagues. In this place there is very little pasturage, and it has no other water than a small tank which is in the same sierra and is not sufficient for the saddle animals.

January 28.—In the morning we continued the march, bearing this range on the left, and traveled three leagues to the west-northwest. Later, changing

---

[1] This place still bears the same name. It is now a little village inhabited by Mexicans and Pápagos.

[2] The Sierra de Cubabi. Camp was made near Piedra Parada.

our direction, we went north to reach the pueblo of San Marcelo de Sonóitac, distant seven leagues from the last camp-site. This is an old mission[1] which was administered by the Jesuit fathers until the year 1751, when its Pápago inhabitants, having risen in rebellion, killed its minister, since when it has remained in ruins up to the present. This pueblo has about thirty families of that tribe who regularly live scattered about, suffering extreme misery and poverty. There is a permanent arroyo[2] here with which crops sufficient for its support might be irrigated, but the soil is very scarce and thin. In the neighborhood there are plentiful pastures for the maintenance of some cattle and horses.

January 29.—Having celebrated the holy sacrifice of the Mass, we began to journey toward the west-northwest,[3] bearing on the right a range in the middle of which is the Cerro de la Sal,[4] so-called because of some ledges of salt rock which are in its cliffs, from which, according to the report they gave us, these natives provide themselves an abundance, taking it out easily during the rainy season. Having traveled six leagues in this direction we left the sierra, which continues its course to the northwest, and went two leagues to the west in order to reach an arroyo called

[1] The old mission site is about a mile and a half east of the present town of Sonóita.

[2] Now called Rio de Sonóita.

[3] They continued down the left side of the Rio de Sonóita.

[4] There are several round peaks in the location described, but my guide, Antonio López, who had lived more than fifty years in the neighborhood, knew nothing of this Cerro de Sal.

254 A ROUTE TO CALIFORNIA

El Carrizal, where we halted.[1] In this place there is some pasturage of little substance, and water sufficient for travelers, although it is bad.[2]

January 30.—Being informed by one of these natives of the difficulty we should have to find water for the pack train and the saddle animals on the next march,[3] the commander decided to divide the company, leaving the pack train to follow on the next day. The rest of us went forward in the afternoon to divide the journey, which is one of fourteen leagues. Having traveled eight of these leagues northwest and north-northwest, we came to the entrance of a valley formed by two rocky sierras, and halted near the one on the right, where we spent the night without water and with very little pasturage.[4]

January 31.—Having celebrated the sacrifice of the Mass we continued our journey, keeping very close to this sierra; and having traveled six leagues to the northwest, with great difficulty because of the heaviness of the road and the little spirit which

[1] Below Quitovaquita the Rio Sonóita swings southwestward, while Sierra del Agua Dulce continues northwest. The place then called El Carrizal corresponds to the present Agua Salada. Here is the place where the road turns sharply northwest.

[2] The bad quality of the water is recorded in the present name, Agua Salada.

[3] To the next watering place (Heart Tank, in Sierra Pinta) it was fourteen leagues (Anza says twelve). Since this tank was left for the pack train, the advance party had to go seven leagues further (Anza says six), to Cabeza Prieta Tanks, a total of about fifty miles.

[4] They went through the southern spur of Sierra Pinta and camped north of the international boundary line. Their route was close to what later became known as the Camino del Diablo. Camp was north of boundary marker No. 179.

the saddle animals had by now, we arrived at a tank of water which is very high up in the same sierra on the right.[1] Seeing that it was very difficult to get water to the horses, mules, and cattle, and that in the vicinity there was no pasturage, of which they were in such need, the commander decided to go forward over a part of the next march, hoping to find some pasturage for the night and to arrive more quickly at the watering place the next day. With this in view we left this sierra and crossed the valley, and having traveled four leagues to the west and west-northwest, we camped at an arroyo which was dry but had some pasturage.[2]

February 1.—At seven o'clock in the morning, going northwest, we continued the journey, entering the sierra which is on the left through some hills, and having traveled three leagues we halted near some tanks of water which we called La Purificación.[3] In them there is sufficient water for travelers, and cattle and horses can drink with ease. Here in this place we decided to await the pack train, because in the vicinity there was some pasturage, of which the riding animals had come so greatly in need.

February 2.—We remained in this place, two Masses being celebrated for the success of the expedition.

[1] Heart Tank, called by Anza Agua Empinado.

[2] Anza crossed the plain and halted at an arroyo in the Tule Range northeast of Tule Well.

[3] They entered the Cabeza Prieta Range and stopped at the Cabeza Prieta Tanks. On the return from the second Anza expedition Father Font called these tanks La Candelaria.

February 3.—Two Masses were celebrated, the same as yesterday. Because the pack train arrived at midday greatly fatigued, the march was not continued until next day.

February 4.—At eight o'clock in the morning we set out toward the west-northwest. Having reached an arroyo which is in the middle of a valley, with little difficulty we found plenty of water in its sands.[1] According to the account given us by a native Pápago who was guiding us, it has water for the greater part of the year, although in small quantity. We made camp in this place, notwithstanding it was very short of pasturage, in order not to experience greater difficulty by going forward. In a sierra ahead of us, which runs from north to south, they say there is a tank of water that might serve in case there is none in this arroyo.[2]

February 5.—In the morning, after Mass, we set out from this place, and having crossed the sierra that lay in front, through a very easy pass,[3] we traveled eight leagues in order to reach Agua Escondida, or Pozo Blando, as these natives call it, where we halted.[4] This water, according to what these Indians

[1] Pozos de en Medio. Anza says they went five leagues to this watering place. It was at or near Coyote Water, in the same arroyo.

[2] He refers to Tinajas Altas, four or five miles to the southwest of Pozos de en Medio. His statement "they say" indicates the indefiniteness of his knowledge of these now famous tanks.

[3] Gila Range. They went through Tinajas Altas Pass, just a short distance northwest of Tinajas Altas.

[4] This was a well in Arroyo San Albino, on the west side of Gila Range, and a few miles south of Fortuna Mine. The arroyo runs south down the east side of a spur of the range, from the neighborhood of San Albino Tank.

Dia 25. Por dimidiar la Jornada, que es grande por escasez de agua, comenzamos à caminar al medio dia, y tomando el mismo Rumbo, hicimos alto en un baxio Sin agua, y de muy poco pasto, que dista de dho charco 5. leguas. Antes de llegar à esto paraje, hace fin la Sierra, que trahiamos à la izquierda; siguiendo la otra su curso asta enfrentarse con la Vancheria, ó Pueblo del Quitobac, en donde finaliza.//

Dia 26. A las 8. de la mañana se comenzó la marcha al mismo Rumbo, y caminadas 2. leguas, Variamos al West-norueste, y alguna parte del camino al oeste. para llegar à dho Pueblo de San Luis de quitobac, que dista 6. leguas del paraje antecedente.// En el havitan algunas familias de Papagos, baxo el mando de un Govor à quien tienen algun respecto, y subordinacion; y no es facil asignar su numero, por su continua Vagacion, y subsistencia ninguna.// Tiene este paraje cinco Veneros de agua immediatos: pero de todos sale con tanta escasez, que apenas pudiera Vegarse una fanega de maix; y esta es la mayor Cantidad, que se pudiera sembrar en la poca tierra, que puede gozar el beneficio del Riego.// Tiene tambien algun pasto en sus immediaciones, con el que pueden mantenerse algun ganado, y Cavallada suelta.// De las qualidades de estos naturales, dire en adelante lo que me ha enseñado la experiencia.//

Dia 27. Al medio dia Salimos de este Pueblo tomando Rumbo al norte, para montar la punta de una Sierra peñascosa; y Variando despues al West-norueste, siguiendo su curso. hicimos alto immediatos à ella; haviendo caminado 5. leguas. Ai en este paraje muy poco pasto; y no tiene mas agua, que una tinaja pequeña, que esta en la misma Sierra. y no es Suficiente para las caballerias.//

Dia 28. Por la mañana perseguimos la marcha, y llebando à la izquierda dha Sierra, caminamos tres leguas al West-norueste.// Despues dexando este Rumbo, tomamos el del norte. para llegar al Pueblo de San Marcelo de Sonoitas distante 7. leguas del paraje antecedente. Mission antigua administrada por los P.P. Jesuitas asta el año de 1751. en el que sublevados los Papagos pobladores de ella adieron la muerte à su Min.ro, y quedó asta el presente arruinada.// Tiene este pueblo como 50 familias de dha nacion, que Vegularmente Viven dispersos padeciendo Summa infelicidad, y miseria. Ai en el un arroyo permanente, con q. pudieran Vegarse las Semillas Suficientes para el abasto; pero Sus tierras son muy escasas, y delgadas.// En sus immediaciones ai bastantes pastos, con los q. pudieran mantenerse algunos Ganados, y cavallada.//

Dia 29. Celebrado el Sto Sacrificio de la Misa, comenzamos à caminar al West-norueste; llebando à la derecha una Sierra. en cuyo comedio esta el cerro de la Sal; assi llamado; por algunas betas de Sal piedra, que ai entre sus peñascos, de la que (Segun el informe que nos hicieron) Se proveen con abundancia, estos naturales, sacandola en tiempo de lluvias consolidada. Caminadas 6. leguas à dho Rumbo, dexamos la Sierra, que Sigue su curso para el norueste, y anduvimos dos leguas al oeste, para llegar a un arroyo llamado el Canvixal, en donde hicimos mansion.// Ai en este paraje algun pasto de poca Sustancia, y agua Suficiente para los pasajeros; aunq mala.//

A page of Díaz's diary to San Gabriel.

tell us, is permanent although very scarce. It is in a deep arroyo, which makes it necessary to travel a quarter of a league, going into a sierra[1] of considerable height to reach the water. By departing from the direction of west-northwest which we have followed, and turning west by west-northwest four leagues before reaching this watering place, this march can be made with greater ease and for the following journey three leagues will be saved, because one can come out to another watering place on the skirts of this same sierra, in whose neighborhood there is much pasturage.[2] At this arroyo we met a Pápago of the old mission of Sonóitac, who was returning from the Colorado River to his pueblo.[3] He warned us that we must proceed with care, because a large part of the Yumas, having already heard of our coming, and failing in obedience to Palma, their captain, were determined to attack us, in order to take from us the goods which we were carrying, in case we should not give them up voluntarily. In view of the grave difficulties which might arise if this report should prove to be true, we decided to send the same Indian who made the report to go and bring Captain Palma, agreeing on the place where he would find us the next day, so that, being well informed by him regarding the disturbance and the situation, the

[1] "Internandose á una sierra de bastante elevación."

[2] In approaching Agua Escondida Anza kept close to the Gila Range. Father Díaz means that by going straight to the southern end of the mountain spur (as the road now runs), and not turning aside to Agua Escondida, one could reach a watering place farther northwest, near Fortuna Mine, and thus save the detour.

[3] In one of the diaries this Indian is called Luís.

measures most conducive to quieting the malcontents might be taken.

February 6.—Having celebrated two Masses because of the present trouble, we set out in the afternoon from this place and went a league and a half to the south, in order to double the sierra[1] in the middle of which is the watering place mentioned. Then, changing our direction, we went four leagues northwest, keeping this sierra on our right, and halted for the night in a dry arroyo in whose neighborhood there is plenty of pasturage.[2]

February 7.—In the morning, having traveled three leagues northwest, we came to a very difficult sandy stretch which is three leagues across by the direction in which we were going; but it extends west and south many leagues, as far as the Gulf and the banks of the Colorado.

To the middle of this sand dune came our messenger to receive us, in company with some Yumas and Pápagos, with demonstrations of joy and contentment, and discounting the report which he had given us the day before. Captain Palma did not come because he was outside of his village hunting. But in view of the friendly welcome given us by these and others who kept coming, we decided to go forward, and having traveled in this direction seven

[1] Anza says they went a league and a quarter south in order to get around the spur. Garcés says that when they got near the end they went over a low gap.

[2] Camp was made in the plain between Fortuna Mine and Yuma, near the former.

leagues for the day, we reached the banks of the Gila
River, where we halted.

After a short while Captain Palma arrived with
a large following, all on horseback, and manifesting
great joy at our coming. Being questioned with
great care concerning the matter mentioned, he assured us that there was no disturbance whatever,
because the few who were hostile and disposed to do
us injury were of other villages, and that in order to
avoid ill-feeling he had sent them to their own lands.
This Indian manifested such capacity and loyalty
that he caused us no little admiration to see such
talent in the midst of such barbarism, and the commander, after having shown him much attention, and
confirmed him in the rank which he enjoyed among
his people, promised him also the bastón and the title
of governor. With his accustomed prudence he instructed him as to the obedience which they owe to
our Catholic king and his representatives, respect
and veneration for the missionaries of the gospel,
and friendly relations, peace, and harmony with the
Spanish nation.[1] The missionary fathers, at the
same time, did not forget to attract his heart and his
inclination to love and desire our Catholic religion.
When night came many of those who live roundabout
went to sleep in their villages, but the captain and
others remained with us.

As far as this Gila River extends the tribe of the
Pápagos, of whom a considerable portion live on its

[1] These ceremonies are described in detail in Anza's diaries.

banks from its junction with the Colorado clear to the Apache frontier. Although this nation has been very numerous in other times, at present it is very much reduced. Indeed, according to the opinion of those most experienced, and who have considered the matter with the closest attention, it does not exceed 2,500 souls, there being included in this estimate all the Gileños, who are so-called because they live near this Gila River.

The estimate of the distance which I have made and set down in the diary, from the pueblo of Caborca to the junction of the rivers near this place where we now are, is ninety-four and one-half leagues. But I think that by avoiding some small detours, which we have made through lack of practice and experience, it may be reduced to ninety leagues.[1] The lands which we have traversed are very dry, thin, and entirely sterile. The sierras which lie between El Carrizal and this river are promontories of large rocks, very bare, and incapable of producing even the smallest plants, and according to the opinion of some men of experience who are with us, they give no promise of either precious or ordinary metals.

The Pápago Indians who dwell in them live in greater misery and poverty than can be imagined. Seldom have they any fixed habitation, because, driven by necessity, they wander almost continually,

[1] This estimated reduction of four and one-half leagues in a total of more than ninety is an indication of the directness of the route followed. Had a direct route from Quitobac to El Carrizal been feasible a number of leagues might have been saved, but even now that stretch is little traveled.

sometimes in the sierras to maintain themselves by hunting deer, wild sheep, rats, and certain roots; at other times in the arroyos to live on the bean of the mesquite, and again in the plains, seeking the pitaya, the tuna, the saguaro and other wild fruits.[1] Sometimes they go to the Colorado River to obtain food amongst the Yumas through their skill in their disorderly dances, and at other times down to the missions of the Pimería where, by the same means and by their tenuous labor, they obtain a little grain, and a few pieces of sayal to cover the most immodest parts of their bodies.

These Pápagos speak the same language as the Pimas and, as I have learned through an experience of six years during which I have dealt with them, they are similar to them in their native qualities; but they are much more vicious in their abuses and evil customs, notwithstanding that many of them are Christians. They are extremely independent and liberty-loving. They care nothing for the conveniences of life which civilized men so much love, although they are very fond of repose. They lack almost completely a sense of honor and shame, which is so fundamental in civilized life. They are ignorant of eternal truths, those who are Christians being so only in name.

And since they lack these and other such principles which might incite them to abandon their disorders and embrace the easy yoke of the divine law, and yield full obedience to our Catholic monarch,

---

[1] The pitaya, tuna, and saguaro are all varieties of cactus.

their complete reduction is made very difficult. Indeed, they could be reduced only by establishing some missions in their own lands at extraordinary expense, for otherwise it is not possible; or, likewise by means of new foundations, cutting off their communication with the Gila and Colorado rivers and with the pueblos of the Pimería. For, lacking the aid which they receive in these places, their very necessity, it seems to me, would oblige them to leave their land, which at present almost serves them as an asylum for their blind liberty.

February 8.—In the morning men, women and children began to assemble to see the novelty. All saluted us in very friendly fashion, and when they saw the kindness and gentleness with which we treated them and humored them they at once manifested great confidence, losing the fear which some had felt before seeing us. Captain Palma, desiring to show us hospitality, begged us to go to his village, which is between the two rivers.[1] Therefore, guided by Palma himself, and accompanied by more than two hundred souls of both sexes, we went about a quarter of a league[2] down the river to reach the ford, by which we crossed on horseback without any danger.[3] We halted on the very bank of the river, and at once there again assembled many natives of different villages, who, together with those who were

[1] Palma then lived on the Island of La Santísima Trinidad, described by Father Díaz below.

[2] Anza says half a league.

[3] Anza describes the crossing, which was not quite so simple as this would indicate.

accompanying us, must have made as many as six
hundred persons. All of them went amongst us with
joy and confidence, and such was their desire to see
us, to touch us, and to examine our clothes, baggage,
and weapons, that to those of little patience they
became a nuisance.[1] Everything caused them won-
derment, and they examined with their hands what
they saw with their eyes. Having finally regaled
them with some beeves, tobacco, and glass beads,
and accepted the gifts which they made us of frijoles,
calabashes and the tornillo bean, which is very abundant in this country, after sunset some of them
returned to their houses, others remaining with the
captain in our company.

At this place the Gila is joined by a small branch
of the Colorado, from which it separates some
leagues farther up, forming a good-sized island
which we call Santísima Trinidad, and on which
lives Captain Palma with part of the Yumas.
Farther down, about a gunshot away, it joins the
principal stream,[2] and from there, according to the
account given by these natives, the two run united
until they empty into the Gulf.

Some Soyopa Indians[3] who were found here, and
who live about forty leagues above the junction
in the neighborhood of the Colorado, have told us
that when the river is in flood, in their country a

[1] Even the patient Anza records in his diaries a note of irritation,
but he did not reveal it to the natives.

[2] This fixes the location of the camp at a gunshot from the junction.

[3] These people were the Mohaves.

very large branch separates, and, running west,
after a short distance enters another large river
which carries very red water, and that afterward
these two are joined by another small river of salt
water, but they do not know whether it empties into
the Gulf or not, nor are we able to form a certain
opinion.[1]

According to the examination which has been
made from here, the Gila River runs from northeast
to southwest until it joins the Colorado.[2] At this
place where we have forded it, after it has been
joined by the little branch mentioned, it appears to
me to be a hundred and twenty-five yards wide and
five spans[3] deep. Its water is a little salty. On its
banks there are many cottonwoods, most of them
small. In the neighborhood there is little pasturage,
but the banks offer very great advantages for fields,
so that these natives, in spite of their natural laziness, get very good harvests of wheat, maize, beans,
calabashes, melons, and watermelons, without the
trouble of irrigating their crops, because with the
moisture and the fertilization which the land receives during the great overflow of the rivers, as
well as because of their proximity, no other irrigation is needed to raise any kind of crop. Even more
fertile lands, Father Fray Francisco Garcés tells
me,[4] are possessed by the tribes who live on these

---

[1] Anza tells the same story. It was in harmony with a belief
current in Sonora at the time.

[2] He means from its source to the junction.

[3] A span was nine inches, or an eighth of a fathom.

[4] Father Garcés had traveled down the Colorado in 1771.

rivers as far down as the neighborhood of their mouth. That this is true for the more than twenty-five leagues which I have seen all down the river, I am able to testify at this writing.

On this island and for twelve leagues down the river below the junction live the tribe of the Yumas.[1] During the great floods, which they say are in April and May, they move away from the banks of the river in order to escape inundation, camping in the nearby uplands until the river returns to its channel and its regular course. These Indians are all heathen, but both from their qualities which I have noted and from the report given of them by the Pápagos, their neighbors, I judge that their reduction will be very easy; and I think the same is true of the other tribes who live along these rivers, for apparently they are not very different from the Yumas. All lack rational civilization, but they appear to be agricultural and little devoted to the chase. They are very care-free and pleasure-loving, docile and friendly, and they manifest singular affection for our nation. The men wear no other cover than their painting or daubing, with which they stripe all the body with various colors. The women wear a kind of short skirt made of strips of the inner bark of the willow and cottonwood, with which they cover themselves from the waist to the knees.[2] They also make blankets woven from

---

[1] The end of the Yuma jurisdiction was reached on the second day's march from the junction. Anza gives the distance as eleven leagues.

[2] For the Yumas, see Hodge, *Handbook of American Indians*.

the same material, and others from the skins of hares and rabbits, which serve them somewhat for shelter and decency. All those who live near these rivers are above medium stature, and there are many who are perhaps nine spans high. Amongst them I had one measured—the one who appeared to me the most gigantic—and he was nine spans and three fingers high.[1] Their habitations are the same as those commonly used by the Pimas, with only the difference that their huts or jacales are lower and larger, so that many families live in a single one.[2]

Upstream from the Yumas along these rivers, I am informed, live the Opas, Cocomaricopas, Soyopas, Tutumaopas, Bagiopas, and Nixoras, all of whom speak the same language as the Yumas and are distinguished from each other only by the different names given them from the places where they live. Below these nations live the Cajuenches or Cojats, who also speak the same language; and then come those whom they call Quicamas,[3] who, according to what they tell us, are very different from the rest. All these tribes or divisions of people seem to be very much like the Yumas in their qualities and wear the same kind of clothing. As a rule they are hostile to each other and do each other a great

[1] Nine spans and three inches would be six feet three. The great height of the Yumas and Cócopas, their neighbors, is a well-known fact. Father Kino wrote that the largest Indian he ever saw was a Yuma.

[2] Their dwellings are described by Anza and Font.

[3] Commonly spelled Quiquimas. They lived on the left bank of the Colorado.

deal of damage, which would be still greater if they were skilled in the use of weapons, of which many, or even most of them, are lacking entirely. I do not know whether this is due to disinclination or to laziness. Because of our coming and of the vigorous efforts and effective means which have been taken, we have succeeded in making peace between some of them, although in view of their barbarity and their lack of laws regulating disruptions, peace is likely to endure for a very short time.[1]

February 9.—Having traveled during the morning a quarter of a league to the west, we crossed to the other bank of the Colorado River by a very good ford, although with many windings, aided and guided by many natives, who made every effort to assist us; and after going a short distance in the same direction, impelled by their great insistence we camped on the bank of this river below its junction with the Gila.[2]

This Colorado River is by itself very large, so that although this is the time of the lowest water, it is about two hundred yards wide and five spans deep, as we saw by the measurement made by the commander. Its magnitude below the junction with the Gila may be inferred. According to the report given by the Indians it has no falls before entering the Gulf. From a small hill which is near this place and which the river cuts in two, making of its two

[1] Anza tells more about these efforts made by him to end war among the tribes.

[2] For the location of the camp site see Anza's diaries.

halves a most beautiful and delightful pass, which we call the Puerto de la Purísima Concepción,[1] we made an examination to determine its course, and we saw that for some leagues which are visible from this little hill it runs from the north-northwest to the west-southwest, until it joins the Gila and enters this pass, but from here it turns to the west.[2] According to what I am told by Father Fray Francisco Garcés, who has examined this country on other occasions, it runs also for some leagues to the south, and I conclude that its disemboguement into the Gulf may be to the southwest. Its banks and adjacent lands are very thickly grown with cottonwoods, which would serve for any kind of building. I have not been able to learn with certainty how far the Gulf is from the junction, but judging from reports it would seem to be not more than forty leagues.

February 10.—In the morning, after Mass, we set out from this place toward the west and west-southwest, and having traveled six leagues downstream we halted at a village of Yumas called San Pablo.[3] Here more than eight hundred persons assembled, in addition to the many of both sexes who were accompanying us with their Captain Palma. They

[1] The hill is just above the Southern Pacific Railroad bridge across the Colorado.

[2] It runs west and northwest about ten miles, then swings sharply southward, near Pilot Knob.

[3] Anza called Pilot Knob Cerro de San Pablo. The village of San Pablo was about a league below, just over the present international boundary line. Anza gives the distance as five leagues.

all made us the same gifts as the preceding ones, and they were presented with a great quantity of tobacco and glass beads. When night came many of them went away, but others remained with us.

February 11.—After Mass we began the march toward the west,[1] passing through other villages of the same tribe, accompanied and guided by a large number of persons, all of whom invited us and begged us to stop at their houses, desiring to look at us to their heart's content. Having traveled six leagues we halted at a small lake not far from the river, in a place with plentiful pasturage. Here ends the Yuma tribe and here begins that of the Cajuenches, who are more numerous than any of the others, according to what the natives say.

February 12.—Having celebrated the holy sacrifice of the Mass, we set out from this lake toward the south-southwest, in which direction also the river runs, coming to a lake or ditch which is four[2] leagues distant from the preceding one, and which we called Santa Olaya. This lake is permanent and has an abundance of water and plenty of pasturage in its environs. Its lands are very fertile and well grown with trees. Very near here there is a good-

[1] All the diaries state that this day's march was to the west, but it clearly must have been southwest. The route was close to the river.

[2] Anza records four, and four and one-half leagues, and Garcés five. The statement that this is a lake or ditch shows that the body of water was a part of an arroyo. It was evidently in or near the channel of Rio de las Abejas, or Bee River. Father Font adds important data here. Santa Olaya was twenty-five or more miles from Pilot Knob, and not far above Pescadero Dam.

sized village of Cajuenches which has the name of Our Holy Father San Francisco.[1]

February 13.—Having said goodbye to Captain Palma, who shed tears and caused us to shed some at his farewell, and accompanied by some Cajuenches, we set out from this lake. Having traveled six leagues west-northwest we came to a little well called El Rosario,[2] but because it had very little water, and no pasturage whatever, we continued on our way, guided by two natives, whom the commander promised good pay if they would accompany us. Having traveled three leagues to the northwest, we halted at an arroyo called El Carrizal.[3] This is a place of little and bad pasturage, and the water, which is contained in several lagoons, is salty, but in a well which is in the very arroyo fairly good water for the men was found.

February 14.—After Mass we set out from this Carrizal, and having traveled two leagues to the west we halted on the same arroyo,[4] where there is a little well of better water than the last, and some carrizo for the cattle and riding animals. Here we remained all day, because the natives who were with us told us there was no other convenient wateringplace farther on where we could camp, but that by setting out early the next day we should be able

[1] This name was given to the village by Father Garcés in 1771.

[2] Garcés had passed El Rosario in 1771 on his way back to the Colorado River.

[3] This arroyo was evidently the Paredones of today.

[4] At Pozos de en Medio. Evidently on the Arroyo de Paredones.

to reach water and pasturage for the night. They said they could not go with us any farther, because the natives who lived in that country were their enemies, and their minds were so possessed with fear that we were not able even by means of urging, presents, or promises to induce them to go any further.[1]

February 15.—We set forth at daybreak in the direction which they had indicated to us, following a well-beaten trail, and having traveled for three leagues we came to a well which is within the same arroyo in the same direction.[2] Since the pack train had experienced such difficulty during the preceding days, it arrived at this well very badly shot to pieces; and seeing that in all this vicinity there was no pasturage whatever, and that the water was very scarce, the commander decided to leave half of the cargo here, in order that the mules, thus relieved, might reach the next watering place.

Putting this plan into effect, we continued the journey, following the same trail, which led toward a peak[3] where they had told us the camping place was, but having traveled three leagues to the west-northwest we came to a very wide sandy stretch, such that we concluded that it was morally impossible to take the pack train and the riding animals forward

[1] Anza says they refused to cross the arroyo.

[2] Anza calls this a "deep well." Another name for it was Pozo de las Angustias. From the diary it appears that all of the last three wells were on the same arroyo.

[3] *Cerro.* This was Signal Mountain, twelve miles west of Mexicali.

in their present condition. While we were deliber-
ating over the decision which we ought to make, the
Reverend Father Fray Francisco Garcés told us
that not very far from another little hill,[1] four
leagues to the south from where we were, there was
a village of Cajuenches, which he called San Jacome,
and that it was the last watering place which he saw
in these parts in the course of his peregrination.[2]
Therefore, guided by the reverend father we went
toward the hill, hoping that, the pack train being
recuperated there, we should be able afterward to
continue our journey. We arrived after nightfall
opposite the hill, but, having made an effort to find
the village we were not able to discover it or any
of the signs which the father gave us. The commander then decided that we should pass the night
in the vicinity of the hill,[3] although entirely without pasturage or water. According to what we have
subsequently seen, the village of San Jacome was
abandoned because the well from which the natives
got their water had dried up, and this was why we
were unable to find it that night; and in any case
it never would have served to remedy our need at
that time.

[1] This was Cerro Prieto, near the Cocopah Range, some thirty miles
southeast of Mexicali. Father Garcés says they went south-southeast
to find San Xacome. Anza and Díaz say that Cerro Prieto was south
of the turning back point, and San Xacome close to it.

[2] During his journey of 1771.

[3] This is evidence that the village was near Cerro Prieto, or that
here is where they were expecting to find it. A few days later
Garcés saw vestiges of it some two leagues southeast of Cerro Prieto.

Yegaɾandonos á ella, Son 449 u z̄: peɾo, exijɾando algunos Rodeos, q̄
me paɾece pueden omitiɾse; he foɾmado Juicio, que pueden quedan en
100 leguas de Camino.=

Dia 5. de Abɾil Viniexon los Haxxiexos de san Diego con algunos Vivexes, q̄
no exan Suficientes, paɾa que todo el cuexpo de la Expedicion pasase
á Montexxey: poɾ cuyo motivo, y el de nohavex Caballexias expeditos
paɾa todos; pues las que Venian, estan̄ inhabiles paɾa tan laɾga joɾ-
nada; detexminó el Sōx Commandᵗᵉ pasax con pocos Soldados á d̄ho.
Puexto, saliendo los demas con uno de los Padxes á espeɾaxle en el Rio
Colorado. Y paɾa q̄ con mayoɾ pɾomptitud llegase al Emᵒ Sōx Vixxey
la noticia de nᵒ feliz axxibo á estos nuevos establecimientos detexminó tambien, dax desde aqui paxte á Su Exᵃ poɾ medio de un
extraoxdinaxio. Pox loque—

Incluye, y finaliza este diaɾia en esta Nueva Mission del Glo-
ɾioso Axcángel Sōx San Gabriel en 8. dias del mes de Abɾil de
1772 á.=

Fɾ. Juan Diaz

Last page of Díaz's diary to San Gabriel.

February 16.—Concluding that by no means would it be possible for us to go forward conveniently, we decided to return, over the same route which we had followed, to the lake of Santa Olalla, in order that the riding animals and pack train might recuperate, and that we might afterward resume the march and conquer this stretch. For this purpose we set out from the camp, and having traveled five leagues we arrived at the last well, where the rest of the cargo had remained.[1]

February 17.—The horse herd and the pack train were moved to the next watering place, since in this one pasturage was lacking, and therefore we were unable to set out until noon. Then, going east, we marched three leagues to reach it, and halted there.

February 18.—The muleteers remaining in this place to take the cargo to the lake in several trips, as necessity required, the rest of us set forth and came to pass the night near a salty lake which is two leagues from that of Santa Eulalia.[2]

February 19.—At eight o'clock in the morning we reached that lake, where we halted, but the pack-train, on account of its bad condition, was not able to bring all of the packs until the 23rd, at midnight, when the muleteers and the guard arrived safely, although with the loss of some mules which died from exhaustion and lack of food.

[1] This distance of five leagues instead of four was due in part to the detour to meet the pack train. It may also indicate that the Deep Well of Little Water (Las Angustias) was farther than the sand dunes from the Cerro. See pp. 63–66.

[2] Santa Olaya or Olalla.

Until the 2d of March we remained at this lake of Santa Olalla in the company of Captain Palma, who came as soon as he learned of our return, and of many natives, who, drawn by their affection, curiosity, self-interest, and desire for glass beads, tobacco, and other such things as were given them, stayed with us, employing themselves each day more and more in our service. There was opportunity during these days to impress upon them some knowledge of God, although it was not as we wished, through lack of a good interpreter. Some of them brought the idols which they have and delivered them voluntarily, in order that we might smash them to pieces. Nearly all of them acquired the habit of repeating those sweetest names of Jesus and Mary, and some of them learned how to make the sign of the Cross, although very imperfectly.

The commander, seeing that even after several days of rest the riding animals were not getting stronger, and were not fit to undertake so long and difficult a journey, decided to leave the greater part of the cargo, cattle, and pack train in the care of Captain Palma, in whom all of us had come to have great confidence, and to set out with the strongest riding animals, or rather the least weak ones, and with only the provisions necessary to reach the new establishments.[1] This captain accepted the responsibility with great pleasure, promising to care for everything with the greatest vigilance, and mani-

[1] The new establishments in California.

festing such fidelity and care in the matter that none of us had any distrust of his conduct.

But the muleteer, fearful of the loss which might occur, offered to remain, together with two servants, to care for everything. For this purpose three soldiers remained in his company, with the most unfit of the riding animals, to prevent the natives from committing any excess. We were obliged to adopt this plan because we saw that only twelve mules were able to undertake the journey, and that these would not be able to carry all the necessaries for all the men, a reason which, aided by the fear and the insistence of the muleteer, induced and obliged us to make this decision, which, although it was risky, was the only one by which it was possible to absolve the obligation to fulfill our orders.

On the 24th of February the Reverend Father Francisco Garcés set out to visit the natives who live in this vicinity, and on the 1st day of March he returned in safety.

March 2.—Having said goodbyes to those who remained with the rest of the cargo, the riding animals, and the cattle, and having learned from the natives of the most convenient stopping places in this stretch, to enable us to reach our destination, we set out after midday, and having traveled four leagues to the west we came to a lake of fresh water called La Merced,[1] halting near it in a place of good and abundant pasturage. Many Cajuenches

---

[1] Called El Predicador by Anza. Father Garcés had been here on his former journey.

who live near this lake assembled here and made us great demonstrations of love and affection.

March 3.—After Mass had been said we set out accompanied by many natives, and having traveled three leagues to the south-southwest we came to a lake of good and permanent water, where we halted, because the natives had told us there was no other convenient watering place for many leagues. This is a place of abundant pasturage and the lands in its vicinity are very fertile. The lake is a little more than three leagues from San Jacome,[1] already mentioned. Here the natives told us that it was at present deserted for lack of water, and for the same reason it was necessary for us to set out from here to divide the next journey, which was very long and difficult.

March 4.—After midday we set forth from this lake, accompanied by three natives, one of whom promised to guide us to the next watering place, the others going solely for the love of it, and having traveled seven leagues to the west-northwest[2] we halted in a plain near the little hill from which we turned back on the 16th of February, where there is neither water nor pasturage.

March 5.—At daybreak we continued the journey and traveled ten leagues to the west-northwest, in order to ascend the sierra of San Gerónimo,[3] which

[1] Father Garcés after again traveling the distance to San Xacome, said it was over four leagues.

[2] This would put the last camp southward of Volcano Lake, and would give a turn to the northward next day.

[3] The Sierra de San Gerónimo was Cocopah Mountains. They crossed it at the Lower Pass, just below Signal Mountain.

we had borne on our left. After descending by a
dry arroyo for about a league to the southwest, we
crossed a small sand hill. Then, changing our direction to the west and west-northwest, we crossed a
very wide, dry lake to reach a little marsh, which
we called San Eusevio, where we halted.[1] In this
small marsh there are several little wells of salty
water, and in the midst of them there is one of fresh
water, which, although scanty, was sufficient to relieve our need. In its vicinity there is also some
pasturage, although of bad quality. The lake which
is near here extends the whole length of a valley[2]
formed by the sierra of San Gerónimo and another
chain of very high mountains which comes from
California and runs past here to the north, and
afterwards, making a semi-circle, changes its direction to the east and southeast, until it reaches the
Colorado River seven or eight leagues above the
junction. In the same valley, ten or twelve leagues
farther down, is the place where the reverend
father Fray Francisco Garcés saw the Agua Amarilla, as he says in his diary.[3] From this information and from a very large school of sea-fish which
we have found on the beach in this place all along
the banks of the lake, together with many other

[1] The dry lake was the upper end of Laguna Salada or Lake
Maquata. San Eusebio was on the western side of it.

[2] From this we might infer that only the upper end of the lake
was dry. This is inferred also from the statement about the fish
just below.

[3] During his journey of 1771 Father Garcés thought this was the
Colorado River, not knowing that he had crossed that stream.

signs which show clearly that it is water from the
sea which it has received at some other time, we
have inferred that the Agua Amarilla of the father
is some large estuary formed in time of heavy rains,
or perhaps by the sea during some extraordinary
overflow, aided by the drainage of these mountains,
and that it extends the full length of this valley and
afterwards returns to its regular state.

March 6.—In the morning we had the news that
the Indian whom we had with us as a guide had fled.
For this reason, after Mass the commander dispatched a corporal with three men to go and find
out if there was water in the place of which he had
told us the day before. Then, after midday, following the trail of the corporal, we set out from the
little marsh, and having traveled three leagues west-
northwest and west, we were told that he had found
both water and pasturage. We resumed the march,
entering the mountain chain mentioned, and having
traveled two leagues to the southwest and then one
to the south along a canyon or very deep vale, following an arroyo which runs out of it,[1] we reached
the watering place. It consists of two little springs
of fresh water and some others that are salty.
Here we passed the night, having traveled six
leagues in the course of the day. We named this
place Santo Thomás.

[1] This arroyo was in Pinto Canyon, up which the highway to
Tijuana now runs. Anza entered it some ten miles below the inter-
national boundary line. The stream running through it was Pinto
Wash. Santo Tomás was therefore several miles up the canyon.

March 7.—Having taken the same measure of sending the corporal ahead, we set out after noon, and having traveled four leagues to the north,[1] bearing the same mountain chain on the left, we were told that a league away there were some wells of fresh water. Because there was plentiful pasturage at the place where we were, and not a great abundance of it at the watering place, we decided to pass the night here.

March 8.—In the morning we set out for the wells, where we arrived after traveling a league and a half to the northeast. These little wells, which we called Santa Rosa,[2] apparently must be permanent. The water is very good and clear and flows out in abundance. Since he found plentiful pasturage not very far from the watering place, the commander decided to give the riding animals a day's rest. So we remained here until the afternoon of the next day.

March 9.—At two in the afternoon we set out from this place, traveled five leagues to the north, and halted at a dry arroyo in which we found some pasturage.[3] Here we were assured by the Indian Sebastián Tarabal that on the next day he would

[1] These four leagues were traveled after emerging from the canyon. Anza says he went half a league northeast to get away from the mountain, then three and one-half more leagues.

[2] Yuha Well, called by Anza Santa Rosa de las Lajas, on account of the flat rocks there.

[3] This distance north would take them to one of the south flowing forks of Coyote Wash, a few miles north of Plaster City. Eldredge's identification of the Arroyo Seco with Carrizo Creek is untenable.

lead us to a watering place at which he stopped when he went out to Sonora.[1] This was the first place he was able to recognize, for this is the stretch of country where he was lost for three days, which was the cause of the death of his wife and a relative of his who were with him, because they did not find any water until they reached the Colorado River.

March 10.—At dawn we set out from this arroyo, guided by Tarabal, having at the left the great sierra, and at the right a little mountain which we passed after going four leagues.[2] Then crossing a very difficult sand dune for two leagues and traveling seven leagues in all, we arrived at the place of which the Indian told us, and here we halted. In this place there is a spring of very good and plentiful water. Very close to it is a salt marsh in which there is plentiful pasturage, but of bad quality.[3] Here in the neighborhood live some families of the Cajuenche tribe who in their method of speaking are little different from those of the river. They live on mesquite beans, together with the mescal which they bring from the sierra, and the rabbits which they hunt, which for them is very easy. Although they fled, borne by fear, afterwards, losing their terror, they came to visit us and stayed with us until we departed. They told us of two other watering places which are to the southeast, and we concluded

[1] See p. 248.   [2] This small range was Superstition Mountain.

[3] This camp, called San Sebastián, in honor of the guide Sebastián (also called El Peregrino in allusion to his wanderings) was at San Felipe Creek, near its junction with Carrizo Creek. The site is now marked by Harper's Well.

that on our return we might be able to discover by
way of them a more direct and less difficult route
across the stretch which lies between here and the
river, which is the hardest in all this journey, according to what the Indian Tarabal tells us.

March 11.—Saying goodbye to the natives, at
two o'clock in the afternoon we set out from this
place, which we called San Sebastián, and having
traveled two leagues to the west we halted at a
village of the same Cajuenche tribe.[1] We found
neither water nor pasturage here, but we were
obliged to halt by the delay of the pack train, which
took a long time to get out of the marsh, because
it was very miry.

March 12.—At four o'clock in the morning we set
forth toward the west-northwest, and, doubling some
small peaks which come before the mountains, we
entered a valley formed by these hills and another
sierra of great elevation.[2] At the entry to the valley
we halted at a place with abundant pasturage,
where there is a well of plentiful water which we
called San Gregorio, having traveled during the day
eight leagues.[3]

March 13.—For the purpose of allowing the pack
train and the riding animals to rest we remained
here all day.

[1] West of Harper's Well.

[2] The small hills were Red or Borrego Mountain. The valley was
Borrego Valley. Anza was practically on the road now running from
Kane Spring to Beatty's Ranch.

[3] Anza swung to the right of Borrego Mountain, camp being on
San Felipe Creek, just west of the mountain.

March 14.—At five o'clock in the morning we set out from this place, and, having traveled five leagues to the northwest, we entered a valley formed by the sierras already mentioned, through which runs a small arroyo which rises from several springs in the same valley. After going a league along the arroyo we halted at the head of the first springs. At this place, which we called Santa Catalina,[1] there is some pasturage, and also some small willows. The water appears to be permanent, although it is scarce during the dry season.

Some of the natives who live in this vicinity are of the Cajuenche tribe, but most of them are of another tribe who, according to the report given by the Indian Tarabal, and to what we have seen at the time of this writing, live all through this mountain in the direction toward which we are going, but we have not been able to ascertain its name. I have formed the opinion that they speak the same idiom, although with some differences, as the Indians of the mission of San Gabriel, newly established near the coast by the apostolic fathers of San Fernando de Mexico.[2] This opinion comes from seeing that the Indian Tarabal, who lived for some time in that mission, understands them and speaks some words of that language, although in one village it seems

[1] The Arroyo was Coyote Creek. The Springs of Santa Catalina were Reed's Springs, or Lower Willows, about four miles above Beatty's Ranch.

[2] Serra and his companions were from the College of San Fernando de Mexico. Díaz and Garcés were from the sister college of Santa Cruz de Querétaro.

they were not able to understand anything that he said. But this may very well be, because of the very slight knowledge which he has of the language, and because the natives of this village may have corrupted or changed more than others some words or terms of the idiom, a usual thing in the barbarism of these nations, as experience has taught us. To this place many came to visit us after they had lost the fear which at first they entertained, and having given us some heads of very good mescal and received our gifts of tobacco and some gewgaws, they withdrew to their houses.

These Indians of the sierra are less robust and prosperous than those of the river. We have seen no other weapons here than a club which they make in the shape of a sickle and use for hunting hares and rabbits,[1] to which it seems they are greatly inclined. We have not learned that they plant any crops. They sustain themselves solely from the chase, and from mescal, pinenuts, and acorns, which abound in these mountains. For this reason, as I have noted, the sierra is more thickly populated than the plains. The dress of these natives is almost the same as that of the river people, but it differs in that the men wear sandals which they make from the fiber of the mescal or maguey,[2] of which material they also make some nets which they regularly wear around the head. The women also wear skirts of deerskin.

[1] Sometimes called rabbit-sticks.
[2] The Yumas and Cajuenches called these the Sandal Wearers.

March 15.—At three o'clock in the morning we set out from Santa Cathalina, following the valley and the principal arroyo, and seeing many natives, whom we tried to humor and befriend as much as possible. Having traveled two leagues to the north-west and the north-northwest we ascended to the top of the mountain by a ridge that is not at all difficult. Then we continued our journey along the same plateau, which is quite wide, and having traveled a league toward the north we halted, before going through the pass, in a little valley where there is plenty of pasturage and running water.[1] All this mountain and those which can be seen from here appear to be very moist and fertile. They are well grown with brush and with some pasturage, and in the highest altitudes and in the canyons are seen many pines, and large oaks, which seem to be more plentiful the farther north the mountains run. The snow covering some of the heights and in the canyons is very deep and, as I am informed, it remains in them until the beginning of May.[2]

March 16.—Day dawned raining, and we were not able to set forth until one in the afternoon. Then, going northwest, we ascended the pass, which we

[1] They followed Coyote Canyon, the narrow valley through which runs Coyote Creek. At the forks they made a stiff climb out of the valley between Nance and Tule canyons, traveled about five miles to the head of Nance Canyon, and camped in the little valley right behind Fred Clark's corral. Here there are several springs and fine grass.

[2] He means those to the north, farther along the trail, not those which they have just left behind.

called San Carlos, and without any special descent
entered a small valley with much pasturage, formed
by some small hills.[1] After going a short distance
we came to another and much wider valley, and having traveled two leagues and a half altogether in
this direction we halted in this valley, which we
called El Príncipe. This valley is formed by two
sierras of considerable elevation, well grown with
pines and oaks and other trees of little importance.
In it there are some springs of water, and a very
large lake which I judge must be permanent.[2] Its
lands are very fertile and thickly grown with pasturage, and I think it would be possible to establish
here a good-sized settlement which could exist without scarcity. The soldiers with us who are versed
in metals say that these sierras and others which
they have seen in these parts may in time be of
great value and richness, although up to the present
no vein whatever has been discovered, nor have I
seen that they have made any special effort.

March 17.—On account of a heavy rain we remained here until the afternoon, then, going northwest, we came to a very deep-gorged and narrow
arroyo which rises in a spring in a small valley
which we had at our left, and which runs with good
flow for about six leagues in that direction until it
disappears in the sand.[3] Near this arroyo we halted,
having traveled three and a half leagues. There is

[1] Cahuilla Valley.   [2] Dry Lake on Contreras's ranch.
[3] Bautista Canyon.

some pasturage on all its banks, and although it is
so narrow anyone may travel by it unless the arroyo
becomes very full of water, and it does not appear
that there is any other road more convenient in this
direction.

March 18.—In the morning we set out from
camp, following the same direction along the arroyo,
which we called San Patricio. After two leagues
it gets very much wider, forming between its two
ridges a very fertile and delightful valley, which
ends three leagues farther down. Here begins a
broad valley which we called Señor San Joseph, in
which we halted, having traveled seven leagues for
the day.[1] This valley is formed by a very high
sierra which we have on the right, and a chain of
small hills which we have borne on the left. From
the drainage of the sierra there is formed a good-
sized arroyo,[2] thickly covered with cottonwoods.
According to appearances it must be permanent,
and because there is no outlet it forms in the middle
of the valley some very large lakes, to which contributes, likewise, a very wide marsh, the great
quantity of water which runs from its channel
emptying into them. The lands of this valley are
extremely fertile and enough, it appears to me, to
raise crops and support stock for a settlement of
the largest kind. The valley is very delightful to
the sight. The nearby sierras are thickly grown
with pines, and all appear to be mineral bearing.

[1] Above San Jacinto.   [2] San Jacinto River.

March 19.—After celebrating two Masses we left this place and traveled three leagues, arriving at the marsh mentioned, which we called San Antonio.[1] We continued our journey along the same valley, and before leaving it we halted near a small hill, having traveled during the day six leagues to the northwest.

March 20.—Now leaving the valley and continuing in the same direction, we traveled over plains well grown with pasturage, bearing on the right a snow-covered mountain which depends on the preceding one. Then, having ascended a small ridge through a very easy pass, we entered a most beautiful and broad valley in the middle of which runs a river well grown with cottonwoods, which was crossed by the first discoverers about twelve leagues lower down, and called by them Santa Ana, as we are told by the two experienced men who are with us.[2] Having traveled eight leagues for the day, we halted at the bank of this river, which, being at high water and much boxed in, we were not able to cross this afternoon, and it was necessary to make a bridge of cottonwoods in order to cross over the next day. On the bank of this river we saw some natives, who, by their great gentleness and the confidence with which they began to deal with us, manifested that they already had knowledge of our people.

[1] San Jacinto Lake, now drained.   [2] Valdés and Sebastián.

March 21.—After Mass we crossed to the other side of the river by the bridge. Then, keeping the Sierra Nevada on the right, we traveled seven leagues to the northwest over very fertile plains with much pasturage, halting near an arroyo which rises in this sierra and which may be permanent, judging from the large growth of trees along its banks.[1]

March 22.—We set out in the morning from this arroyo and traveled two leagues to the northwest, with great difficulty because of the heavy nature of the land. Then, turning to the west and west-north-west, we traveled five leagues in order to reach the arroyo of San Gabriel. It cost much time and trouble to find a ford free by which to cross it. But this difficulty having been overcome, we continued in the same direction and arrived a little before night at the mission of the Glorious Archangel, having traveled during the day eight leagues.[2]

Our arrival at this mission was an occasion of great rejoicing for everybody. Its ministers and the soldiers who guard it welcomed us with many volleys and repeated "Victorias!" and did whatever was in their power for our entertainment. On the next day Mass was chanted with all the solemnity possible, as an act of thanksgiving to the Infinite Majesty, who deigns to reward with full hands the

[1] This was San Antonio Creek, and camp was about at Ontario.

[2] A few months later the mission was moved some three miles northward to its present site.

Catholic zeal, constant piety, and religion of our invincible and most amiable monarch, enlarging his dominion so easily, exalting his arms, and trusting to his fervent charity the task of converting so vast a heathendom to the fold of our sacred religion.

Since we had left the greater part of our provisions at the Colorado River, we reached this mission without any whatever. Having told the reverend father ministers of our need, they offered with great generosity whatever they had, but it was so little withal that it was not possible to supply us so that we might go on to the port of Monterrey. But, it being learned now that a frigate had just arrived with provisions at the port of San Diego, the commander decided to repair thither in order that we might be supplied with what was necessary. For this purpose he dispatched some soldiers and muleteers on the 25th of the present month, we remaining in this mission to celebrate Holy Week.

The number of leagues which we have traveled from the junction of the rivers to this mission of San Gabriel, not counting those which we covered from the lake of Santa Olalla and retraced in going back to it, are one hundred and nineteen and a half. But omitting some detours which it seems to me might be avoided, I have concluded that the distance would be one hundred leagues of travel.

April 5.—The muleteers returned from San Diego with some provisions, but they were not sufficient to enable the whole body of the expedition to go to Monterrey. For this reason, and since there were not enough suitable riding animals for all, as those which came with us are unfit for so long a journey, the commander decided to go with a few soldiers to that port, the rest of the men going out with one of the fathers to await him at the Colorado River. And in order that with greater promptitude his Excellency the Viceroy might get the news of our happy arrival at these new establishments, he decided also to send a report to his Excellency from here, by means of an extraordinary courier.[1] This concludes and ends this diary, in this new mission of the Glorious Archangel San Gabriel, on the 8th day of the month of April, 1774.

FRAY JUAN DÍAZ (Rubric).

[1] This courier was Juan Bautista Valdés. With this diary Father Díaz sent a letter dated April 8. See Volume V of this work.

DIAZ'S RETURN DIARY

1774

DIARY KEPT BY FATHER FRAY JUAN DIAS,
APOSTOLIC MISSIONARY OF THE HOLY CROSS
OF QUERETARO, DURING THE JOURNEY WHICH
HE MADE FROM THE MISSION OF SAN GABRIEL,
IN NORTHERN CALIFORNIA, TO THE PRESIDIO
OF SAN YGNACIO DE TUBAC, IN THE PROVINCE
OF SONORA, IN COMPANY WITH THE SENOR
CAPTAIN DON JUAN BAPTISTA DE ANSA, COM-
MANDER OF THE EXPEDITION.[1]

The Reverend Father Fray Junípero Serra, who
on his return from Mexico had just landed at the port
of San Diego, distant from this place forty leagues
to the southeast, having arrived at this mission
of San Gabriel, his Reverence told me that in that
port there was a friar who had the necessary instruments for observing latitudes.[2] And, thinking that
it would be of great importance to give to the superior government an exact report of the latitudes
of the principal places which we have discovered
during this expedition, I decided to go in person to
try to procure those instruments. Therefore, having
said goodbye to my companion, the Reverend Father

[1] Diario, que formó el Padre Fr. Juan Dias . . . en Compañia
del S.ᵒʳ Capitan D.ⁿ Juan Baptista de Ansa Comandante de la Expedicion. A. G. I., 104–6–17.

[2] Father Serra was on his way back from Mexico City to Monterey, having come by sea to San Diego in the *Nueva Galicia.*

Fray Francisco Garcés, who with part of the soldiers had departed the day before to await us at the Colorado River, I set forth for the port of San Diego.

During the journey, through the observations which I made of the country, I saw that it would be of little or no use to make our return by way of that port, as formerly had been planned; for, on account of the great roughness and the height of the sierra, it appeared to me to be indispensable in going from Sonora to any one of these new establishments to go by way of the Pass of San Carlos. This opinion has been confirmed subsequently by those experienced in the country, who give assurance that there is no other pass suitable for surmounting that sierra. With this conviction I returned to the mission of San Gabriel, where, on the first of May of this present year of 1774, the commander Don Juan Baptista de Ansa arrived on his return from Monterey.

We being agreed that it was more important to straighten out as much as possible the road which had already been discovered, and everything necessary being made ready, and accompanied by six soldiers who came with us to learn about the road, we set out in the afternoon on the 3d of the present month from this mission of San Gabriel, and having traveled six leagues to the east we halted at a stream called Arroyo de los Alisos.[1]

On the 4th of the same May, having traveled five leagues in the same direction, we arrived at the Santa Ana River, which we were able to ford without

[1] Arroyo de San Antonio. Camp was near Ontario.

any danger. Continuing the journey in the afternoon, and traveling six leagues in the same direction, we arrived to spend the night at a little pass which is near the marsh[1] of San Antonio, where we were on the 19th of last March.

May 5.—Traveling in the morning five leagues to the east by south we came to the arroyo which waters the valley of San José; and having made an observation of its latitude I found it to be in 33° 46'. In the afternoon we continued the journey and having traveled six leagues to the southeast we arrived to pass the night in a small valley where the Arroyo de San Patricio rises.[2]

May 6.—Traveling four leagues to the east-southeast we came to the Pass of San Carlos, and having observed its latitude at high noon I found it to be in 33° 42'. In the afternoon, having continued four leagues to the southeast, we halted at the Arroyo de Santa Catalina. The heathen who inhabit this range, although at first they manifested themselves very friendly and obsequious, afterward came secretly and shot two or three riding animals with arrows,[3] and according to the note from the Reverend Father Fray Francisco Garcés which we found at this place, they did the same when his Reverence passed through with the detachment of soldiers who accompanied him.

[1] Elsewhere called the Lake of San Antonio. It was San Jacinto Lake.

[2] Anza gives the distance traveled as four leagues and the latitude as 33° 46½'. Camp was near Tripp Flat, in Cahuilla Valley.

[3] Anza tells us that one of the offenders was given a beating.

May 7.—Having traveled in the morning five leagues to the east-southeast we arrived at the well of San Gregorio where we took our siesta. Then, continuing the journey in the afternoon, and traveling seven leagues to the east, we arrived at the watering place of San Sebastián. Here we found a letter from the Reverend Father Fray Francisco Garcés, informing us that, guided by a heathen of this village, he had gone forward by a different route, with the hope of finding some watering place which would equalize the marches as far as the Colorado River, and avoid the excessive detour which we had made to cover this stretch when we came.[1]

Therefore on the 8th, in the morning, we set out from this place, following the trail of the reverend father, and having traveled all day to the southeast and covered twenty leagues more or less, we arrived at eleven o'clock at night at the well of El Carrizal, where we were on the 14th of February, not having found a single watering place during the whole march. It would appear that this journey could be accomplished by setting out in the afternoon from this Carrizal in order to arrive the next day before noon at Santa Rosa de las Lajas, which is distant from here about fourteen leagues to the northwest by west, as the pack trains are accustomed to do in similar marches.[2]

[1] Anza gives the day's march as ten or eleven leagues, and a less eastward direction than that assigned by Díaz. He does not tell of finding the letter from Garcés at San Sebastián.

[2] Anza says they traveled seventeen leagues to Pozo de las Angustias on the 8th and five in the night to Santa Olaya. He does not mention El Carrizal. I conclude that Anza by mistake wrote Las Angustias instead of El Carrizal.

May 9.—Traveling in the morning six leagues to the east-southeast, we arrived at the lake of Santa Olalla where, having made an observation at noon, I saw that the place was in 32° 34′. In the afternoon, having traveled five leagues northeast, we came to pass the night at one of the villages of San Pablo.

May 10.—Having traveled in the morning six leagues in the same direction, straightening the road as much as possible, we arrived at the Puerto de la Purísima Concepción and passed the siesta near the junction of the rivers.[1] Captain Palma and all his tribe have felt great jubilation at our successful return, and have exerted themselves as formerly to assist us to the full extent of their ability. Because the Colorado River had begun to rise, they made a very large raft, on which this same afternoon they took us over to the other side, and we halted at the place where the Reverend Father Fray Francisco Garcés had established his camp.[2] Notwithstanding what was said in the first diary concerning the floods of the Colorado River, it appears from what we have seen that they are not the same every year nor at the same time; for, since the cause of them is the melting of the snows, the deeper the snows the greater the floods, and the time of the floods likewise varies according to whether the melting of the snows is early or late.

[1] Anza says that on the 10th they traveled eight leagues to San Dionisio.

[2] This incident is given in greater detail by Anza.

On two different days I have observed this place where the Gila and Colorado rivers join, and both times I have found it to be in 32° 44′. I cannot explain the great difference between this observation and the one which the book called *Afanes Apostólicos* says was made by Father Kino at this same place. But, giving attention to the directions and distances which are assigned, and the latitudes which recently have been observed in the establishments of California Alta, it will be manifest to every intelligent person that this place can not be in the latitude which that book gives.

The natives of the villages of San Pablo, not being acquainted with the soldiers who have accompanied us from Monterey to learn about the road, and giving the frivolous pretext that they were from the land of their enemies, attempted to steal from them the riding animals and some cattle which the commander had given them. Therefore it was necessary for us to remain at this place until the 15th, so that, through fear of the troops, they might not go to the excess of carrying out their plan. But Captain Palma, with all his village, persevered in his proved fidelity; and in order to prevent the deed which the rest were planning, he set out in company with the soldiers to conduct them in safety and free them from the assault which threatened them. On account of this occurrence, and of other circumstances which I have observed with careful reflection, I have formed the opinion that passage through these lands will not be

easy unless our nation establishes itself at some
points on these rivers, for the fickleness of the
Indians is well known, their inclination to thievery
is patent, their consideration is none, and the passage of the river very difficult. And if they should
come to be discontented, and disinclined to coöperate
in the crossing with their aid, and on the contrary
should attempt to impede it, a large force of arms
would be necessary to vanquish so numerous although
so uncivilized a heathendom.[1]

The muleteers and soldiers who remained here
with the rest of the cargo, the riding animals, and
cattle, on account of a vague report which these natives gave them, telling them that we were all killed,
abandoned the place, returning to Caborca with
everything which was in their care, except some
beeves and provisions which they left in charge of
Captain Palma. For the purpose of reconnoitering
the tribes who live on the Gila River, observing the
principal sites along it, and examining the qualities
of this road to Sonora, the commander decided to
turn from the road by way of the coast and make his
way along the banks of this river.

Therefore, on the 15th, in the afternoon, we
started, and having traveled four leagues east-northeast we halted on the banks of the river where some
pasturage for the riding animals was found.[2]

---

[1] In evidence of the soundness of this opinion, Father Díaz himself, some six years later, suffered martyrdom at the hands of the
Yumas at San Pablo, below Pilot Knob.

[2] Camp was up the river about half way to the Gila Range.

May 16.—After celebrating the holy sacrifice of the Mass we began the march, and having traveled nine leagues in the same direction we came to pass the night near a lake which is distant from the river a quarter of a league, at a place extremely short of pasturage.[1]

May 17.—In the morning, after Mass, we traveled six leagues to the northeast by east and came to pass the siesta near a peak by the river which we called San Pasqual. In the afternoon, having traveled three leagues in the same direction, we halted at a place with plentiful pasturage.[2]

May 18.—After Mass we set forth from this place, and having traveled four leagues in the same direction we halted at a village of Cocomaricopas, near the river and by us called San Bernardino. This is the first village of the tribe found upstream between the junction of the rivers and this place. The reason why this stretch of country is uninhabited is the continuous war waged by this tribe with that of the Yumas, although now, as a result of our exhortation, they have promised to maintain mutual peace. I made an observation at this place at high noon and found it to be in 33° 3′ north latitude.[3]

May 19.—After celebrating two Masses we set out from this village, and having traveled ten leagues

---

[1] This lake evidently was Laguna Salobre.

[2] The Cerro de San Pasqual was Mohawk Peak. Anza says they camped two leagues farther upstream.

[3] San Bernardino was near the present town of Palomas. Anza gives the latitude as 33° 2′.

east by north we came to pass the night at a place with plentiful pasturage called El Aritoac.[1]

May 20.—In the morning, having traveled four leagues east by north, we halted at a village of Opas. It is a place of plentiful pasturage and has an abundance of land for planting crops. In the afternoon, having traveled four leagues in the same direction, we came to pass the night at another village of the same tribe, in whose vicinity plentiful crops for these natives are raised.

May 21.—In the morning, having traveled a league to the east, we arrived at San Simón y Judas de Upasoitac,[2] which is a village of the same tribe, although some Pimas ordinarily live in it. Its environs are very fertile and these Indians harvest every year plentiful wheat, maize, and other grains and vegetables. Having made an observation here at noon I found the place to be in latitude 33° 15′. Between the village of San Bernardino and this one of Upasoitac, this river and its adjacent watering places are inhabited by Opas, Tutumaopas, and Cocomaricopas, none of which are different from the Yumas in anything, either in language or in any of their native qualities. The clothing worn by the women is the same. The men wear their tápalo, which serves the requirements of modesty, in which respect, as well as in the management of arms, they are superior to the Yumas, on account of the

1 Anza mentions passing Ojo Caliente three leagues before making camp, which was at the river opposite Oatman's Flat.

2 Upasoitac was at Gila Bend.

union and continual commerce which they have with the Gila Pimas. In this village the Reverend Father Fray Francisco Garcés remained to attempt, by means of these heathen, to send a letter to the missionary fathers of New Mexico, to do which he told me he was charged by the reverend father guardian of our College.

Therefore, having entrusted to the natives the care and assistance of this father, who thought it was not advisable that any escort should remain with him, we set out in the afternoon, and having traveled eight leagues to the east-northeast we halted at an arroyo without water and with very little pasturage.[1] At a distance of three leagues from this place toward the north-northwest the Gila River joins that of La Asumpción,[2] which apparently is of equal or even greater volume. We have not examined the junction close to hand, in order to avoid a detour which would be necessary to follow the course of the river, which at this place makes a long turn toward the north.

May 22.—After celebrating the holy sacrifice of the Mass we set forth on the way, and having traveled seven leagues to the east we arrived at the first pueblo of the heathen Pimas, called Sutaquison,[3]

---

[1] Camp was about half way between Maricopa Range and Sierra Estrella.

[2] Salt River. The distance was much more than three leagues.

[3] Sutaquison was near the bend of the Gila east of Sierra Estrella. Anza tells us that it had more than two thousand inhabitants, and mentions ancient ruins in the vicinity. These are now called Casa Blanca.

where the natives received us with great demonstrations of joy, serving us in every way they could, and the commander, at their request and mine, confirmed one of the natives in the office of governor, impressing upon him with his accustomed prudence the obligations of his office and exhorting him to their due fulfillment.

May 23.—We set out in the morning from this village, and having traveled three leagues in the same direction we arrived at the last pueblo occupied by these heathen, where they received us with the same or even greater hospitality. Here a governor and an alcalde were installed, and they immediately gave proofs of their good conduct. At noon I observed the latitude of this place and found it to be in 33° 24'.[1] These are the Pimas whom we call the Gileños, all of whom are confined to the space of three leagues on one bank of the river and the other, because thus united they are better able to withstand the continuous assaults of the Apaches. The lands which they possess on both banks of the river are very fertile, and, aided by the irrigation, they produce in plenty all sorts of crops, but they do not fail to suffer from the scarcity of pasturage which is experienced all along this river and in all the stretch of the Colorado River which we have explored. I have formed the opinion that in all the region examined it will not be possible to support more cattle

[1] This town was called Uturituc, or Juturitucan. Anza says the inhabitants numbered three thousand. Anza gives this latitude as for Sutaquison. See p. 240.

than are necessary for the maintenance and sustenance of the Indians, and for the riding animals which are necessary for communication with the pueblos.

These natives are of the same qualities as the reduced Pimas, with whom and with the Pápagos, Opas, and Cocomaricopas they have close relations. According to appearances they are very industrious, for in the short space of three leagues which they have settled with six villages, each village plants in common so large a field of wheat, maize and other crops that they have filled us with admiration. The fields of wheat which they are just now harvesting, according to our computation may have a hundred fanegas planted in each one, and according to the testimony of the Indians themselves one of them has one hundred and twenty fanegas. All these fields the Indians cultivate with no more oxen and no other implements than a wooden stick, with which they make holes in the ground and go slowly burying the seed. Yet, by means of such slight cultivation the Indians produce crops with such abundance that they served as a great delight to all of us who saw them. The clothing of these natives is the same as that worn by those already reduced in our missions, and they are accustomed even to obtain a greater abundance of goods through the commerce in their crops which they maintain, now with the Papaguería and now with other heathen who lack them in their own lands. Among them there are some Christians and, from what I have observed from communicating

Diario, que formo el P. Fr. Juan Diaz Misionero Appº. de la Sta Cruz de Queretaro en el Viage, que hizo desde la Mision de Sn. Gabriel en la California Septentrional hasta el Presidio de Sn. Ygnº. de Tubac el Govierno de Sonora en Compañia del Sor. Capn. Dn. Juan Baptista de Anza Comandante de la Expedicion.

Haviendo llegado a esta Mision de Sn. Gabriel el R. P. Fr. Junipero Serra, que de vuelta de Mexico acababa de desembarcar en el Puerto de Sn. Diego, distante de este Parage quarenta leguas al vez=este me dixo su Ra. quedaba en dho Puerto un Religioso, que para el fin de observar las alturas del Polo tenia los instrumentos necesarios. Y considerando seria de mucha importancia dar al Superior Gobno. exacta noticia de la altura en que se hallan los Parages principales, que hemos descubierto en esta expedicion; determiné pasar personalmente en solicitud

First page of Díaz's return diary.

with them, all would gladly become Christians, and it would be at the cost of very little labor, if only for this purpose the necessary provisions were made.

May 24.—In the morning we set out from this pueblo, and having traveled three leagues to the east we passed the siesta at a place of plentiful pasturage close by the river.[1] In the afternoon, now leaving the course of the stream, which comes from the east, we began the march, going directly toward the pueblo of Tuquisón, a *visita* of the mission of San Xavier del Bac, and distant from this place twenty-five leagues to the southeast. On this stretch at this season no watering place whatever is found, but in order not to expose ourselves to the risk of some incursion of the Apaches, it was decided to begin the march at once. Therefore, having traveled in this direction all night, we arrived on the next day about eleven o'clock in the morning at an arroyo of water near the pueblo of Tuquisón, to which we went in the afternoon.

May 25.—In the morning, having traveled three leagues in the same direction, we arrived at the pueblo of San Xavier del Bac. After passing the siesta here, we set out in the afternoon for the presidio of Tubac, distant from this mission fifteen leagues in the same direction.

The following day, in the church of this presidio, Mass was chanted as an act of thanksgiving to our patrons, who have deigned to bring us to our des-

[1] Anza says camp was two leagues below the Palace of Moctezuma, or Casa Grande.

tination with such felicity after having achieved the purpose of our expedition.

This diary was finished at this presidio of San Ygnacio del Tubac on the 26th day of May, 1774.

FRAY JUAN DIAS, apostolic missionary.

I certify that this is a copy of the original which remains in this Secretaría de Cámara y Virreynato of New Spain in my charge. Mexico, September 26, 1774.   MELCHOR DE PERAMÁS (Rubric).

GARCES'S DIARY FROM TUBAC TO
SAN GABRIEL
1774

(F)

DIARY OF THE EXPEDITION WHICH IS BEING
MADE BY ORDER OF HIS EXCELLENCY THE
VICEROY, DON ANTONIO MARIA BUCARELI Y
URSUA, DECIDED UPON IN COUNCIL OF WAR
AND ROYAL EXCHEQUER, TO OPEN A ROAD BY
WAY OF THE GILA AND COLORADO RIVERS TO
THE NEW ESTABLISHMENTS OF SAN DIEGO AND
MONTE REY, UNDER COMMAND OF CAPTAIN
DON JUAN BAPTISTA DE ANSA.[1]

According to orders there are going two friars,
the Reverend Father Fray Juan Díaz and I, Fray
Francisco Garcés, twenty soldiers, a person who
knows the roads of California, an interpreter of the
Pima language, a California Indian who came out
on the 26th of December to the presidio of Altar, an
Indian carpenter, five muleteers, and two servants
of the commander—total, thirty-four persons; and
thirty-three pack loads of baggage, sixty-five cattle
on foot, and one hundred and forty riding animals.

[1] Diario de la entrada que se practica . . . el R. P. Fr. Juan
Díaz y yo, Fr. Fran.ᶜᵒ Garces. A. G. P. M., Historia, Tomo 52.

The expedition had arranged to assemble at my mission[1] to go by way of the Gileños and their allies, and to ascend the Colorado River[2] in order if possible to avoid the sand dunes and bad stretches which I had seen in my last journey. But the theft of the riding animals at Tubac by the Apaches and our inability to supply ourselves promptly except in the west, and the coming out of the Indian Sebastián and Captain Palma of the Yumas,[3] who assured the commander that the road was good, caused him to direct the journey by way of Caborca, making a detour of fifty-two leagues. Some Gila Indians had come to inform me and to go with us, but having received a letter from Father Fray Juan Díaz, who said that he had one from the commander himself telling what had happened and had been decided upon, I sent a message to the Gila Indians telling them not to wait for me.

January 6.—I set out from my mission of San Xavier del Vac, and having traveled fifteen leagues arrived at night at Tubac. On the 7th everything was arranged for the journey, and from the 8th to the 21st we spent on the road from Tubac to Caborca, which is seven leagues from El Altar. Five of these leagues are traveled to the west-northwest and the remaining two to the west. Of all this region the superior government is well informed, and I will

[1] San Xavier del Bac, thirty-six miles north of Tubac.

[2] That is, they were to go to the Gila River and cut across to the Colorado at some point above the Yumas.

[3] Salvador Palma, the Yuma head chief, escorted Sebastián to Altar shortly before the expedition set forth.

therefore note only that Captain Don Bernardo de Urrea and the gentleman of La Siénega[1] and two father missionaries, enthusiastic for the enterprise, assisted with some presents to be given to the Indians. Several Masses were chanted to the Most Holy Trinity, and to the Immaculate Conception as prelate of my college and patroness of my religion and of Spain. Indeed, this expedition and others which have been made and will be made during the happy reign of our great monarch, Carlos III, ought to be considered as a reward for his great devotion to the Immaculate Conception. For my part I take also as patron St. Peter the Apostle.

January 22.—At twelve o'clock we started from Caborca toward the northwest, and, having traveled six leagues, at eight o'clock we camped for the night. We did not set out over the road which I followed on my return from the Colorado River, because it is difficult for the animals, and it appears that we went roundabout. The place where we halted is without water although it has some pasturage. We called it San Yldefonso.[2]

January 23.—We traveled eight leagues in the same direction and reached San Eduardo del Arivaypia,[3] which has a vateque or well in a dry arroyo,

[1] Ciénega, then commonly called Cieneguilla, was a mining town a few leagues south of Altar. It is still on the map.

[2] San Ildefonso was near Cerro Babura, a little more than half way from Caborca to Tajitos. Garcés alludes to his return from Sonóita to San Xavier by way of Caborca in 1771.

[3] Arivaipa is on Arroyo El Coyote, about forty miles northwest of Caborca.

where by digging in the sand the water seeps out so that with some labor the animals can drink. Within a circuit of a league there are three small villages. The one which has the most Indians is the one which I called Santa Coleta de Cuboitac,[1] and does not have more than twenty-five families.

January 24.—We set out at noon in the same direction, traveled four leagues, and came to halt for the night at a lake or pond, which is not permanent except in the rainy season, like the preceding days when rain has been abundant. It is called San Juan de Mata.[2]

January 25.—We broke camp at noon and traveled until eight o'clock at night, the greater part of the way to the northwest and the rest to the north. In the neighborhood of a little pool there are some Indians, and plenty of grass and some jojoba.[3] The Indians who were going in our company lived at the place where a viper bit my horse on my last journey out. To the east of San Yldefonso begins a large mountain chain which continues to the west.[4] There is another, a black one, which ends in some hills at the pool mentioned.[5] The day's march must have been as much as six good leagues.

[1] This village, visited by Father Garcés in 1771, was evidently the same as modern Cubo, on Arroyo de Cubo, a few miles east of Arivaipa.

[2] This place was at or near Temporales.

[3] Camp was in the plain about two-thirds of the way between Costa Rica ranch and Chujubabi ranchería.

[4] Sierra de Chupurate, called by Anza Buccomari.

[5] Cerro del Cozón ends about three miles south of the camp site. This is evidently the range that he refers to.

January 26.—We broke camp about eight o'clock in the morning. Starting toward the northwest and then turning north, we came to some hills where there is permanent water in a well, at which there were some Indians when I came out from the river on my last journey.[1] Then we turned west and west-northwest and came to San Luís de Quitovac, where we saw three springs of water, which I mention in my diary, and some other veins which have been caused by the rains, and also some pasturage.[2] Today the Indians were scattered, but when I passed through here there were twenty-five families. The day's march was four leagues. No mission could be founded in this village because of the poor land.

January 27.—At noon we marched north, keeping a rocky sierra on the left. At nightfall we came to a rancho and the spring of the topil of Sonóyta, where I camped for the night on my return. Then we stole two hours of the night and made camp near a tank where the animals were not able to drink.[3] On the right there are small hills. The mountain chain ends here and two others begin. The Peñon of Vabuquíburi[4] is visible from here, and it is plain

[1] These are the hills at the left of the road just beyond Chujubabi ranchería. In that neighborhood there are two or three good-sized arroyos, generally dry.

[2] Quitobac is now a little pueblo of Pápago Indians and Mexicans. The brooks have been dammed and there is a small lake right in the town.

[3] The topil was an officer of the Indian village. This camp was on the skirts of Sierra de Cubabi.

[4] Babuquíburi Peak, in Babuquíburi Range, west of Tubac, is visible and imposing for a long distance in every direction. Father Kino called it Noah's Ark.

how short and direct is the road from here to the presidio of Tubac. During the two hours which we traveled after nightfall our direction was west-northwest, and the day's journey was six leagues.

January 28.—At eight o'clock in the morning we set forth in the same direction; having traveled three leagues we swung to the north, and then going five more we reached San Marcelo, formerly a mission of the Jesuit fathers. It has a spring and pasturage but bad soil. The people are very much scattered. By first establishing missions on the Colorado and Gila rivers one could be founded at this place, but otherwise I could not guarantee progress in this foundation, which will have to be effected by other means than those employed on the rivers. To the right and to the northwest there runs a sierra containing salt. I told the commander that the Indian official here was the most experienced in the road to the rivers, so we employed him and he accompanied us thither.

January 29.—At half past eight we set out between the sierra on the right and the rocky one which runs through here to the southwest, and having traveled eight leagues to the west, with minor deviations, we came to the watering place of El Carrizal, which has little pasturage, bad water, and some carrizo.¹ They told us that by continuing,

¹ The road ran west-northwest along the south side of Sonóita River, turning southwest opposite Quitovaquita. El Carrizal, or the carrizo marsh, was evidently at the present Agua Salada, where the road turns sharply northwest.

good water is found in wells as far as the sea,[1] and that the coast is inhabited by Pima Indians, enemies of the Quiquimas and of those who took me across the Colorado River during my last journey. Having several times asked the guide concerning the watering places, he mentioned no others than those which I saw on my return from the Colorado River, and I recognized that we were taking a bad road because of the situation of the tanks and the scarcity of pasturage, which was bad along the road by which I returned.[2] It is also bad the way I went, but it was the report made by Palma and Sevastián that caused us to come this way.

January 30.—We set out toward the northwest. After passing some hills we kept on the right a sierra which runs toward the north, and on the left another which we crossed at night by a white pass,[3] halting at the beginning of a valley with little or no water. The day's march would be about seven leagues, a part of it being made to the north-north-west.

[1] He means continuing southwest down Sonóita River to the sea. Father Kino attempted to reach the head of the Gulf by that route, but did not succeed.

[2] Garcés means that they were now taking the route by which he had returned in 1771. His route to the Colorado was farther west for a part of the way.

[3] The "white pass" was just north of the international boundary line near monument No. 179 on the Camino del Diablo, as it was later called. Garcés's recording of the "white pass" and the Sierra which "in part is black and afterward white" makes the route certain. This was Sierra Pinta, or Pinto Range, so-called because of the different colored rocks. See p. 154.

January 31.—At seven o'clock in the morning we began to travel northwest. Keeping on the right a sierra which in part is black and afterward white, and on the left the same sierra as yesterday, we reached an extremely high tank,[1] having traveled about five leagues, during which we crossed a short stretch of sand dunes that greatly molested the riding animals and the cattle. In order not to leave the pack train without water, the riding animals and the cattle which we had with us were not allowed to drink. Continuing the journey to the west-northwest, after going three leagues we halted near sunset at a dry arroyo which had some fairly good grass to meet the extreme necessity of the riding animals.[2] This same grass is found in the sand dunes, and these lands, being so dry, have no other.

February 1.—At half past seven in the morning we set out to the northwest through some hills, and having traveled three leagues we came to the watering place of the tanks which are placed one above another and are called La Purificación.[3] Here the commander decided to wait for the pack train, and some pasturage was found a little distance away.

[1] Aguaje Empinado. This was the Heart Tank in the Sierra Pinta or Pinto Range. Father Kino called it Aguaje de la Luna.

[2] Camp was made in the hills of the Tule Range just northeast of Tule Well.

[3] Cabeza Prieta Tanks, in the Cabeza Prieta Range, about seven miles northwest by trail from Tule Well. Having walked them I can testify that they are good long miles. On the return from the second Anza expedition these tanks were called La Candelaria, in reference to Candlemas Day, Feast of the Purification.

February 4.—We set out, changing our direction, although we went principally to the west-northwest, and having traveled five leagues we came to an arroyo which has water when it rains, pools soon being formed in it.[1] The preceding watering places I saw during my return from the last journey. To the west-southwest of this one, in the sierra which runs to the north, is the Tinaja de Eusebio, of which I make mention in my diary; and there are other small watering-places in that sierra, but none of them are convenient for this journey.

February 5.—At five o'clock in the morning we set forth west-northwest, and, having crossed the sierra,[2] at a distance of eight leagues we reached Pozo Blando,[3] which on my last journeys I thought was Agua Escondida. This march was difficult. During the forenoon we came to the road which goes to the Gila, and the soldiers saw the groves,[4] so we

[1] Called by Anza Pozos de en Medio, or Half-way Wells. They are now called Coyote Water, which is in an arroyo in the plain in front of Tinajas Altas, which Garcés called the Tinaja de Eusebio. This paragraph gives a clue to Garcés's return route on his previous journey. Tinajas Altas were called by Kino Agua Escondida.

[2] They went through the Gila Range by Tinajas Altas Pass, a fact which Anza does not state, but this entry and one in Díaz's diary establish the fact, and make intelligible the rest of Anza's itinerary.

[3] This was called Agua Escondida by Anza, he erroneously thinking it was the tank to which Kino gave this name. It was a well in Arroyo San Albino, on the west side of the Gila Range, and a few miles south of Fortuna Mine.

[4] These groves of the Gila were seen in the morning before going through Tinajas Altas Pass. The Sierra del Bonete, or Sierra de la Campana, was north of the Gila and is now called Chimney Peak. This gives us another clue to Garcés former itinerary.

left to the north the Sierra del Bonete, near which I came out on my last journey. At the watering place we met a Pima Indian who told us that part of the Yumas were awaiting us to steal our animals and to kill us, especially the fathers. He said that downstream from Palma's village the people were good, but not those upstream. Since I learned that upstream from the house of Palma there are few Yumas, those living there being Cocomaricopas and their allies, I thought this to be a fiction, and I proposed to the commander that I should go to see both the good and the bad, and talk with them concerning our coming. He did not think this plan a prudent one, so we sent the Indian with a message for the Captain, asking him to come, in order to make arrangements concerning the case.[1]

February 6.—We set out south, traveling a league and a half, in order to double a range.[2] We crossed it by a short and narrow pass, which the commander ordered repaired, and then keeping on the right a range which runs to the north, we went four leagues to the northwest and halted late at night at a dry arroyo with some grass. We saw that the principal range forms a point to the south-southwest which appears to be near the Gulf.[3]

[1] The messenger was Luís, an Indian from Sonóita.

[2] From Pozo Blando they back-tracked a league and a half (Anza says a league and a quarter) down Arroyo San Albino, to get around the spur of the mountains that runs south, skirting the west bank of the arroyo. They evidently crossed the spur near its lower end. They then continued along the Gila Range and camped in the plain in front of Fortuna Mine.

[3] He probably refers to Sierra del Rosario.

February 7.—Traveling five hard leagues across the sand dunes, we reached the Gila River near the villages which I called San Pedro,[1] where I slept during my last journey on the night of August 23d. This stretch of sand abounds in pasturage of the kind which I have mentioned. Although when seen at a distance it looks like a beautiful and vast plain that these sand wastes occupy, certain it is that it would be difficult to find a worse piece of country.[2] It cannot be denied that the Gila River is short of pasturage, nevertheless the road which runs by way of it is better than this, and two things appear to me to be clear. The first is that this road is not a desirable route in the rainy season, because at that time one may go conveniently to the Gila at any point. The second is that if this road has such defects during the rainy season, what must it be during the time of heat and drought?

Concerning these Pápagos I have stated both in my diaries[3] and in my reports that if measures were taken to give them ministers in their lands, there would be no difficulty in their complete reduction. Although this tribe or portion of Pimas has been very numerous, now, on account of the number who have attached themselves to the pueblos or have gone to the Gila and Colorado rivers, it may be that the population does not reach four thousand souls, though it does not lack much of it. Their lands have

[1] Near the present Yuma.

[2] Water accomplishes marvels. The bench lands in this vicinity are now flourishing fruit orchards.

[3] He refers to the diaries and reports of his former expeditions.

some sites with good pasturage, and when the rains
of winter and summer are regular they harvest sufficient provisions, and have the necessary water in
pools. In all their lands there are no trees worth
mentioning, except jediondillas, palo de guaro, palo
verde, nopales, and saguaros, which produce fruit
like that of the pitayas.[1] Besides these there are
some gomas and jojovas and various roots similar
to the camote and the covena. There grow in some
parts also some yellow-green worms, which they eat
and which they dry to keep. In this region seeds
of various kinds of grass are found, but not as
abundantly as on the rivers. Since the country is
so poverty stricken, the Indians grow more energetic
and active than those of the rivers, and they have
rare devices for getting provisions, both from the
Indians of the missions, who for the greater part
are born in their lands, and from those of the Gila
and Colorado rivers.[2] They are very industrious
and have a quicker intelligence than those of the
rivers. All wear clothing, and they have a great
abundance of Moqui blankets which they get from
the rivers. The western Pápagos are hostile to the
Quiquimas,[3] but are ancient friends of the Yumas,
whom they have aided in their campaigns. The
eastern Pápagos are allied with the Gileños[4] and

[1] Garcés means that the nopales and saguaros produce fruit like
the pitayas. The nopal is the common prickly pear.

[2] Díaz's diary clarifies this statement. See p. 261.

[3] The Quiquimas lived along the lower Colorado River, on the left
bank.

[4] The Gila Pimas.

First page of Garcés's diary to San Gabriel.

their friends, and they take part in the campaigns which they make. As a consequence they are becoming more dexterous in arms every day, with the result that on a campaign one Pápago is worth many Yumas and Opas.

The Pimas and Yumas came out very joyfully to welcome us, and on our arrival they assembled in great numbers, which kept getting larger each of the succeeding days. Their affability and familiarity are insufferable for those who do not like them, because they are excessively curious. Captain Palma, the chief Indian of this country, of whom I make mention in my last diary for the 24th, 25th and 26th of August, begged that we should have patience, because his people had a keen desire to touch us and examine us, to satisfy their simplicity, and they did so without distinction as to sex. Although Palma told them that they must not steal, they did not fail to display the dexterity of every Indian in pilfering trifles. One of the laughable things is to see their skill and slyness in stealing and taking things with their feet, which they use as well as we manage our hands. With this way of doing things one can understand what molestation and rudeness I must have suffered in my journey when I went alone, and how well they have conducted themselves in matters of honesty.

When we asked the Indian Palma if he was one of the malcontents, he replied that his children were good, but that the Opas, who had come with the embassy asking us to go through their lands[1] to the junction of the rivers, on learning that we had changed our route had become discontented and returned to their lands, but that he was at peace with them, as I had counseled him to be,[2] and likewise with the Quiquimas and Axagueches who lived down the river, but that he was at war with the Cocomaricopas living up the Colorado River and in its neighborhood, because he did not wish peace with them, but I did not believe him.

The commander comported himself with this Indian and his followers with the prudence, liberality, and good conduct which is so characteristic of him, and we tried to fulfill the ministry, although the interpreters were incompetent and served only with regard to very ordinary things, because the Pimas who are mixed with the Yumas corrupt the language greatly, and we had with us no Castilian speaking Indian, thinking that the Indian Sebastián Tarabal[3] would serve. To this lack of an interpreter I attribute in part the setbacks which we have experienced in the journey.[4]

February 8.—I crossed the Gila River by the ford which was a league away, in the arms of Indians, and the rest of the company crossed it on horseback. The river is large, for besides being so itself it is

1 That is, down the Gila River.

2 During his former expedition.

3 Sebastián was a Lower California Indian who had lived at San Gabriel.

4 This last comment probably refers to the whole journey and was written at the conclusion.

joined a little above the ford by a branch of the
Colorado River. It would not be much to say that
it is as large as the Guadalajara River. Nearly all
the Indians recognized me, since during my last
journey I had come down the Gila River from the
place fourteen leagues above here where the river
has in its bed so many cottonwoods that its water
can hardly be seen.[1]

February 9.—After dinner, going a quarter of
a league, I crossed the Colorado River in the arms
of Indians, because I did not trust the horse. Most
of the company went over on horseback, and without
any mishap, by a shorter ford which the river forms
in the shape of this figure ʃ . Having measured
the river it was found to be ninety-five fathoms wide.
And from the goodness of the people and from the
land so suitable for crops, all members of the expedition formed a very favorable opinion, seeing the
fields of wheat and the stubble of maize and tepari,[2]
which is a small, hard bean, all of which is raised
without irrigation. After crossing the river we continued a little more than a quarter of a league and
halted near the river below its junction with the
Gila. Seeing the junction of these rivers, which I
did not recognize on my last journey although I
slept so near it, we at once climbed a hill which, with
another opposite it on the other bank of the river,
forms a pass through which the river flows very

[1] This place was above the Gila Range.
[2] The Yumas raised several kinds of beans.

majestically.[1] These two hills are lookouts which afford an exquisite view, embracing admirable sites for settlements, although this vicinity is short of pasturage. From all these beaches one can see the Peñol del Babuquíburi, which has the shape of a head, and which we now call the Giant's Head,[2] and another which we call La Campana, because it is shaped like a bell. They are very conspicuous, and for this reason I made mention of them in my last diary.

February 10.—At half past seven in the morning we set out to the west-southwest, and having traveled six leagues we reached the villages opposite the one which I called San Pablo, leaving to the right the village of El Llanto.[3]

February 11.—Going west we traveled six leagues.[4] In this vicinity on my last journey I came out from the sand dunes and the well of El Rosario,[5] and recrossed the river. The Yumas and their good lands and wide river bottoms reach as far as here.

[1] These hills are just above the Southern Pacific Railroad bridge across the Colorado River.

[2] Cabeza del Gigante. This is not the Babuquíburi mentioned by Father Garcés further back. The Cerro de la Campana is also called El Bonete in the diaries.

[3] San Pablo was just south of the present international line. During his former journey he visited a village which he called San Pablo on the opposite bank of the river. During Anza's expeditions they all called this one San Pablo. El Llanto means "The Weeping."

[4] All the diaries say west, but the direction must have been southwest. This is borne out by the records of the subsequent journeys over this stretch.

[5] Mentioned in the entry for February 13.

I estimate that they must number nearly 3500, but I do not give many names to the ranches because eventually they will unite and few will remain.

February 12.—Going south-southwest we traveled five leagues with some Yumas and some Cajuenches, who are the tribe which comes next, and are somewhat different in language and in their mode of speaking. This tribe has various names. The Pimas call them Cojat; those who live in the sierra call them the tribe of the mescal sandals, or more properly guaraches;[1] and the Yumas call them Axagueches; but they themselves say that their tribe is the Cajuen. It reaches clear to San Diego, as I saw when I was at that mission and presidio.[2] We halted at a lagoon which we crossed dryshod, naming it Santa Olalla. It has good pasturage and water, and is near the villages which I called Our Father San Francisco.[3] Here we saw several Indians from Our Father San Francisco and La Merced,[4] but for lack of an interpreter we could not get exact information as to the route which we ought to travel, although a Yuma started with us saying that he would guide us, and we hoped that he would direct us until the Indian Sevastián could get his bearings.

February 13.—Having said goodbye to Captain Palma, who rained tears, we traveled six leagues to the west-northwest and came to the green well which

[1] A kind of sandal worn in Mexico.

[2] When Father Garcés reached San Gabriel Mission he went to San Diego. This entry was made after that event.

[3] During the former journey.

[4] A village to the west mentioned in the entry for March 2.

I called El Rosario.[1] Immediately I told all the
company that San Xacome[2] was to the west-southwest by west, and that the sierra to the west of us
was called San Gerónimo. I told them that in its
vicinity I had seen no water, but that I had seen
some watering places in the sand dunes, though they
were salty and those lands lacked pasturage. In
spite of this the Indian said that there was another
watering place, and we reached it after a little more
than three leagues of travel. We found a lake with
some carrizo grass and with water of very bad color
and very salty, but on the bank there was a small
well of fair water.[3] Since I am little practiced in
matters of out-door life I did not notice it, and
although in my last journey I saw this and other
similar watering places, neither I nor the horse
drank. The Yuma Indian as well as the Cajuenches
told also of other watering places and people near
the Sierra de San Gerónimo who, they said, were
their enemies.

February 14.—The Yuma and two of the Cajuenches turned back, but with some coaxing two
remained. They led us west to another watering
place very much like the preceding one, and we
halted because they said that the next one had no
pasturage.

[1] On his former journey.

[2] San Xacome, formerly visited by Father Garcés, was near Cerro
Prieto, one of the permanent landmarks, and this statement is an
important clue to the location of El Rosario. The Sierra de San
Gerónimo was the Cocopah Range.

[3] El Carrizal, also called La Alegría.

February 15.—The two Indians who had remained with us now turned back, but they told of water and people and of the road. When the countrymen saw the road and the sierra apparently not very far away, they thought the journey could be made, although the pack train and the riding animals were so worn-out. The Indian Sevastián recognized the pass which is one of the two openings which I mention in my diary.[1] Having traveled, then, two leagues to the west, we found a deep well with a little water,[2] though it was somewhat bad, and there was very little pasturage. The muleteer reported that the pack train was in bad shape and could no longer carry the cargo.

The commander at once thought of dividing the expedition, continuing with part of it and sending the rest back to the river with one of the fathers. I did not think this decision wise, because we did not know what people we might meet if the expedition should take so small a force, and because we could pasture our animals along the river for as long a time as might be necessary.[3] The commander, therefore, decided to go with half the cargo to cross the stretch of country between here and the

[1] Apparently a pass in the main California range, north of Signal Mountain. Perhaps the opening through Borrego Valley, by which Anza crossed the mountains a few days later.

[2] Called also Pozo de las Angustias, or Well of Tribulations, for reasons which will appear.

[3] Father Garcés means that it would be better to give the horses time to recuperate at the Colorado River and then go on with the whole expedition.

sierra, and so the vanguard set forth to the west-northwest.

We must have traveled about three leagues when we discovered a vast plain which appeared to have many sand dunes. Seeing this we all concluded that it was impossible to reach the sierra. In order that the riding animals might not again drink the preceding water and eat the tule which had injured them, I told the commander that near San Xacome and near a black hill[1] there was a well of fresh water which it seemed to me we would be able to reach. Turning south-southeast, and sending a message to the effect that the pack train should go straight to San Xacome, we traveled as fast as we could, but the horses could not hurry as was desired in order that we might reach and reconnoiter the site of the village by daylight.[2] So we were unable to find the well, the village, or the lagoons, although I went out with two soldiers, and we saw a light but they said it was a fire. The mules smelled the foul water of a lagoon and we perceived the scent, and the soldiers said that it was very strong, and they did not believe that any such San Xacome could be located there, thinking that I must be greatly mistaken, and so we returned. Since I had evidence that San Xacome was in this vicinity and that La Merced was further on[3] I proposed to go alone, and

[1] This was Cerro Prieto, whose name means "Black Peak."

[2] Anza's diary B gives the distance as four leagues to Cerro Prieto from the place where he turned south.

[3] That is, further southeastward. The foul water which the mules smelled was in Volcano Lake.

that if I should find the village I would signal with smokes or send the Indians. But he did not think well of this plan, fearing that I might get lost.

February 16.—And so before daylight, setting out northeast to meet the pack train and to go by direct road to the last well which we had seen, and where we had left half of the cargo, we traveled five leagues.

February 17.—On account of having taken the riding animals to another watering place in order that they might eat and drink, we did not start until noon. Then, naming this the Well of Las Angustias, we returned to the watering place whence we had set forth on the 15th;[1] and because the soldiers were very happy even though they were going on foot, we called this watering place La Alegría.

February 18.—At midday we set out from this watering place, and going past the well of El Rosario we halted at nightfall at a salty lagoon without pasturage which we had seen on going.

* February 19.—With about two hours' travel we reached the lake of Santa Olaya, where we halted with the intention of pasturing the riding animals. The pack train remained at El Carrizal and on the 21st it arrived with half of the cargo.

February 24.—Today the rest of the cargo arrived, and because I thought that we should be

[1] El Carrizal.

* From here to p. 341 the MS. was copied for Father Garcés by the corporal of San Gabriel. See his letter of April 27, 1774. A.G.P.M., Historia, Tomo 52.

detained for many days on account of the bad condition of the animals, I consulted with the commander about going to see the people living down the
river whom I already knew. I desired also to see
if by going to the lake of San Matheo and to the
Agua Amarilla[1] I might find Indians from the sierra
who could give us information about the watering
places in the neighborhood. In order that I might
regulate my movements accordingly, the commander
said that his departure must be on the 1st or the 2d
of March.

February 24.—The same day at one o'clock in
the afternoon I set forth accompanied by three Indians, taking a small quantity of glass beads and
half a roll of tobacco. I traveled to the south about
three and one-half leagues, seeing some ranchos.
The Indians there live on the mesquite bean and on
another bean which has the shape of a screw.[2] Some
Indians who are more particular still, had calabashes, and a very special seed which they begin to
eat near the last of August. Others were eating also
the seed of the chamiso. At sunset I saw a lake
which I called San Mathías.

February 25.—I set out toward the west to see
some ranchos and then going southeast and having
traveled two leagues I came to the river. On its
banks I met a very old chief, who regaled us, and

[1] The lake of San Matheo was down the river. The Agua Amarilla
was Lake Maquata (now called Laguna Salada) west of Cocopah
Mountains. On his former journey Garcés thought this lake might
be the Colorado River, not realizing that he had crossed that stream.

[2] The tornillo bean.

when I saluted him he said, "Usu!" The guides told me that this chief and his Indians greeted each other by saying "Mulay!" Going two leagues to the southwest I came to other ranchos, and then making some turns I stopped at the house of a bald, old, and very venerable chief whom I had seen on the other side of the river during my last journey. He regaled us with beans and other foods.

February 26.—Traveling a quarter of a league, I again reached the river and saw many people on the other bank. The chief and the old men urged me to cross over, and in order to please them and to see what place the one on the other side was, I crossed on a raft which the old men promptly made. I recognized these villages to be those of Santa Rosa.[1] Now, leaving the westward direction in which the river flows at this place, I went four leagues to the south, accompanied by some Indians. Seeing that I was now leaving their lands, they sat down, saying that the people below were their enemies, as I had experienced in the last journey. Neither the horse nor the present circumstances permitted repeating the operations of my last journey, so I returned in all haste with the same Indians.

February 27.—I recrossed the river at the same place. Twice the Indians swam while taking the raft across, but for the most part the river must be only five spans deep. Then, following its current, I traveled along, seeing many people and good lands planted with wheat. Generally they saluted me by

[1] So-called on his former visit.

saying "Yñels!" About five o'clock in the afternoon
they wished me to recross the river, but I refused.
They told me that farther down they now had
enemies, and, knowing that the horse was tired, I
decided to return, going back directly to Santa
Olaya. That afternoon and night I traveled about
three leagues to the east-southeast on foot through
great thickets.

February 28.—Some Indians, very much like
those of San Xacome, who made signs that they had
seen me during my last journey, wished to lead me
to the west, but I did not wish to go, for I was now
traveling on foot because the horse was tired. That
day I saw other ranchos of Cajuenches, and I set out
north, reaching a lagoon which is now inhabited by
the Indians of the old chief. They saluted me by
saying "Mulai!" A goodly portion of them assembled and I decided to continue the journey with some
of them. They led me to a village, one of those belonging to Our Father San Francisco. All day I
traveled toward the north, covering about five
leagues.

March[1] 1.—Having traveled four leagues in the
same direction, before dinner I came out at the Lake
of Santa Olaya. Here I met the Pima who served
me as an interpreter among the Yumas, and from
him I learned that those people who say "Mulai"
and "Yñelse," and the villages which I called Santa
Rosa, are the ones whom they call Quiquimas, and
that those who took me across the river on my last

[1] By a slip Garcés here wrote February for March.

journey were another people, but I think that the language of the Cajuenches differs from the Yuma more than that of these others. It is certain that although they differ very little in language, they are made distinct by their names and wars and customs. The Cajuenche tribe count only those who live near the river, and contained in the villages of our Father San Francisco, La Merced, and the sierra near to the Agua Amarilla. The Yumas say that the Cajuenches comprise a number of Indians greater than their own, and I know that in the villages of Las Yagas,[1] San Ustaquio, San Matheo and Jesús María they will comprise a number equal to the Yumas, and still farther down below Las Yagas near the sierra I saw some smokes. The Quiquimas included in the villages of Santa Rosa and in the people of the two chiefs whom I have just seen will reach two thousand. From having seen on the 26th of last month that the river is very narrow, I conclude that in that region it forms an island, but I was not able to verify this opinion through lack of interpreters.

Today the commander told me what had been decided in conference with Father Juan[2] and all the troops, namely that the expedition must be made in light order of marching, since most of the pack train would be unable to go forward even though it should pasture for a long time. Although I have wished

[1] Las Llagas, or the Wounds of Our Father San Francisco. These were villages visited by him in 1771.

[2] Fray Juan Díaz.

that since now we are not going by a higher latitude[1] we might at least return that way, to which purpose this plan might be an obstacle, yet, the prudent persons assuring me that there was no other way by which this expedition could be accomplished, I bowed my head. The muleteer remained behind with three of his companions and three soldiers, all being willing to do so, and instructed in what they must do by the commander, who made this decision.

March 2.—Having said goodbye to those who were returning to the junction of the rivers, and having traveled four leagues to the west with some declination to the southwest, we came to a lake belonging to La Merced,[2] where there are many stubble fields of maize and good groves.

March 3.—Going south-southwest with three hours of travel, making some turns through the groves, we came to another lake. Here assembled a vast number of Indians and I saw some of those whom I had seen at San Xacome. I inquired for the town, and they told me that because the well had dried up it was abandoned. I regaled an Indian and inquired through two others who together with him had accompanied me, and they said that the people of San Xacome were in the sierra, near the sea, or estuary, where they obtained very large fish. They also replied to the inquiry if there were rivers to the west, that there were two, both being salty and not large. They were greatly undecided about

---

[1] Father Garcés was keenly interested in finding a more northern route.

[2] By Anza called El Predicador.

accompanying us, but finally two others joined a Cajuenche who lived with the Yumas in order that all
three might come with us.

March 4.—After midday we set out from the lake,
and going a league to the west-northwest we saw a
well. Having traveled another league we came to
another well, likewise of good water, the lands nearby
being well grown with pasturage. Here the Indians
wished us to halt for the night, saying that the next
journey was very long. This proposal was not considered desirable, and so, traveling another league
in the same direction, we came to a village of eighteen or twenty persons, who saluted by saying "Jesús María." A little more than a league farther on
we came to the blind well and the abandoned site of
San Xacome, all recognizing by the signs how great
a number of people had lived here and how close we
had been to it on the night when we sought the place.
We saw one of the salty lakes, and although the Indians insisted that we should camp there for the
night, this was not done, because there was no other
pasturage than the dry canes of the wild amaranth,
and so we traveled in the night three more leagues
in the same direction.

March 5.—At dawn we set out in the same direction, and going ten leagues we reached the sierra of
San Gerónimo. Then traveling a league and a half
along an arroyo, we crossed the sierra and came out,
after passing a small sand dune, to a dry lake[1] which

[1] Laguna Salada or Lake Maquata. Garcés in 1771 called it
Maqueque. Where Anza now crossed it was dry, but the finding of
fish indicates that it was not all dry.

covers almost an entire valley, having many fish of various sizes on the beach. All of us were of the opinion that this lake had communication with the sea and was the same as the Agua Amarilla of which I make mention in my diary on the 21st of September. Since the soil of these lands is very salty, and likewise the arroyo of San Lino and the other, for they say it also is excessively salty, it may be that this is the reason why the large fish come up from the sea to this lake. Not so many come up the Colorado River, for in my last journey when I asked for the large fish, the Indians always answered me by pointing below the sierra. They also have said that a sierra enters the sea and is greatly cut up, the water communicating from one part to another. And so it may be true that behind the sierra and this estuary the sea comes farther up than at the place where the Colorado River empties, and it is possible that this estuary or lagoon which we passed has no connection with the sea in the dry season,[1] although it was miry.

Going a distance of two leagues we found on its banks, in the middle of another salt one a well of fresh water which we called San Eusebio.[2] This march was certainly very difficult, and although it can be shortened by two leagues or even four by opening the well of San Xacome, and drinking water somewhat salty, it is not of the right distance. On

[1] It has connection now in wet seasons.

[2] The other diaries say they crossed the dry lake, evidently at its head.

coming out at the sierra of San Gerónimo we saw another blind well, and if there should be water in it, two more leagues could be saved.[1]

March 6.—The guide and some animals having fled, we were not able to set forth in the morning. Since we did not know with certainty where the next watering place was, the commander sent ahead some soldiers to reconnoiter the country which the guide had indicated. After dinner we set out to the west, and having gone three leagues along the trail we learned of the watering place called Santo Thomás. There is little pasturage, and one enters between two sierras, the direction changing so that we advanced but a short distance, although we traveled five leagues that afternoon.[2]

March 7.—We took the same measures as yesterday, and having traveled four leagues to the north and northeast we learned that some Indians had told the corporal of a well which was thereabouts. We kept on the left the large mountain chain and on the right the sand dunes and plains, because the sierra of San Gerónimo had ended.[3]

March 8.—With a league's journey to the northeast we came out to the wells called Santa Rosa de

[1] This would imply that San Xacome was two leagues from the place where they reached the Sierra de San Gerónimo.

[2] The other diaries tell us that they turned southwest into the mountains. Santo Thomás was in Pinto Canyon, a league or more southwest of the point where they entered it.

[3] The Sierra de San Gerónimo ends in Signal Mountain, west of Calexico.

las Lajas, and here we remained until the next afternoon. Indeed, the animals required it. On my journey on the 29th of September I arrived at a point about three leagues east of this place.[1] Here also the Indian Sebastián recognized the pass and the route which he followed when he went out to the river.

March 9.—About two in the afternoon we set out to the north, and having traveled five leagues we halted. Although at Santa Rosa there is a scarcity of pasturage, here we lacked it entirely.

March 10.—We set out at daybreak and, going seven leagues, now over good terrain and now over sand dunes, we arrived at midday at the watering place called San Sebastián.[2] Here there is some pasturage, but because the soil is salty it is not good for the animals. There is a very large marsh through which run some little arroyos of excessively salty water, but there is a little lake and a well that are quite fresh. The Indians are Cajuenches. They saluted us by saying "Natajaguaque." The greater part of them recognized me, for they saw me in San Xacome during my last journey.

They also told us that soldiers had traveled through here. We did not know whether it was Don Pedro Fajes or the deserters, or whether both had

[1] This gives a definite clue to the place where Father Garcés turned back on his 1771 journey. The Wells of Santa Rosa were at Yuha Well, in the same wash.

[2] They passed between Superstition Mountain and the main range. San Sebastián was at San Felipe Creek near where it is joined by Carrizo Creek. Harper's Well is near the spot.

passed successively.[1] Here all the Indians recognized Sebastián, and told of two watering places,
which, if they were convenient, would greatly shorten
the road for the return. Indeed, it has always appeared to me desirable that an exit should be sought
to this place of San Sebastián or to another of those
farther on, where now there is no difficulty. If Don
Pedro Fajes or the deserters reached this vicinity
the road from San Diego is already known, and if,
as they say, he came out at San Luís, the road from
San Luís is already discovered. I judge that by
making the attempt the most direct road to Monterrey will be found, even though the Soyopas said the
road was bad. Before knowing who these Soyopas
were, and the nature of the people who live above
them, there was reason for being afraid to go much
higher up the Colorado River with a small number
of men, but now it is known that the Soyopas and the
rest farther up, as well as those of the sierra, are
Indians of the same quality as the Yumas.

Oh, what a vast heathendom! Oh! what lands so
suitable for missions! Oh! what a heathendom so

[1] In the year 1772 Pedro Fages crossed the mountains from San
Diego in pursuit of deserters. Being forced by the desert to seek
water, he entered the mountains, crossed over, reëntered them by
Cajon Pass, northwest of San Bernardino, skirted the Mojave Desert,
entered the San Joaquin Valley by a pass at its southern end (evidently threading Tejon Pass), went to Buena Vista Lake, thence west
to Mission San Luís Obispo. This we have directly from Fages
himself. Father Garcés must have learned of Fages's expedition at
San Gabriel or San Diego, or possibly from Sebastián, who was from
San Gabriel. From all the circumstances it is inferred that Fages
crossed the mountains by essentially Anza's route. See p. 343.

docile! How fine it would be if the wise and pious
Don Carlos III might see these lands! And oh, if
at least we might bring it about that the one who so
worthily governs these kingdoms might see these
provinces! What vigorous measures they would take,
because, indeed, seeing a thing is very different
from hearing about it! In such a case we would see
renewed those conquests which were made in the
time of Carlos V, and the fiscal would not complain,
and with reason, of the little progress which we make
in these times. Now we shall see who is to blame that
there should be no great progress in the spiritual
and temporal conquest, for the piety of the king is
not responsible. Neither will the great spirit of his
Excellency, Don Antonio María Bucareli, permit the
obstruction of these great services to both majesties.
Indeed, I am sure that the providence of God will
aid the gifted ministers. And then if it does not
succeed it must be attributed to what is well known
to the señor fiscal, and which I state in the report
which I sent concerning the matter, where in large
part I attribute the retardation of these provinces
to the lack of commerce, which the superior government has so restricted in these provinces.

Pardon this digression, for my feelings have not
allowed me to restrain myself. It appears to me,
also, that by way of the estuary and the lake of San
Matheo a good road might be opened to San Diego,
avoiding the sand dunes, but some kind of a canoe
will always be necessary.

The Cajuen Indians who live away from the river are ordinarily small of body and weak. They make some guaraches, or sandals of mescal fiber, and some nets with which they bind now the head, and now the stomach. Some wear their wigs, while on the river many go bald. They also carry a macana of the shape of a sickle.[1] These Indians inhabit the whole sierra which runs from here to the mouth of the river and extends, as I have said, as far as the Gulf.

March 11.—At two o'clock in the afternoon we set out to the west. All the afternoon was spent in finding a way through the mire, and by nightfall we had traveled only two leagues.

March 12.—Going west-northwest and through small hills we came to a valley, and after passing a red hill we halted, having traveled five leagues, at some wells and salty marshes called San Gregorio,[2] a place which has much pasturage and is in a very narrow valley between two ranges.* To this point came many Cajuenches, and here we saw another tribe. These Cajuenches do not paint themselves as much as the Yumas. With their macanas they are accustomed to kill many rabbits and some deer, with whose skins the women cover themselves behind, but

---

[1] *Macana* was a word widely used for some kind of wooden ax or club. He refers here to the rabbit sticks.

[2] From San Sebastián they turned sharply west, and went into Borrego Valley through the gap just north of Borrego Mountain. San Gregorio was west of Borrego Mountain, on San Felipe Creek. The "red hill" was Borrego Mountain.

* Here ends the corporal's handwriting

in front they wear aprons of the fiber of *arria,* made of the inner bark of trees. These multitudes of fibers some wear like a net and others loose, but all cover themselves well, and even the little girls three years old or even infants are never seen naked. In these regions the women use the nets to carry wood, herbs[1] and the ollas in which they carry water, and also to carry their little children. The men build corrals with the nets, stakes and flat rocks, and, driving the game from long distance toward a corral, they kill it in abundance. Since these mountain Indians eat much mescal and in some parts the roots of the tule, their teeth are very badly decayed and damaged. Some carry a lance with a good point, which appears to be a weapon for war, and even the women carry poles that are shorter and thicker. They eat a great quantity of wild onions, which abound in these parts. Although these Cajuenches are not such people as the Yumas they are friendly and more timid.

March 13.—We rested because the pack train had become badly fatigued on the previous day.

March 14.—Going northwest, and having crossed a stretch of sand dunes and level land, we came to an arroyo which runs for about a league and has some trees along its banks, where we camped, having traveled five leagues.[2] Here we saw many Indians of another tribe, and although there were still

---

[1] Quelites.

[2] They continued northwest across Borrego Valley, and entered Coyote Canyon. Santa Catarina was at Reed's, or the Lower Willows, just at the lower end of Collins Valley. Here there are excellent springs. The arroyo runs in summer nearly to Beatty's ranch.

a few Cajuenches, it caused me a great deal of trouble to induce the Indians to approach the commander, who wished to give them presents. This place we called Santa Catarina. Near here we saw traces of mules and horses, and here the Indian Sebastián had been in the course of his journey to the river.[1] He was of the opinion that we should not follow the route by which he had come, and we did as he advised.[2]

March 15.—Having traveled two leagues to the north-northwest, following the arroyo which is dry in that part, we came to the source of another water.[3] And we saw many Indians, who in dress are very little different from the Cajuenches, but they are distinct in language and in their method of speaking, for when these people speak they move their feet, raising them high behind, and wave the arms as though complaining and grumbling; and they likewise raise their voices, speaking in tones like some little crows which abound in this region. It certainly is laughable. We did not see that they carried any weapons, which appear to be useless to them. They are scrawny, and they live on the same kinds of food as the mountain Cajuenches.

Having traveled two more leagues to the northwest and north-northwest, we halted at the foot of

[1] This would indicate that Fages may have ascended Coyote Canyon. But no mention is made of horse tracks further up the valley.

[2] "Que no siguieramos el camino que el traxo i assi lo executamos."

[3] At two distinct places above Santa Catarina, Middle Willows and Upper Willows (the Fig Tree), there are springs in the arroyo.

the ridge. The Indian Sevastián went to reconnoiter from a height, and it appeared to him that there was no outlet. But the Indians by signs persuaded us that we would get through, and the corporal went and found a way out. By a short climb we ascended the ridge, and having gone about a league toward the north along the height which forms a good plain, we halted.[1]

March 16.—Because it rained we could not set out before one in the afternoon. Then, going northwest, we climbed for a short distance and reached the pass called San Carlos; then, having crossed a small valley we came out to another and larger one called El Príncipe, and halted at a lake, having gone three leagues.[2] Because we had traveled over roads so dry and lacking in pasturage, it caused us much pleasure to see these lands so well grown with pasturage; and it seemed to the men that since it was raining this country must be suitable for all kinds of grain and good for settlements, although it may be that in the dry season it would not appear so good. Therefore this goodness needs more experience and proof.

March 17.—Going northwest between two sierras which seem to have some pines on their crests, we

[1] Coyote Canyon forks into Horse Canyon, Nance Canyon, and Tule Canyon. Keeping straight ahead, Anza climbed the ridge between the two last-named, and, having traveled some five miles, camped in a flat just before emerging through the pass, which opens into Fred Clark's fields. The flat is just east of his horse corral; it has excellent springs. The gap at Clark's is still known as La Puerta.

[2] Laguna del Príncipe was Dry Lake at Contreras's ranch, about six miles northwest of the Puerto de San Carlos.

came to the canyon and arroyo of San Patricio, which is very narrow, but not so narrow as to impede passage. There are some live oaks, jucaros, cottonwoods, and other dilapidated trees, but no cedars are seen.[1]

March 18.—Going seven leagues to the northwest, we came to the beautiful valley of San Joseph, which has all the qualities for a good settlement.[2] There is a great abundance of good quelites which the Indians eat in season, sour cane which they call sotole, and a little palm which bears dates which are not like those of Spain, but very different. These are found also in Pimería Alta. There is a large cottonwood grove, a very large marsh with much pasturage, a lake, and a river which probably is permanent. We saw a countless multitude of white geese like those which I saw at Agua Amarilla. It appeared to the men of experience that the soil along the river mentioned, in some very high hills near the large Sierra Nevada, is mineral bearing, and a stone which they got that day appeared to them to contain metal.

March 19.—Winding around by a very miry road, we came to a hill,[3] having traveled about four and a half leagues almost to the northwest but with many windings, because the hills as well as the plains

[1] Thomas Mountain was on the right and Cahuilla Mountain on the left. Arroyo de San Patricio was Bautista Creek. Camp was at the end of the Cahuilla Valley, near Tripp Flat.

[2] Valle de San Joseph was San Jacinto Valley. Camp was on San Jacinto River above San Jacinto. The lake, called by Anza San Antonio Bucareli, was San Jacinto Lake (or Mystic Lake). It was drained about fifteen years ago.

[3] This was evidently Mt. Russell, southeast of Moreno.

are so boggy. The groves are thickly grown with grass, one species of which bears a seed very much like rye. I have no doubt this is the grain which the Gileños call wheat, for they told me that near the sea there was wheat which they harvested without planting it. Throughout all these lands there are bears, rosemary, sage better than that of Guadalaxara, cobenas, and chia.

March 20.—Traveling six leagues to the northwest, we came to the Santa Ana River.[1] After following the current for a league and a half to find a ford we halted, and a bridge was made on which to take over the cargoes. The place offers fair advantages for stock and crops, but there is little timber. There are few Indians in the neighborhood. Having examined a hut I saw a number of little baskets, very similar to those of Pimería Alta, and a good many of the beads or corals which they trade with the tribes of the rivers and pass as far as the missions,[2] where we have always heard that these corals came from this region.

March 21.—Going seven leagues to the northwest, we came to an arroyo called San Antonio.[3] Here there are many bears and sycamores. The Sierra Nevada now turns toward the west-northwest. In it

[1] Still so-called. They entered the valley near Riverside, evidently descending Sycamore Canyon. The bridge was built west of Riverside, some distance below Rubidoux Mountain.

[2] He means the missions of Pimería Alta.

[3] Still so-called. The other diaries call it Arroyo de los Osos (Bears) or Arroyo de los Alisos (Sycamores). They crossed the arroyo near Ontario.

there is a pass which, according to what they say, leads out to the mission of San Luís.[1]

March 22.—Having traveled three leagues, we found ourselves in sight of San Gabriel, and ran upon the trail of the horses and cattle. To find the ford cost us a great deal of time; then we crossed the river and arrived at the mission of San Gabriel. The direction traveled this day was much varied, especially in order to enter, but the principal direction seems to be west-northwest.[2] The day's march was five leagues.

This establishment of San Gabriel has everything to make it one of the best in these provinces. We found the mission in extreme poverty, as is true of all the rest. The day when we arrived our provisions for the soldiers gave out, putting us in great need because of the scarcity here, and the account would be more melancholy if the news had not come that the frigate *La Galicia* had put in at San Diego. The missionary fathers were delighted at our arrival, and they succored us with what little they had. We were sorry on both sides, the fathers at having so little to give, either of animals or of provisions, and we at having brought nothing to relieve them of their want.

[1] The San Bernardino Mountains. The pass was Cajón Pass. Through it Fages went on his way from Imperial Valley to San Luís Obispo in 1772. See p. 339.

[2] After swinging round the hills at San Dimas the direction was a little south of west. Mission San Gabriel at that time was about a league south of its present site, to which it was moved a few months later.

The commander and I decided to go to San Diego to make a personal effort to get provisions and a pilot to make observations, but the overflow of the river prevented acting on this plan, and so the pack train went for provisions. The river went down, and on Palm Sunday, after conference with the commander and Father Juan,[1] I decided to go to San Diego in order to get what has been mentioned, and that the very reverend father might assist in the observation by the aid of a father in case a pilot could not be obtained. The commander told me that if the very reverend father president, Fray Junípero Serra,[2] should come, he would send the pack train ahead, and that he would wait three days and afterward we should continue our journey to Monte Rey.

I set out for San Diego on the 27th and arrived on the morning of the 30th. On the 1st of April we dispatched the pack train, the corporal being ordered to spend a week in getting back to San Gabriel, because the mules had to return at once for provisions. The very reverend father president planned to set out on Monday, and for this reason he did not reply to the commander. The corporal reached San Gabriel in five days. The very reverend father president did not set out until Wednesday, the 6th, and I could return no earlier because there was no escort.

[1] He means Father Juan Díaz.

[2] Father Serra was in San Diego, on his way back from Mexico to Monterey. Garcés means that Anza promised to wait for him three days after Serra should arrive at San Gabriel. Garcés accompanied Serra to San Gabriel, whence Anza had already departed for Monterey.

Although we traveled in light order of marching, it rained on us for two days and the road was very bad, so we did not reach San Gabriel till the 11th.

Here we learned the decision of the commander, who doubtless through lack of animals and provisions and for other solid reasons determined to go in light order of marching to Monte Rey. He invited Father Juan Díaz to go with him, but knowing that the speed of the truly tireless commander, when he was on horseback, meant twenty or twenty-five leagues a day, he wisely excused himself; and I would have done the same, having no hope of returning by another road in order to send some useful reports to the government.[1] I have been very sorry that advantage has not been taken of this occasion, so opportune for discovering the course of the San Francisco River, which I believe is connected with the Colorado, and both with some very large lakes or a water which is still and is very large, as the Gileños have told me.[2] Likewise, I presume that the deserting soldiers or those who have sought them were near the Colorado River, for the Indians of the river told us that the people up the river had said so.

Since there was no certainty of the observation, in order that it might be made Father Juan and I agreed to go to San Diego to see if the chaplain of the frigate, who had remained, infirm, would lend the instrument and instruct Father Juan, who under-

[1] He alludes to his desire to return from Monterey directly to the Colorado, coming out above the Yuma villages.

[2] By the San Francisco River Father Garcés meant the San Joaquin.

stands its principles and has good capacity. But
the soldiers made many objections, and so Father
Juan decided that he could make the observations
by himself, going first to San Diego for the instruc-
tion and the instrument, thinking that perhaps the
commander might arrange to have the Reverend
Father Crespi[1] accompany him on his return. And
I, according to what the commander had ordered,
decided to return with the troop and the rest of
the pack train, the six soldiers and three servants
remaining to come with the commander.

April 13.—At three o'clock we set out over the
same road, with the same turns. We halted at eight
o'clock at night before reaching the arroyo of San
Antonio.

April 14.—We saw some bears, and the soldiers
killed one. We traveled the same road on which we
had come, from seven in the morning until three in
the afternoon, when we reached the Santa Ana River.

April 15.—At four o'clock in the afternoon we
set out to the east by a new and direct road, and at
ten o'clock at night came to a pass which we called
San Rafael, having traveled six leagues.[2]

April 16.—Thinking that we might go by a direct
road, we encountered a marsh or mire, because with

[1] Father Crespi was at Mission San Carlos (Carmel) near Monterey. Father Díaz went to San Diego and returned to San Gabriel
with the instrument to await Anza.

[2] Father Garcés's diary is too indefinite to enable me to map his
route with precision from the Santa Ana River to Bautista Canyon.
Evidently he went through the hills between Allesandro Valley and
Lakeview, encountering the San Jacinto River in flood where it flows
south, and then was forced to swing northeast to the old trail.

the rains the water of the lake and the river San Joseph had greatly overflown. For this reason we wound around for more than a league and a half, and by a road close to the sierra we came to another bad stretch, where we halted and they carried over the packs on their shoulders. We saw a great many Indians, who were now less afraid than when we came. Among others came a very droll Indian singing a lively tune and with measured tread. Then, keeping the step, and taking the posture of one sitting on a low bench, he ended the song. All out of breath, he continued in plaintive key, still keeping the step, amusing us greatly. These Indians also use for their dance a calabash with pebbles inside, like the people of the river.

From six until twelve we traveled four leagues, a league and a half to the northeast and the rest to the southeast. We did not succeed in shortening the road because it was much more flooded than on going. At two in the afternoon the corporal of the mission of San Gabriel came to get a Christian boy who has heathen parents. He had joined us, asking me to take him to see other lands, leaving his relatives and his natural and spiritual parents. This corporal and the experts said that this place of San Joseph was opposite Santa Margarita on the road to San Diego.[1]

April 17.—We crossed another mire with great difficulty, and between half past eight in the morning

---

[1] It was at this time that the corporal copied eight pages of Garcés's diary for him. Camp was evidently below San Jacinto.

and sunset we traveled eight leagues to the southeast, camping for the night in the canyon and arroyo of San Patricio, a little higher up than where we camped in going. I saw some stone instruments for cutting, and they gave me mescal and quelites. There was a dance in this manner: the Indian, as if in great distress, cried out, moving his arms and legs wildly and acting like a maniac, while a crouching woman made turns around him, and beckoned with her hands like our Spanish women. This tribe is of the same tongue as the Indians of San Gabriel, although they differ in some words, and in customs and dress they are the same as the mountain Cajuenches whom I have already described.

April 18.—At one in the afternoon we began the journey, and by a straight route not at all miry, and without seeing the lake which we had seen on going in the valley of El Príncipe, at half past five o'clock we reached the entrance to the Pass of San Carlos, having traveled four and a half leagues to the southeast, although the last league was to the east-southeast.[1] The men who are experienced in the road from San Diego to San Gabriel said that the valley of El Príncipe is close to San Juan Capistrano, and an opening is seen through which apparently there might be a good pass.[2]

[1] I conclude that Father Garcés kept to the right of the former trail.

[2] There is an easy pass from Cahuilla Valley past Lake Elsinore down Temecula Valley, thence either to Riverside or to San Luís Rey, on the river then called San Juan Capistrano.

Computo de leguas
De tubac a Caborca 52
El Caborca à Sonoyta 48.
De Sonoyta a la Junta de los Ríos 50
De la Junta a Sn Gabriel por la ida 122
A la buelta emos salido a la Laguna
de Sta Olalla con 72 leg de camino
i con el mismo camino se puede salir
à Sn Pablo. assi si pudieramos mejorarlo uno mis viajes.

de la Junta de los Ríos a las
immediaciones del de en vo
que del colorado en el Golfo
abra por camino derecho algo
mas de quarenta leguas.
el Agua Amarilla es tan ola
guna ô Río en tiempo de Aguas
que por algunos arroyos que se le
agreguen sube como 2 a leguas
o algunas partes) es tan hondo en
mis viajes.

se quede aun tan el tramo de tierra que ay desde el Río colorado asta el
Aguaje de Sn Sevastian. La expedicion se a echo sin contra tiempo de hasta la cargazon
à los indios y aunque el gobernador de Sn Pablo o capitan Yuma
de aquellas Rancherias quiso vendernos la fineza y Desvervid de que avia
mandado a la Muger de uno que se mato una mula y la viuda pero yo crei ser ficcion
i mas llevando el Sr bradurу colgada que no solto. Algunas ve
ces an perecido i dos an muerto los indios Almenos no an llegado a noti
cia de muerte o hurto de otras vestias. No ay duda que todo bien proce
de de la bondad de Dios pero su majestad se vale de sus caminos y asi se sigue
el buen orte que el Sr comandante a tenido con los indios sujetan estas con
los soldados disciplinandolos u sabstemente i con los PP respetandolos
i su fantandonos noble con los precios si tambien con el regalo obra
movido de la piedad Divina para que se aya echo la expedicion pacifico mien
te i con un abio fatal sin n i por caminos malos asta que llegamos donde
ya encontramos mucho zacate aunque en el Río ay tan lejaño si hay una
medianira pues sus gentes son afables, allegre i amigos de los españoles, ya
ramente la proporcion para los siembras excede a los Seranos immedia
to ala mar, segun lo que evito. Especial mente suedo el Río en el sentio
assi lo siento i firmo a 26 Abril en las immediaciones de la junta de
los Ríos en Domisio año 1774
Fr Francisco Garcés

April 19.—Because a horse had run away we did not start until nine o'clock. We descended through the pass and traversed the canyon, seeing many Indians, who regaled us with an abundance of mescal. The women now came down from the sierra with less fear than when we went, but after they had regaled us for a short time with chomites, cuentas, etc., an Indian shot an arrow at our fattest horse, wounding him, but we did not see who did it nor did we pay any attention to it. After night fell some Indians came and finished killing the same horse without making any other demonstration. The deed was done so quietly that the men on horseback did not see them, and it seems that it was committed through a hankering for meat. We reached Santa Catarina at half past three.

April 20.—Because of what happened the day before we set out cautiously, but there was not the least disturbance. Following our own trail we reached the wells of San Gregorio at noon.

April 21.—We started at two o'clock in the afternoon, and, following our same trail, at half past nine at night we reached the little lake of San Sevastián, whose Indians heard us coming and welcomed us very joyously. They told us that they would take us out by a direct road. I would have liked to pasture the animals two days in San Gregorio or here, but the soldiers did not wish it. Indeed, my plan was first to send someone to examine the water holes and the road, to see if it could be improved and made

permanently convenient. To this they replied that
the riding animals were getting in bad condition and
that the provisions were nearly exhausted.

April 22.—We set out at three in the afternoon,
going east, in sight of some low hills which lie somewhat between the plains and the sand dunes and which
we kept on our right at a distance of about a quarter
of a league. On the left we kept at a distance of
about four leagues the chain of mountains which begins at the Yumas and runs to the northwest.[1] Near
San Sevastián it makes an opening somewhat larger
than the one which we took to go to the Pass of San
Carlos. Thus, between the range which ascends
from the Gulf, which I suppose may be the California range, and one which begins in sight of San
Sevastián,[2] is the opening and pass which we have
followed. And, according to appearances, between
this Sierra Nevada which we have had on the right
in this journey, and which reaches and passes beyond
San Gabriel, and another which begins at the Yumas, there is another opening or pass. But as far
as one can see this range which begins at the river
always follows the same direction as the Sierra Nevada, in front of which it lies, and so either they
join or else the valley between them is not very
wide.[3] And I believe, until the contrary is seen,
that by that opening or pass which we have seen, or

[1] These mountains were much more than four leagues away.

[2] The Santa Rosa Mountains.

[3] Between these ranges the Southern Pacific Railroad runs, through
San Gorgonio Pass.

on the other side of the chain which today we have on our left, there ought to be a more direct road to Monte Rey.[1]

We halted at seven in the afternoon, having gone a league and a half to the east, and the rest, which would be another two and a half leagues, to the southeast. At a league and a half from San Sevastián we saw another small water hole and a little tule. We called the place San Anselmo. The old man who guided us said that we ought to camp there, but the soldiers said that the journey ought to be divided, whereupon the old man stopped, and according to what was said by those who came behind, there was no way to make him go any farther. A young man came but after nightfall he said that we must halt because at night he did not know the roads. We halted and he fled.

April 23.—I wished to return to the lake of San Sevastián because, although we knew that we could go out to the carrizales and to the Pozo de las Angustias, yet I did not wish so much to go as to ascertain if there is a fairly good watering place between San Sevastián and Las Angustias or the well of La Alegría. But the soldiers said that the food was nearly exhausted and that if they returned their horses would not make it. Therefore we decided to go straight to Pozo de las Angustias. I released

1 That is, beyond the range that is northeast of Imperial Valley. Probably Salton Sea was dry at this time, for Garcés passed close to it and did not mention it. San Anselmo was Kane Spring.

two soldiers to see if they could find a way around
the sand dunes, and before night fell they explored
the road well. This investigation was made in the
afternoon.[1]

In the morning of this same day we set out at
half past five and traveled until nine o'clock, going
three and a half leagues to the southeast; and in the
afternoon we set out at half past three and traveled
until three o'clock in the morning to reach the Pozo
de las Angustias, having covered more than eleven
leagues and a half, because the pack animals were
carrying scarcely any load and the riding animals
are fat because they have pastured at San Gabriel.
We traveled five leagues southeast by south-southeast and east-southeast, and the rest to the east.[2]
The Pozo de las Angustias had no grass, and so we
went on to La Alegría, now by our old road. Water
and pasture were very scarce here and so we went
on to the first Carrizal; and since the animals were
strong and there the water was bad and the pasturage scarce, we set out at sunset on the 24th by our
old road, and arrived at midnight at the lake of
Santa Olalla, having saved nineteen leagues solely
from San Sevastián to Santa Olalla, by the short
cut made on the return. And this road could be
made even shorter. But I cannot say with certainty
whether or not it is passable with pack trains, because to me the road from Sonóyta to the Colorado

[1] The afternoon of the 22d, I take it.

[2] They swung east of Superstition Mountain to the vicinity of El
Centro, thence southeastward to their old trail.

appeared bad, but some have said that it can be traveled, and so the countrymen will say whether this is good or bad, for to them credence must be given in this matter, although to me they have responded with some variety of opinion.

April 25.—About three in the afternoon we set out from the lake and halted at another small one, where we had camped for the night on going.[1] I carried a watch and a compass, otherwise I should have been lost. We heard sinister reports, because we did not understand the Indians, but having arrived near the junction of the rivers, today the 26th, we have learned what really happened. It is that the Indians came to say that the mountain Cajuenches had killed us, and for this reason the soldiers and the muleteers went home taking most of the provisions, bundles, and boxes of tobacco, knives, and the riding animals, but we found here sixteen beeves, etc.

The Yuma Indians, as always, are famous for their coiffure, their games and other things which might be noted down, but there is no time for telling about them now, and it seems to me that in the first diary which I sent to my prelates I said something about these things. And I suppose that the commander and the Reverend Father Fray Juan Díaz will write at length about everything. Both have good diction and good handwriting, and so it will not be necessary in this diary, which only has the merit of referring in some parts to my former journeys.

---

[1] Evidently the lake at the Yuma border. See p. 269.

Whoever reads the diary of the Jesuit Father Consag[1] of Californias and sees that of my last journey will believe that I was in the neighborhood of the mouth of the Colorado River, and that the islands which form the river are those which I saw forming the river and the lakes, for when it overflows its banks the water runs into them and into the Agua Amarillo or the estuary. Until a few days ago I had not read the diary of this Jesuit, and then I came to know about this. Now, with the flood, the water of the river is red, but before the flood it is not red. Nor do I think that this river is as large as the Danube during the whole year, though reports of it had caused me to form an exaggerated idea of it. Likewise, during the preceding days the rains had been heavy and the rivers were in remarkably high flood, and as I went first to the Gila River and it was then running so high I expected to see in the Colorado an immeasurable river, but this was my mistake. Being ignorant of the location of the junction, and thinking that the Indians were deceiving me, I did not wish to affirm what I did not know for a certainty. Above all, I assure you that if I had known for certain that I had reached the junction of the rivers I should not have gone farther down, and so this ignorance was the reason for my having taken the trouble to go farther downstream.[2]

[1] Father Consag, a Jesuit missionary from Lower California, made famous explorations to the head of the Gulf in the middle of the eighteenth century.

[2] In 1771 Garcés traveled thirteen days down the Colorado thinking that he was still on the Gila.

Even though these Indians might have made way with the cattle and the provisions which we left in their keeping it would not have been surprising; indeed, how much more surprising it is that they behaved themselves well!

Estimate of Leagues

From Tubac to Caborca, fifty-two leagues.

From Caborca to Sonóyta, forty-eight leagues.

From Sonóyta to the junction of the rivers, fifty leagues.

From the junction going to San Gabriel one hundred and twelve leagues.

On the return we have come out to the lake of Santa Olalla in seventy-two leagues of travel, and by the same road one can come to San Pablo, and in this way we might improve it, just as it is possible to shorten the stretch of road between the Colorado River and the watering place of San Sevastián.

From the junction of the rivers to the neighborhood of the disemboguement of the Colorado in the Gulf, by direct route, it must be somewhat more than forty leagues. During the rainy season the Agua Amarilla, estuary, or lake, or river, or some arroyos which join it, come up about twenty-four leagues or somewhat more, from what I have seen in my journeys.

The expedition has been made without molesting or vexing the Indians. And although the governor of San Pablo or the Yuma captain of those villages

wished to palm off on us the hoax and barbarity
that he had killed the wife of one who had killed a
stray mule, I believed it to be a fiction, especially
since he was wearing the mule's shoes suspended
from his neck and did not give them up.[1] Some
animals have died and the Indians have killed two.
At least I have not learned of the death or theft of
any others.

There is no doubt that all good proceeds from
the goodness of God. But his Majesty makes use of
his creatures, and so I think the good conduct which
the commander has shown, bearing with the Indians,
disciplining the soldiers gently, and respecting and
sustaining the fathers, not only with what is necessary, but also with the presents, must have moved
the divine mercy to the end that the expedition
should be made peacefully, although with impossible
equipment, and over bad roads until we arrived at
a place where we found much grass. 'Tis true, there
is fairly good grass on the river in some places, and
its people in personal matters are joyful and friendly
to the Spaniards; likewise the river people excel
the mountain people in conveniences for planting
crops. Especially near the sea, according to what I
have seen, does the river excel in population.

And thus, I write this down and sign it on April
26, in the year 1774, near the junction of the rivers
at San Dionisio.

Fr. Francisco Garcés (Rubric).

[1] This story is told in Anza's diaries.

GARCES'S BRIEF ACCOUNT

1774

(G)

GARCES'S BRIEF ACCOUNT[1]

Señor Lieutenant General Don Antonio María
Bucareli.

Most Excellent Sir:

Having arrived with all felicity on the 22d of
March at the mission of San Gabriel of this California Septentrional, with the expedition destined for
the exploration of roads from the Pimería Alta to
these new establishments, and having come to the
port of San Diego for the purpose of getting some
provisions and to talk with the very reverend father
president, Fray Junípero Serra, concerning matters
relative to the expedition, it has come to my notice
that an extraordinary courier is setting out, and this
has impelled me to give some information to your
Excellency concerning what has happened on the
journey, deferring the sending of the diaries till I
arrive at the port of Monterrey, whence (at least
this is my advice) we shall return by a direct road
to the Colorado River in order to accomplish on the
return what has not been done in coming.

[1] Expediente formado á consequencia de Representacion del P.ᵉ
Fr. Francisco Garces con que acompaña el Diario de su expedicion á
los Rios Gila y Colorado; en que expone su dictámen sobre fundacion
de Misiones en estos parages. A.G.P.M., Provincias Internas,
Tomo 23.

The journey has been made with all success, without illness or fear of the tribes, although some toils and difficulties have not been lacking. Your Excellency will already have learned the reason why the expedition did not go through the Gileños, in order to take a much higher latitude on the Colorado River, and go from there directly to Monterrey, and that we went instead by way of the mission of Cabohorca,[1] which is distant from Tubac fifty-four leagues, all this journey being purely a detour for the purpose of supplying ourselves with the animals which we lacked.

On the 8th of January we set out from Tubac, going by road as far as El Altar, which is well known in Mexico. From El Altar to Cabohorca it is seven leagues. From there we set forth on the 22d for Sonóita, going by almost the same road over which I returned from my last journey, and arriving there on the 28th. On the 29th we left Sonóita, and by almost the same road that I took on my return we reached the Gila River at a place very close to its junction with the Colorado.

The Indians conducted themselves as well as could be desired, and here lives Captain Palma, of whom your Excellency will already have good accounts, he being the same one whom I mentioned in my diary[2] on the 24th and 25th of August. We crossed the river without any risk, in the neighborhood of the junction of the two streams, and saw

[1] *Sic.*   [2] Of the journey of 1771.

that an arm of the Colorado joins the Gila a little above the junction, leaving an island in the middle. We also learned through a Soyopa, whose tribe lives about forty leagues above the Iumas, that another branch separates and, turning in various directions, empties into the sea toward the west. The Colorado was measured, and it is ninety-five fathoms wide, not counting the arm which runs into the Gila above the junction of the two rivers. The lands and the people are better than I said in my last diary, in which there are some errors in consequence of my not having seen the junction of these rivers, which I have seen on this occasion. For I was at the junction of these rivers on the 24th of August at eight o'clock in the morning, and therefore all that I say in the diaries about lands and people is to be understood as referring to the Colorado River and lagoons adjacent to it.

I came with urgent instructions from my prelate to write to New Mexico, for which purpose I interrogated two Soyopas, who are the tribe who bring the colored blankets and some blue cloth of very durable sayal, and blue chomite, and other things which they acquire from the people of Moqui, and from missions where, according to the account, it is to be understood there are oxen and small stock. They replied to me, assuring me that they had communication with those people, but the commander having examined one of them, who doubtless presumed that we would go that way, he talked very differently with respect to Moqui and also with respect

to Monterrey. Indeed, he admitted that by a large
sierra they went out from their country and came
to the road which the Spaniards travel in these new
establishments, and that the road was short of water
and very bad for traveling with animals. This was
the reason why the commander did not go straight
to the destination to which he was ordered, although
I, because of my experience with the Indians, knew
that what he said was untrue, and that they intended
that we should not go through the country of the
Cocomaricopas and Niforas, their enemies.

Likewise we were greatly handicapped in getting
information for lack of a good interpreter, which
we might have brought but did not because we
assumed that this lack would be supplied by the
Indian Sebastián Taraval, who had come out from
San Gabriel to Sonora.

From the junction of the rivers we traveled six
leagues to the southwest, six to the west, and five
southwest, and arrived at the Laguna de Santa
Olalla, belonging to the villages of Our Father San
Francisco, which I mention in my diaries on the
4th and 5th of October. On the 13th of February
we set out with some guides for the green well which
I called Pozo del Rosario. I saw that San Jácome
was to the west and likewise the Sierra de San
Gerónimo, and I called this to the attention of the
commander and his company, telling them of the
difficulties which I had experienced in my former
journey. We had traveled that day eight leagues[1]

---

[1] His diary says nine leagues. See pp. 325–326.

to the west-northwest, and there was no grass whatever in those regions, so we halted at another watering place which was very bad, but had some carrizo for the animals. On the next day, at a distance of two leagues to the west, we came to another watering place of the same qualities. On the 14th the Indians turned back for fear of the people in the country through which we were to pass, but they said that there was a road and water. The latter we found, although with some scarcity, in a well. But such were the inconveniences which the pack train had suffered at the watering places, and those which we expected to encounter in some sand dunes which we had in sight, that it was necessary to return to Santa Olalla, leaving behind half of the load, whose transportation to the laguna was not completed until the 24th of February.

Since a long time was necessary in which to permit the pack train and the cavallada to pasture, and since the commander decided not to ascend the river, I decided to go downstream to see if the Indians of the lake of San Mateo could give me favorable notices regarding any watering place which there might be in the Sierra de San Gerónimo or in its vicinity. My idea was approved by Father Fray Juan and the commander, but the latter informed me that he had decided to start on the first of March.

I traveled two days downstream. The Indians urged me to cross the river on rafts, which I did in order not to displease them. I examined the villages which I had already seen in my last journey, and which I then called Santa Rosa. I wished to go to see the Indians who took me over the Colorado River in my last journey, but they deserted me, saying that they were their enemies. I now gave up this plan, and recrossed the river, which has no ford in this vicinity. Having traveled southwest all that day, and the horse being tired, I returned on foot by direct road. Traveling all that night and all the next day, at noon on the 1st of March I reached the village of Santa Olalla, accompanied by Indian headmen, and very well pleased and satisfied with those people who so greatly assisted me.

On the 2d of this month of March we set out from the Laguna de Santa Olalla. The first day's journey was four leagues to the village of La Merced; the second three leagues to the south-southwest through the same villages. On the 3d, 4th, and 5th, passing through San Jacome, we traveled twenty leagues to the west-northwest, crossing the Sierra de San Gerónimo. Here we saw a dry lake which fills nearly all the valley and had a large amount of fish stranded on its banks, a sure indication that the sea must have some connection with it. If this is not the case, it must be a lake of formidable size, for it had these fish, and of this same kind, it seems to me, must be those which in my diary I say the Agua Amarilla had. And it may have become dry in this region through the high providence of God, for the place which I saw it was two and a half days' travel from here.

cneganales, que teniamos ala vista,
que fue precisa la buelta á santa Olalla, dejando tirada la mitad dela
Carga que se acavó detransportar
hasta la Laguna; El Dia 24 de Febre-
ro, como se necesitaba mucho tiempo para que Agostase de Yegua, y
Cavallada, yno determinava el señor
Comandante suvir Rio arriva, determiné irme rio avaxo paraver
silos Indios dela Laguna de san
Crateó me davan alguna noticia
favorable de algun Aguaje, que huvie-
se enla sierra de san Geronimo, ō̃.

A page from Garcés's Brief Account.

From this place we went five leagues to the west, this being the sixth journey. The seventh was four leagues north and northeast. Here there are some wells which we called Santa Rosa de las Laxas, and I may note that on my last journey I came to a place four leagues east of this watering place, when I saw the two openings. The eighth march was five leagues, directed or traveled to the north; the ninth was seven leagues to the north. Here they told us that Don Pedro Fages and the deserters had passed that way, and the Indians recognized Sevastián and me, for most of them were at San Jacome at the time of my last journey.[1]

From this place we traveled seven leagues west-northwest, this being the tenth march. Then, the eleventh was five leagues northwest, the twelfth five leagues northwest, and the thirteenth five leagues northwest. From here we traveled five leagues northwest and north-northwest. On the fifteenth march, in the afternoon, we halted at a lake, having traveled three leagues northwest. The sixteenth we went three leagues in the same direction to an arroyo called San Patricio. The eighteenth day, which was the seventeenth march, we traveled eight leagues in the same direction. On the nineteenth, changing the direction because of the mires, we traveled north by west four leagues. On the twentieth we traveled seven leagues, six to the west-northwest and then one to the west. The twenty-first march we traveled

[1] Garcés's summary does not exactly follow the diary as to journeys and distances, and it contains a few errors.

five leagues west-northwest, and on the twenty-second four leagues in the same direction and succeeded in reaching the mission of San Gabriel, which is distant from San Diego forty leagues, a little more or less.

And so, most Excellent Sir, according to the directions and the distances covered, San Gabriel is one hundred and twenty-six leagues from the Colorado River. From this is to be subtracted the distance covered from the junction of the rivers to Santa Olalla, and then the direct distance remains ninety-nine leagues, for the laguna is close to the river, bearing in mind that many long detours have been made for lack of guides and interpreters, from whom to inquire of the Indians the correct road.

We struck the trail of Don Pedro Fajes and threaded the pass by which the Indian Sevastián had come out, although not by the same cañada.[1] From this I conclude that in time the road to these new establishments will be greatly shortened, notwithstanding that now, having cut the trail of Don Pedro Fages, two roads are already opened, one to San Gabriel and the other to San Diego, and I trust in God that the commander will return directly to the Colorado River from Monterrey, and that the intentions of your Excellency will thus be carried out.

We have asked for a pilot to make observations on our return, and although there is none in the frigate which we found in this harbor, because there are only the captain and his second pilot, it may be

1 See pp. 338, 343.

that this may be done by some father of these new
establishments who may be granted us by the very
reverend father Fray Junípero Serra, with whom I
have talked about the matter. And if this is not
possible, perhaps some one of the expedition, or the
reverend father Fray Juan Díaz, may be instructed
to make this observation, which is so important, for
I think there will be no difficulty in borrowing the
instrument.

I have desired that the affair might come out
with entire success, but a thousand difficulties have
interfered with my good wishes. What is certain is
that your Excellency, continuing with your measures, so appropriate, will make these two provinces
of Monterrey and the Rio Colorado extremely desirable. The latter excels in people and opportunities
for agriculture, but the other is superior in pasturage for the raising of stock.

The commander's dealings with the Indians have
been all that might be desired, and he has given
evidence of his prudence and perseverence in over-
coming difficulties. The soldiers, in spite of coming
for several days on foot, have been most willing and
have edified me with their patience and obedience.
This results from the fact that both the chief and the
soldiers have come voluntarily. The observation
made by Father Quino, putting the junction of the
rivers in 35° 30', is not exact, according to the road,
the starting point, and the terminus.

From Monterrey I shall write to your Excellency
at length everything that has happened, for now I

have not the opportunity, nor does the time permit me, but the commander and Father Fray Juan, who have taken great pains with their diaries, will send them. May God spare your Excellency many years for the service of both Majesties, as I desire. San Diego, April 2, 1774.

Most Excellent Sir, the hand of your Excellency is kissed by your humblest chaplain and servant.

FRANCISCO GARCÉS.

Most Excellent Señor Baylio Frey Don Antonio María Bucareli y Ursua.

GARCES'S DIARY OF HIS DETOUR
TO THE JALCHEDUNES

1774

(H)

GARCES'S DIARY OF HIS DETOUR TO THE JALCHEDUNES[1]

After the extraordinary courier set out with the reports of the expedition down to the 25th of last April, I continued my stay in the neighborhood of the junction of the Gila and Colorado rivers, awaiting the señor commander and the father companion. Their arrival was most welcome to me, for it enabled me to see made the observation which was so urgently charged and so much desired by the curious, and which would have been made at the mouth of the river and at other places if there had been an opportunity.

I do not wish to molest by repeating the story of our return up the Gila, for this has been told by the commander and Father Fray Juan Díaz. I will only say that if the Yumas are good the Opas are better, but this is not true of their lands, which, however, are good for planting all kinds of crops. I have observed this tribe very leisurely on one side of the river and the other, and it appears to me that they number no less than 2500 souls between Agua Caliente and the villages of La Pasión de Tucavi.

[1] Expediente formado á consequencia de Representacion del P.ᵉ Fr. Francisco Garces con que acompaña el Diario de su expedicion á los Rios Gila y Colorado; en que expone su dictámen sobre fundacion de Misiones en estos parages. A.G.P.M., Provincias Internas, Tomo 23.

They have two sites which are the best for founding missions. One is Agua Caliente; the other is San Simón y Judas de Uparsoytac, in whose neighborhood there are opportunities for tapping the river as much as might be wished.[1]

In this pueblo I remained the 21st of May in company with a servant of the señor commander, who invited himself to stay. My purpose was to go to the Niforas Indians who have the red hematite with which most of these tribes paint themselves, a reason why they maintain friendship with them. I was not able to carry out my plan by a direct road, for the Opas and Pimas are at war with other Niforas near to themselves.[2] But they advised me that I should go to Agua Caliente, whose Indians perhaps would carry the letter. And so I did, returning on the 22d and 23d of May by way of the same Opas as far as El Aricurittoac,[3] and on the 24th as far as a village distant from Agua Caliente about a league and a half.

Here they raised insuperable objections to my going to the Niforas Indians. They said especially that it was impossible to go with the horse which I had because I would be so closely watched, but they persuaded me to give them the letter which I

[1] On his return Garcés reached Tucavi after ascending the Gila nine leagues above Uparsoytac, at Gila Bend. The villages extended along the river two and one-half leagues. See entries for June 19th to 21st. Agua Caliente is still so-called.

[2] These Niforas were evidently the Yavapais or Yabipais.

[3] Aricurittoac was evidently the same as Aritoac, which was east of Agua Caliente, and across the river from Oatman's Flat.

wished to send to the fathers of New Mexico, in order that it might be carried by two Jalchedunes Indians of the Colorado. I talked with these Jalchedunes and in the conversation, through the misunderstanding of the Pima interpreter, they said that there was a father on the Colorado River, who I thought might be some deserter from among the soldiers of Monte Rey. They said that they were friendly with the Niforas and with the people of Moqui. And since, on the other hand, these two Jalchedunes manifested great affection for me, and since for a long time I had wished to go to their lands, I decided to go in their company, leaving the servant of the señor commander in charge of the Pimas, because he would serve me rather as a burden than as an advantage, he being so timid and pusillanimous, and since I was carrying nothing to eat, for we went, indeed, trusting almost to providence.

This Spaniard and a little Indian whom the Yumas had given me started back with all felicity and well supplied by the Indians, and I on the 24th of May from the same place, which must be in the latitude 33° 15' more or less, set out at noon to the west-northwest, and traveled until eight o'clock at night, covering five leagues. In the first league I saw large patches of pasture.[1]

On the 25th we started at half past four in the morning. Going in the same direction, at half past

[1] Garcés's route was generally west-northwest, between Eagle Tail Mountains and Castle Dome Mountains.

eleven I arrived at the sierra which I called San Venancio, having traveled six leagues. In order to get water at this place, which is in very large tinajas, it is necessary to labor to carry it to the place which can be reached by the animals. In the afternoon I traveled three leagues and a half in the same direction and halted in a cañada which is in sight of another sierra in a valley.

On the 26th we set forth at half past four in the morning, and after traveling four and a half leagues in the same direction we arrived at a tank which is in a large sierra that runs to the west and which I called San Phelipe. This sierra has plentiful pasturage, although it is not near the watering place.

On the 27th we set forth at half past six in the morning, traveled two leagues to the west and north-west, and arrived at some wells called Espíritu Santo. Before reaching the place we passed near a cliff which looks like a castle, and saw another having the shape of a bell with some graceful carvings,[1] and this is not the bell which we saw at the Yumas. After midday we set forth and traveled west and northwest until eleven o'clock at night, covering seven leagues. On the way there is pasturage but a complete lack of water. At a distance of two leagues and a half, when the sierra ends, one can see the Peñol Gigante of the Yumas rising in the south.

On the 28th I set forth at four o'clock in the morning, and, traveling northwest, with some short

---

[1] *Cortados ayros.*

turns to the west, I arrived at eleven o'clock in the forenoon at the beaches and the groves of the Colorado, halting at a very long and narrow lagoon where there were many huts of the Jalchedunes, who assembled in very joyful mood.[1]

I have not made mention of the pleasure and willingness with which the two Jalchedunes served me on the way and the attention with which they cared for me, giving me of what they carried for their sustenance and saving the water so that I might not lack, the patience with which they beat the horse in order to hurry him up, and the care with which they made stops in order that I might eat. However, I believe that all this will be kept in mind by His Divine Majesty, and will cause Him to show His mercy with these people.

This day's march was seven leagues toward a sierra called San Hermenegildo.[2] On the same day in the afternoon I traveled two leagues west-southwest to the house of the Indian chief, where assembled many Jalchedunes who lived down the river.[3] The groves and beaches enter far to the southwest, and so it appears that these beaches are situated to the north-northeast of San Sebastián.[4] Indeed, it may be true that even the Indians who sell it the corals or cuentas are not more than four days distant, although this is to be understood as refer-

---

[1] Garcés reached the Colorado in the vicinity of Ehrenberg.

[2] Sierra de San Hermenegildo was evidently Chemehuevi Mountain.

[3] Garcés called this settlement Santísima Trinidad.

[4] San Sebastián was at Harper's Well on San Felipe Creek in California.

ring to those of the Santa Anna River and others near to them. What is certain is that, keeping the Sierras Nevadas immediately at the left, they will guide travelers directly to the missions near Monte Rey, and that the branch which separates from the Colorado or some of those large rivers which come out to the coasts of Monte Rey may also be of much aid for such transit. I say this because, although there are sierras near the Colorado River, yet they are not of the greatest size and they have openings of great width.

On the 29th, starting at three o'clock in the afternoon and going north, I traveled two and a half leagues, and having passed a lagoon I halted at some ranchos which I called Santa Coleta. Those downstream and the other lagoon I called La Santísima Trinidad.[1]

On the 30th I went out to the Colorado River, going a league and a half to the north. Afterward, going another league and a half to the northwest and west, I came to the famous fields and villages of San Antonio, which appeared to me the best favored for a mission of all that I have seen on the Colorado River.[2]

---

[1] From Santísima Trinidad Garcés traveled up the river 2½ leagues to Santa Coleta, 3 leagues to San Antonio, thence 2 leagues to the dry lagoon and 4 more to Lagunas de Santa Petronila, where he talked with the Yabipais. Thence he went 3 leagues plus some two hours (perhaps two leagues) to the hill north of Chemehuevi Mountain where he turned back. Thus from Santísima Trinidad he ascended the Colorado about 16½ leagues, or perhaps forty miles.

[2] San Antonio was near the southern edge of Chemehuevi Mountain.

On the 31st I traveled two leagues to the north-east, coming out to a dry lagoon where they were cutting and trampling a grain called *equiesa,* admirable for making atole and bread. Some people may laugh at these expressions, but if they had lived during recent years at Monte Rey they would know that they are the strict truth. The same day, traveling four leagues north-northwest, I arrived at the Lagunas de Santa Petronila,[1] where there were a few Jalchedunes and four Yabipais or Niforas, who in dress, language, features, and other circumstances are Apaches, although they are hostile to them, according to what was said by the Pimas, who make it appear that the Moquis and Siurs are also enemies of the Apaches.

As soon as they saw me these Yabipais asked me for some awls with which to sew sandals with three fringes which they wear, but, telling them that I had none, I offered them the spurs and some scissors if they would take me to their land. To this they agreed, but the Jalchedunes, because of the bad condition of the horse, persuaded me not to go.[2] Indeed, the lack of water and the great heat might make it somewhat risky, although with respect to the Yabipais there was no risk whatever, for they are intimate friends of the Jalchedunes who have such frequent dealings that some of them speak familiarly

[1] Santa Petronila was near the northern edge of Chemehuevi Mountain.

[2] The Jalchedunes may have been sincere in their argument, but it was no uncommon experience for one tribe through self-interest to try to keep white men from visiting other tribes.

in the language[1] of these Niforas. However, the old man of the Yabipais gave me to understand that there was water on the road to his country.[2] He said also that they did not plant there, but that they maintained themselves by hunting deer and wild sheep and on mescal. He told of many bands of people who were their friends, especially the Yumas whom all these people call Cutchanas, which is the same name by which they call themselves. When I asked this old man how many days' journey it was to those who make the colored blankets, he made five lines on the ground and gave me to understand that they were his friends. The advantage of the peace which these Niforas enjoy is due to the red hematite. The same benefit is enjoyed by the Moquinos because of the commerce in these blankets.

From this reply and that which he says later it appears to me that it is easy to make the mistake (for it is always easy when there is not a good interpreter) which is contained in the reports which I have given with respect to the distance from the Yumas of the junction and those higher up to the pueblos of New Mexico. It seems to me that the distance must be more than four days, and it must be that what they say of the four days' journey has reference to these Niforas or Cuilsniovrs or Naxi, for another name, or to the Soyopas,[3] for they confuse the people of Moqui, the Niforas, and the neophytes

---

1 Hablan oppoditamente.

2 The Yabipais (Yavapais) lived northeast of the Jalchedunes in the vicinity of Rio Verde.

3. The Soyopas were the Mohaves.

of the fathers of New Mexico. There is a kind of
people called Yabipais,[1] although it is also true
that they are distinguished by other names, because
some are called Yabipais Guichi, others Yabipais
Mogchi, others Yabipais Geecóche, and others Yabipais Apagueche, and still others who live on the
same river higher up are called Yabipaya. The first
are the Niforas. The second appear to be the people
of Moqui, and the third those of the converted pueblos of New Mexico, for they called me Geecochi, and
of these they gave me to understand that they had
cows. The fourth I think are the Apaches who molest us, and the fifth the Soyopas from above.

The first of the month I spent in the same con-
versations with the Jalchedunes and Yabipais. The
former said that there had arrived at their lands
people from the northeast who wore ribbons on their
heads and who had given them some little gifts. I
then remembered the reports which had been given
me by the Gileños, and I concluded that it would be
useless to attempt to send the letter to New Mexico,
but in order not to lose any opportunity I decided
to leave the letter with an old Jalchedun, in order
that he might send it at the first occasion, which,
according to what they said, would be when the mesquite bean was ripe. I added to the letter for the

---

[1] Garcés shows that Yabipais was a descriptive term applied to
various tribes. In its more special usage it refers to the Yuman
people who were sometimes called Mohave Apaches because of their
warlike qualities. Their early habitat was between the upper Rio
Verde and the Colorado. Recently they have lived on a reservation
on the upper Rio Verde in the vicinity of Camp McDowell.

fathers that now I would return as soon as possible, because I had written in it that I would await the reply, and that if there should be some neophytes I would go in company with them as far as the first mission if there was no objection.

Now that I had given up the plan which looked to New Mexico, seeing myself so high up on the beaches of the Colorado River, and knowing that I would be well received by the Soyopas (for they had sent me a message when I was with the Yumas, saying that the father must pass by these lands and they would give him food) and since the Cuirsniurs[1] also have knowledge of me, for I saw one of them in my other journey, I made a test to see if the Jalchedunes who refused to accompany me upstream lied through fear.

On the 2d of the month I set out alone with the idea of returning at once to the lagunas if they would not go with me. In a short time a Jalchedun came on horseback and took me to a watering place three leagues to the north with some turns to the northeast. We took a siesta, and then, about four o'clock in the afternoon, we set out in the same direction. He stopped and then turned back with great speed, or on the gallop. Seeing myself alone and on a road very thickly grown and with many trails, I continued until sunset toward the north. Then, as a goodbye, I ascended a high hill to look around. I saw that the

---

[1] This name is evidently an equivalent for the Cosninas, or Havasupai, although Garcés was not clear as to its application. The name is retained in Coconino County, in which the *s* or *ç* has been erroneously replaced by hard *c*.

mas acerca de la Mudanza de Presidios hace sin duda a estos Indios los mas acreedores a la Piedad del Rey.

Dia 8: anduve tres leguas pasando por tierras de Pima despobladas, y llegue a la Rancheria que se llamo Pitac; y viendo assi, que abajo no corria el rio, aqui habia mucha agua, y tambien pasto en los alrededores, y siguiendo la Corriente del Rio, long por los ni antes de llegar al Subtuquison, y en este sitio sigamente se puede poner Presidio. Por la tarde sali casi a las cinco, y a poco mas de una legua encontre un pozo grande, y con dos mas rumbe al Sueste, y doce leg. al Sur. llegue a los pozos Salados muy escasos de agua a las nueve del otro dia. habiendo descansado quatro veces, y medio dormido breves intervalos. Con dos leg. al Sudueste. Deste Sudueste llegue al pozo amargo, que tiene mucha agua, y es asilo de los Papagos de esta parte, quando se les acaban sus Jagueyes, o charcos de agua. Avia en el una numerosa Rancheria, y bestias, y con todo esso esta el agua muy abundante, pues mana mucho el Pozo, que aunque da agua algo amarga, pero no es nociva. El mismo dia llovio, y el dia 10 por tierras muy empoluadas, y que tenian algunos Jagueyes, o charcos de agua habiendo salido a las ocho de la mañana y parado dos veces llegue a las cinco de la tarde a mi Pueblo de S. Xavier del Bac, andadas cinco leguas al Sueste, pies a la luz huyendo del Monte, y dos al Oeste. tambien a distancia de quatro leg. del Pozo amargo queda otro al Poniente del tucson, llamado Cubava y su puesto, que en tiempo de Saguaza, y de la seca se ranchean muchos en su immediacion hago Juicio que sea abundante de agua, y con esto en todo tiempo, se podra salir por el Hornueste de S.n Xavier asta el Rio Sta, y tiene este camino la ventaja, de pastos muy buenos. Es muy creible que el Camino para Monte-Rey dirigido por el Hornueste de los Pimas Pueblos sea mas breve, y mejor, y no arriesgado pues no son Apaches sino tiernas los que pueden hacer algun mes. Esto desee, y por aqui estaba dirigida la Expedicion, pero la Salida del Indio Sebastian mudo todo el proyecto, y despues la guerra de los Jumas con los Jalchedunes con las noticias de los Cuyopas impidieron mi designio, y de el S.r Comandante, pues era preciso obedecer pudiendo. Y por lo que a mi toca, con este sso. la suma repugnancia, que tenia, para ir a experimentar los trabajos passados en mi ultimo viage en aquellos horribles Arenales; por que aunque Sebastian, y Valdes facilitaban el passo, una vez, que estuvieran de la otra vanda del Colorado, pero aviendo perecido la Muger y Hermano de dicho Sebastian, y experimentado yo los trabajos por ser dos siempre la casa dificultosa, como lo fue. No obstante, que aten didas las circunstancias de la Salida del Indio, y poca gente de la Expedicion, fue conforme a prudencia la resolucion que se toma. El Cabo de Monte-Rey que vino con el P.e Comandante, me dijo se via sa lido de S. Diego por la Sierra asta muy cerca de los Pozos de Sta Rosa de las tija y que despues me a. S. Gregorio mastumbo su Sierra, de la derecha, y pasado un chico valle subio a otra Sierra desde donde diviso arboledas, y playas, que creo son del Colorado Fray Francisco Garces

sierra which begins apparently near San Antonio
and runs to the northwest, makes a turn to the north
and comes to the north-northeast and does not run
any further.[1] In the vicinity of the sierra I saw much
water, groves, and large beaches, which must be
those of the Colorado River. To the northeast and
east there is seen a very large opening which indicates level land. To the south lay the Sierra de San
Hermenegildo, and to the southeast that of San
Phelipe.

Father Juan had ordered me not to put myself
in manifest danger, and not being accompanied by
Indians it is very doubtful if I lacked this. And considering that in a government so active there is no
need for doing any more foolish things than those
already done, I returned to the Jalchedunes. The
sierra on the other side of the river I called Corpus
Christi.

My return to the Jalchedunes was very much
celebrated, because they had concluded that I must
have gone out to their enemies and that these must
have done me some injury. They added that a white
man (he must be a deserter from Californias) had
gone toward the north and not returned. They also
told me that they had friends on the same river, but
that they were very far away, and because of the
Cuirsniurs it was necessary to travel through lands
lacking in water, in order to flee from these Cuirsniurs.

[1] This was clearly Chemehuevi Mountain. The spur to the north
where it ends is called Old Woman Mountain on early maps.

An Indian made me a very furious harangue like
the dancers of the sierra.[1] I having arrived at a village, a very old woman sang with various ceremonies
and then began to weep bitterly, and the Jalchedunes
said that she was from there toward the west. I
heard two Indians talk who had come from the northwest of these Jalchedunes. They spoke a different
language and had different arrows from those which
I had seen. The Jalchedunes said they had still
other friends, and so I am not surprised that cotton
blankets like those of the Pimas should have reached
the missions of Monte Rey or that they told the soldiers of Monte Rey that those who made them were
distant five days, for the soldiers heard this at those
great lakes which they say are about thirty leagues
from San Luís.[2]

Among these Jalchedunes I also saw better fields,
and recognized in the tribe some advantages which
they have over the Yumas. The majority of them go
dressed with blankets and blue cloth from Moqui and
from the Pimería. They plant cotton, have better
arrows, and the climate is cooler and better. I observed that in the season of such heat it was necessary to have shelter at night, and for this reason
they have better and larger houses than any I have
seen. As soon as I arrived they gave me another
horse which, because it was not very gentle, I did not
accept because I was afraid to mount it. Since they

---

[1] The Danzantes or Dancers were seen by the Anza expedition in
Coyote Canyon, above Borrego Valley, in California.

[2] These were the lakes and tulares in southern San Joaquin Valley.

call the principal Indian Gedecoche and called me the same, I saw that this was due to the mistake of the Pima interpreter. They are very friendly with the Cajuen tribe, and I saw many Indians from the Laguna de San Matheo and farther down who still remembered the Jesus María.

Finally, the great assistance given me by these Indians, the joy which they manifested on my arrival at any of their houses, the care to give me abundant provisions when I set out to return, are worthy of my greatest appreciation. They furnished me some servants to return with me, but since I had nothing with which to repay them (a thing the most embarrassing for any one who receives favors from such people), I chose one who alone accompanied me to the Tutumaopas near Agua Caliente and who served me as cook. He carried a firebrand in one hand all the way, and it did not go out. In the other hand he carried a stick with which to drive the horse, which could not hurry for lack of shoes, especially where there were stones. And besides all this he carried a jug of water on his head, enduring thirst in order that I might not suffer, and all this with a smiling face. Who will say that this Indian is a savage? And who will not praise a service of such qualities?

Before reaching the Gila I traveled four leagues on foot, and afterward the Opas took me from the village to that of San Simón y Judas de Uparsoytac,[1] of which I make mention in the diary of the year '70.

[1] Uparsoytac was at Gila Bend.

From this pueblo, leaving the road taken by the commander,[1] I ascended the river to the north-northeast, and saw the admirable advantage which it has for taking out as much water as might be desired and making most splendid fields. After traveling six leagues on the 19th of June I arrived at Tugsapi.[2] Here they said that the best road to the Jalchedunes led out from there, and that they went in three or four days according to their pace.

On the 20th I traveled three leagues to the north and reached Tucabi. On the 21st, after traveling two and a half leagues, we had left behind the people of La Pasión de Tugabi. As far as these villages the river carries much water, receiving it at this season almost entirely from the Rio Azul and the Salado.

On the 22d I traveled in the morning two leagues to the northeast, and in the afternoon one to the southeast and four to the south-southeast. On the 23d I went half a league southeast and encountered the people of Subtaquisson, who were gathering saguaro, a fruit very much like the pitaya. On the 26th, with five leagues to the southeast, I passed through many pastures and reached the villages of La Encarnación del Subtaquisson. There are three pueblos with many people. Doubtless with its pastures, which are scarce on the Gila, this is the best site. On the 27th I went to the large pueblo called

[1] Anza continued east from Gila Bend past Sierra Estrella, then went northeast to the Gila Pimas.

[2] Garcés gives us new data regarding the Cocomaricopa villages above Gila Bend, as well as regarding the Gila Pimas north of the Gila River.

San Seraphin de Nacub, which is distant a league, following the current of the river, and on the other side. This pueblo was not seen by the expedition. On the 28th I set out and, traveling a little more than another league, I came to Tuburs Cabors, which is on this side and near the river and is very populous. I had never been in this town, and they told me that I must give it the name of some saint, so I called it San Andrés, because its villages are abandoned and attached to San Juan Capistrano de Uturituc, where I went on the 30th with a little more than a league's travel.

This village must have nearly a thousand souls. The governor said to me, "Father, yesterday we arrived from a campaign and the horses are now very much used up. Rest seven days and afterward you shall go out accompanied by myself and my children. You see that there is plenty to eat, and we will bring you fish," and they also brought some game. The excess of these Indians over all the rest along the river, their situation so advantageous for assisting in the subjection of the Apaches, and for direct transit to Monte Rey and New Mexico, their requests for fathers, their urgent offering of their children for baptism, and the measures which I presume are about to be taken concerning the moving of the presidios, without doubt make these Indians the most meritorious of the piety of the king.

On the 8th I traveled three leagues, passing through uninhabited lands of Pimas, and arrived at the village which is called Pitac. Although farther down the river did not run, here there was much water. There is also pasturage in the vicinity and along the current of the river, and so, in view of what I saw before reaching Subtaquisson and in this place, a presidio can be securely established.

In the afternoon I set out just before five o'clock. After going a little more than a league I came to a large well, and with two more leagues to the southeast and twelve leagues to the south I arrived at the Pozos Salados, which were very short of water. Next day, traveling two leagues to the west-southwest, and having rested four times and dozed at brief intervals, at nine o'clock I arrived at Pozo Amargo, which has much water and is an asylum for the Pápagos of this vicinity when their jagueyes or pools of water play out. Near it there was a numerous village and horses, and notwithstanding this the water was very abundant, for the well flows freely, and although the water is somewhat bitter it is not injurious.[1]

The same day it rained. On the 10th I set out at eight in the morning. Passing through lands very well pastured and with some jagueyes or pools of water, and halting twice, I arrived at five in the afternoon at my pueblo of San Javier del Bac, having traveled five leagues to the southeast, three to the south to escape the woods,[2] and two to the east. At a distance of four leagues from Pozo Amargo

---

[1] Garcés evidently swung west of the Tucson Mountains and turned east again about on the latitude of San Xavier del Bac.

[2] *Monte*, a word which usually means woods or brush.

there is another pozo to the west of Tugson called Cubavi. Since in the time of saguaros and of drought many Indians camp in its vicinity, I judge that it must have an abundance of water, and that with this at all times it will be possible to go out to the northwest from San Xavier as far as the Gila River, and this road has the advantage of very good pasturage.

It is easy to believe that the road for Monte Rey directed to the northwest of the Gila Pimas, may be shorter and better and not dangerous, because those who might do some damage are not Apaches, but Niforas. This is what I desired and through here the expedition was directed to go, but the coming of the Indian Sebastián completely changed the plan. Then, afterward, the war of the Yumas with the Jalchedunes, together with the reports given by the Soyopas, frustrated my design and that of the señor commander, for it was necessary to obey since it was possible. But, so far as I am concerned, I confess the extreme repugnance which I had for going to experience the trials suffered during my previous journey in those horrible sand dunes. For, although Sebastián and Valdés facilitated the passage as soon as they were on the other side of the Colorado, yet the wife and brother of this Sebastián having perished and I having experienced the previous hardships, the thing always looked difficult, as it proved to be. Nevertheless, considering the circumstances of the coming of the Indian and the few men of the expedition, the decision made was in keeping with prudence.

The corporal of Monte Rey, who came with the señor commander, told me that he had come out from San Diego over the mountain to a place very near the wells of Santa Rosa de las Lajas, and that afterward he went to San Gregorio, conquered the sierra to the right, passed a small valley, and ascended another sierra from which he descried groves and beaches which I think are those of the Colorado.[1]

FRAY FRANCISCO GARCÉS (Rubric).

[1] A good summary of Father Garcés's journey to the Jalchedunes is contained in the great work by Fray Juan Domingo de Arricivita, *Crónica Seráfica y Apostólica del Colegio de Propaganda Fide de la Santa Cruz de Querétaro en la Nueva España* (Mexico, 1792), 455–456. Father Arricivita was official chronicler of the College of Santa Cruz. He wrote from archive records, and he evidently had at hand Garcés's diary here published. His book is a highly important work on the history of North America in the eighteenth century.

PALOU'S DIARY OF THE EXPEDITION TO SAN FRANCISCO BAY
1774

(*I*)

DIARY OF THE EXPEDITION WHICH, BY
ORDER OF THE MOST EXCELLENT SENOR BAILIO
FREY DON ANTONIO MARIA BUCARELI, VICEROY
OF THIS NEW SPAIN, WAS MADE BY ME, FRAY
FRANCISCO PALOU, IN THE MONTH OF NOVEM-
BER, 1774, TO THE VICINITY OF THE PORT OF
SAN FRANCISCO, ON THE COAST OF THE PACIFIC
OCEAN IN NORTHERN CALIFORNIA, FOR THE
PURPOSE OF OCCUPYING IT WITH NEW MIS-
MIONS ENTRUSTED TO MY APOSTOLIC COLLEGE
OF FRANCISCAN MISSIONARIES OF THE REGU-
LAR OBSERVANCE DE PROPAGANDA FIDE OF
SAN FERNANDO OF THE CITY OF MEXICO.[1]

Since the port of Monte Rey was occupied with
complete success, and there was founded in it the
royal presidio of San Carlos, and, in its vicinity, in
the meadows of Rio Carmelo, the mission of the
same name, and various others on the coast between
this port and that of San Diego, various expeditions
have been made for the purpose of exploring this
new land, and especially toward the port of San
Francisco, to the north of that of Monte Rey, for the

[1] Diario de el viage que . . . hize yò Fr. Francisco Palou por el
mes de Noviembre de 1774 a las cercanias del Puerto de Sn. Francisco. Certified copy. A.G.I. Guadalajara, Legajo 514. 1774–1795
(formerly 106–6–16).

purpose of founding in it a mission dedicated to Our Seraphic Patriarch.[1]

With this purpose Don Pedro Fages, commander of this royal presidio, set out from it in the month of March, 1772, with a suitable escort of soldiers and accompanied by the father preacher Fray Juan Crespi, missionary of the college named and assistant missionary of the mission of San Carlos, who was sent by the Reverend Father Lector Fray Junípero Serra, president of all the missions. Having arrived in the vicinity of the Gulf of the Farallones, in which, according to the histories, that port is situated, near the Punta de Reyes, their passage was cut off by a large estuary or arm of the sea which empties into the Gulf. And although, ascending, they went around it, following its course on the other side as far as the mouth, they found that another, or the same one, succeeded it toward the northnorthwest. This likewise they followed till they came upon a great lake or round bay, and found that into this one there emptied a great river, a quarter of a league wide, which they could not ford. Ascending a high hill they saw this to be divided

[1] Father Palóu tells us that Serra forwarded this diary to the viceroy by the land mail which left Monterey on January 14, 1775, at the same time sending a copy to the College of San Fernando. In his *Noticias de Nueva California* Palóu inserted an account of this expedition which is essentially a copy of the diary, but, besides numerous differences of detail, it omits minor portions of the diary here and there, and adds occasional comments and items of information drawn from his notes or from memory. That version of the diary is translated in Bolton, *Palóu's New California*, III, 248–308. Rivera also kept a diary of the expedition.

in three branches, each one a quarter of a league wide, the same as the river, and they likewise saw that the three branches were formed from a great river which comes down from the south-southeast from some high sierra. Seeing themselves cut off and unable to pass to the Punta de Reyes, they returned to the presidio, giving an account of everything to his Excellency, with the diaries, on the basis of which was formed a map of this estuary and port.[1]

The most Excellent Señor Viceroy, being desirous that this port should be settled and that the immense heathendom which inhabits its vicinity should be reduced to our holy faith, once more ordered the commander of these new establishments, Don Fernando de Rivera y Moncada, to go to make a new examination to determine the source of this river, and to examine the sites most suitable for the founding of the missions which might be considered desirable. The same person likewise addressed the reverend father president of the missions, in a letter of the 25th of May of this year, telling him that with the arrival of the new commander and of the families of soldiers which he had recruited in Cinaloa, the new exploration of the vicinity of the port of San Francisco should be made, in order to occupy it with new missions, in addition to those already projected. His Excellency concluded the letter by charging him

[1] Father Crespi's diary was inserted in Palóu's *Noticias*. A translation of it is in Bolton, *Fray Juan Crespi, Missionary Explorer on the Pacific Coast, 1769–1774*, pp. 275–304.

to report to him in detail and with all individuality whatever in the exploration might be seen.

In view of this superior charge and order, as soon as the soldiers arrived from Cinaloa, notwithstanding that the time was unpropitious for this expedition because of the proximity of the rainy season, the commander decided to set out on the expedition with an escort of sixteen soldiers and one muleteer for the pack train, fixing the 23d of November for the start, and the reverend father president appointed me to go on the expedition, charging me to keep my diary, in order that his Reverence might be able to report everything in detail to his Excellency, as he charges him to do.

November 23.—The captain commander having set the afternoon of the 23d of November for the start from the royal presidio of Monte Rey, and I having received the blessing of the reverend father president, and having said goodbye to the father companions, set out at about half past eleven from the mission of San Carlos with a servant for the service and a boy, a sacristan, to aid me in the Mass. Arriving at the camp about twelve o'clock, I found the captain and the soldiers getting ready for the departure, which took place at half past two in the afternoon. The commander with some soldiers remained at the presidio to finish some odds and ends and to come later to overtake us, and I, with the greater part of the men, and the pack train loaded with provisions for forty days, set out from the presidio at the hour named. Going northeast over hills

in sight of the beach, at half past five we arrived
at the Rio de Santa Delfina, known as the River of
Monte Rey[1] because it empties into the bay of that
name about five leagues from the presidio going
over the road by the beach. We halted on the bank
of the river in a plain which has at hand plentiful
pasturage, and firewood from the heavy growth of
trees with which the bed of the river is covered.
About ten o'clock at night the captain arrived with
the rest of the soldiers.—From the presidio 3 hours.[2]

November 24.—At seven o'clock in the morning
we set out from the camp and immediately crossed
the river. The water reached the stirrups and from
the large channel which it has it is seen that in the
rainy season it must carry a great quantity of water.
Having crossed the river we traveled north, swinging after a short distance to the north-northeast, and
crossing the plain of the great valley of Santa Delfina, which is nearly four leagues wide. After traveling an hour over this plain we came to a long lake of
good water with large tule marshes on its shores.[3]

At half past nine we came to a range of hills
where the plain ends in this direction, and entered
a narrow valley formed by the hills which are all
of pure earth and have good pasturage. Between
them ran a ditch grown with some trees and having

[1] This was the Salinas River. The manuscript, by an obvious slip,
reads ''southeast.'' This would be correct only for the very start,
the general direction to the Salinas River being north-northeast.

[2] The summaries of hours traveled are marginal entries in the
manuscript.

[3] The lake was perhaps Espinosa Lake, near Del Monte Junction.

water which the hills lack. From this water and from various seepages which we saw in several little canyons of the hills we concluded the lake is formed. We ascended between the hills, and along their slopes we climbed to a high pass, although the ascent was not at all rough, because it is entirely of earth grown with grass.[1]

Near the top, not very far from the trail which we were following, we came to a little pack which we judged must belong to some heathen who, on seeing us from a distance, had left it in order with greater lightness to be able to hide from us. The captain approached it and saw that it consisted only of pinole and thick atole in a basket. And in order that those who came behind us with the pack train and the relay herd might not touch it, he halted to await them, while we continued the ascent. From the summit of a high hill somewhat apart a heathen began to call to us, and we at once conjectured that the pack must be his, but seeing on the trail a fresh track of a woman we were made to believe that it must belong to her and that she had hidden.

We descended from the pass, whose slope was very steep and long, although not dangerous, because it had only pure earth with green grass. On the descent we saw a large smoke in the thicket of a little grove of live oaks within a little canyon. The soldier said it was a village of heathen, although we

---

[1] The mountains were the Gabilán Range. They seem to have been crossed by Gabilán Creek and by a route near the highway from Salinas to San Juan, though it is possible that they may have gone up San Miguel Canyon.

Diario de el Viage que de orden de el Exmo Sor Bailio Frai Dn
Antonio Maria Bucareli Virey de esta N.E. hize
yo Fr. Francisco Palou, por el mes de Noviembre de 1774
a las cercanias del Puerto de Sn Francisco en la costa
del Mar pacifico dela California Septentrional, a fin
de ocuparlas con nuebas misiones encomendadas a mi
Apco Colegio de misioneros Franciscanos dela Regular
observancia de Propaganda fide de Sn Fernando dela ciu
dad de Mexico.

    Despues de haverse logrado con toda felicidad el
poblar el Puerto de Monte-Rey, y fundado en el su
Real Presidio de Sn Carlos, y a sus cercanias en
las Vegas del Rio Carmelo la mision del mismo
titulo, y otras varias en la costa intermedia de
dho Puerto, y el de Sn Diego, se han hecho varias
expediciones con el fin de explorar esta nueba tie.
rra; y principalmente asia el Puerto de Sn Fran
cisco al Norte del de Monte-Rey, con el fin de fun.
dar en el una mision dedicada à Nro Serafico
Patriarca.

    Con este fin, por el mes de marzo de 1772
salió de dho Real Presidio su comandante Dn

First page of Palóu's diary.

did not see any nor was I able to discern their houses because of the thickness of the grove.

Having finished the slope we entered a rather narrow valley grown with oaks and live oaks, and in it we saw a ditch of running water with a good flow of more than a buey. It runs through a grove of cottonwood, sycamores, willows, and live oaks, with many briars, and near it there are many Castilian rose bushes. Having crossed the ditch we continued along the same valley, but we soon noticed that the water was not running, for it disappears under the surface, so, in order not to remain without water, and as it was already late, we went back about a gunshot and stopped near the ditch where the water was still running, in a little valley or canyon of considerable extent, grown with live oaks and good pasturage. Here we halted at twelve o'clock, the journey having been five hours at a good pace and without any delay. At this same place the expedition of the year '72 rested, naming this valley the Cañada de San Benito.[1]

Nowhere on the journey, nor at this place, has any other heathen than the one mentioned been seen, but in the plain of Santa Delfina we saw at every step their trails very well worn, and the same on the hills and in this valley. No doubt they must belong to the village of the smoke which we saw, whose people have not come to the camp.—From the presidio 8 hours.

[1] Cañada de San Benito was San Benito Valley. Camp was near the site of Mission San Juan Bautista.

November 25.—About seven o'clock we set out from the camp toward the north-northwest, and after traveling a short distance we were stopped by a great marsh with large tulares where the little vale ends and one enters a spacious valley. This obliged us to turn north-northeast in order to cross the valley, which is about a league wide, and whose terminus we could not see. It is as level as the palm of the hand, has good land for raising crops, and good pasturage. It was called by the expedition, which crossed it, the Valley of San Pasqual Baylón.[1]

After we saw the marsh at the entrance to the valley and the great amount of moist land at the conclusion of the Cañada de San Benito, we judged that the water which we saw in the Cañada disappears and comes underground, emptying into this valley and forming this marsh. And if this is the case, it would be easy to conduct this water by a ditch along the surface of the earth to irrigate the good lands of this valley of San Pasqual, and there might be founded a large mission with many and good lands, both irrigable and with natural moisture, for by cutting off this ditch of water all the land which is now marsh would be moist like that of El Carmelo and would save the labor of having to irrigate it. This site enjoys the advantage of plentiful firewood, both from the Cañada de San Benito as well as from the many live oaks which it has on the hills at the entrance, in which we saw at a dis-

[1] The Valley of San Pasqual Baylón was Hollister Valley. The stream which disappeared underground was San Benito River.

tance many smokes, which are a sign of villages. Likewise it has at hand timber for building, and in the Cañada de San Benito near yesterday's camp site there is plentiful stone and good pasturage for all kinds of stock.

We crossed this plain and found that it ends with a fair-sized river which runs through a heavy growth of cottonwoods, willows, and sycamores, with a good volume of water, but because of the depth at which it runs it does not appear to me that it would be easy to make use of it for irrigating the plain, unless it might be possible to ditch it higher up, toward the east. This river, the soldiers said, is the one which the expedition of '69 crossed at the beach and was called Santa Anna, alias El Pájaro.[1]

Having crossed the river we ascended some hills of land very thickly grown with grass, although with no other trees than now and then a live oak which grows in the canyons of the hills. We spent about half an hour in crossing the range of hills, from which we saw a large lake with plentiful water, two dry lakes, and a pond with plentiful water from a spring. After the ascent of the hills we traveled northwest, and in that direction we descended to a wide, level valley, called since the last expedition, which passed through it, San Bernardino de Sena. This valley runs from southeast to northwest. To the southeast the extremity is unknown and to the northwest the soldiers say that it extends as far as

[1] It still bears the name of Pájaro.

the great estuary of San Francisco. Its width where
we descended must be about four leagues. It is all
level like the palm of the hand and is good soil,
although in places there are patches of bad and salty
land without grass or trees.[1]

After having traveled two hours through this
valley we came to a large grove, heavily grown with
cottonwoods, sycamores, willows, and briars, and
within it there was a large village of more than
thirty houses made of grass. As soon as they saw
us many Indians came out from them armed with
bow and arrows. Since the trail led us to the village
we passed in front of it, distant about a musket shot.
Calling to the Indians, they came at once and presented me with many of the arrows, this among them
being the surest pledge of peace, and I responded
with some strings of glass beads. They did the same
with the commander and with some of the soldiers,
and all reciprocated with strings of glass beads,
which they greatly esteem. We stopped a little while
with them, the Indians manifesting great affability.
On all who approached me I made the sign of the
cross, and no one resisted, being very quiet and
attentive to the ceremony which I performed on
them, as if they were instructed in it. They presented us with some baskets of atole, pinole, and
seeds, and a bag made of wildcat skin. The women
and children, being more timid, did not come near.

----

[1] Rivera evidently went north from the vicinity of Hollister,
crossed the hills north of San Felipe Lake, and descended into the
great valley east of Gilroy.

The men go entirely naked, like all the rest of
the heathen, and now and then one of them carried
his little cape made of skin or of grass, which pro-
tects their shoulders from the cold as far as the
waist, leaving uncovered the rest of the body, including what especially they ought to cover. Some of
them whom I saw were very much bearded, and
most of them had good features and fat bodies. The
women go covered with skins of animals and with
grass in place of skirts, and on their shoulders they
wear their skin capes. Judging from the people
who permitted themselves to be seen, they must not
have been less than three hundred souls of both
sexes, counting big and little. Near the village we
saw a large pool of water, and judging from the
course of the growth of trees there might be a running arroyo there.

Having said goodbye to this village, we continued our journey in the same direction and in the
same valley, and at twelve o'clock we came to some
hills, not very high, with which the valley seemed to
end, although this was not the case, because from
the top of them we saw that it continued toward the
north between the sierra and the point of the hills,
and in it we saw a large grove which ran through the
valley. We descended from the hills and approached
the grove, which was in the bed of a river which has
water only in pools, but it is seen that in the rainy
season it has a large flow and that the rainfall of the
valley must collect in this river. At half past twelve

we halted near the water, the journey having been
five and a half hours, at a good pace, including the
short stop at the village, [a site which was called
Las Llagas de Nuestro Padre San Francisco[1]].--
From the presidio, 13½ hours.

November 26.—Day dawned with a heavy and
damp fog which seemed like mist. For lack of sun
we could not determine the time of day when we set
out, but it must have been about the same time as
on the preceding days, at seven o'clock. We followed
the course of the valley in the same direction of
north-northwest. The heavy fog prevented me from
seeing the width of the valley. Indeed it was so
dark that we could see nothing a few steps away.
I was able to see, however, that the range of hills
on the south side was not very far from the road
which we were traveling, and that the plain through
which we were going was very thickly grown with
oaks and live oaks. Indeed, we came to some very
dense groves of these trees.

At eight o'clock the sky cleared, although the sun
did not appear, and I could now see that the valley
was getting wider and that it was very thickly grown
with oaks and live oaks. At ten o'clock we came to
a large river channel, thickly grown with cottonwoods, sycamores, and willows, but without water.

---

[1] The words in brackets are supplied from the version in Palóu's
Noticias. The arroyo where they camped still bears the name of Las
Llagas. The ridge which they crossed shortly before camping was
the spur that enters the valley from the west just north of San
Martín. Rivera's party were now following the west side of the
valley.

We followed along the channel, and soon saw a village of heathen on a high hill on the north side.

We followed the river bed and came to a thick grove of various kinds of trees and brambles. It was necessary for us to pass through it and within it we came to some little houses of heathen who on hearing the noise deserted their belongings and hid themselves. As we passed through the grove near the village we saw a ditch of running water, but after a short time we saw no more water and I concluded that it disappeared in the sand.[1] On emerging from the grove we came upon some heathen armed with their bows and arrows, very close to the trail which we were following. I called to one of them, who immediately approached and I gave him some glass beads. On seeing this, others came up to me at once and I regaled them likewise, but I did not stop since the place was very incommodious because of the density of the timber and because the pack train and the cavallada were coming through it.

After we had passed through the grove the valley widened out again, with good lands and likewise grown with oaks. At twelve o'clock we came to a range of hills of medium height, of pure earth and grass covered.[2] We ascended it, and from the top we saw a vast plain, in which at the end of the hills

[1] The stream bed which they were following was that of Coyote River. They were now in the narrows near Coyote.

[2] These were the hills west of Hillsdale and south of San José Cemetery. Camp this night was evidently on Guadalupe River west or southwest of the cemetery. The note in my *Palóu's New California*, III, 261, puts the camp too far southeast.

toward the north ran a great line of timber which to us looked like the tree line of some river, along whose banks continues the plain of the valley, communicating with the one which we saw from the top of the hill. From the hill also we saw a high sierra very far away toward the north-northwest and at the foot of it I saw a little round blue peak which the soldiers told me was an island in the estuary.

We descended from the hill and approached the line of timber and found it to be a river which had water only in pools. At half past twelve we halted near them, under some live oaks with which the river bottoms are very thickly grown. Near the camp we found vestiges of a village, which it was seen could not have been moved very long before. About two o'clock in the afternoon it began to rain, although not very hard, but the mist continued until night.—From the presidio, 19 hours.

November 27.—Early in the morning I said Mass, as it was the First Sunday of Advent, and everybody attended. Because the people were wet from the rain of yesterday afternoon the commander decided not to set forth until after dinner in order to dry the clothing with the good sun which rose for us, and so we did not set forth until twelve o'clock. We then followed the spacious plain toward the west-by-northwest,[1] finding that the valley continues of good land with much pasturage and very thickly grown with oaks. In a little grove of these trees,

[1] The explorers had now turned westward, leaving the trail of the earlier expeditions, made by Fages and Crespi.

about one o'clock in the afternoon, we came upon
three heathen with their bows and arrows. They
apparently were hunting, for in all the vicinity we
saw no villages nor smokes, although in the plain
we saw many well beaten trails. On seeing us they
made no sign of fleeing or hiding whatever. We
halted not very far from them, and I called them,
but they did not wish to come near, although I
showed them beads. They gave me to understand
that I should throw them. I did so, but even then
they did not approach. Seeing this the captain
dismounted, took the beads and gave them to them.
Then we continued our journey, leaving them at
their occupation.

About half past one we found in the same plain
a great marsh, with large tulares. It was so miry
that we could not cross it, and it was necessary to go
around, so we swung to the south for nearly half an
hour, when we came to an arroyo with much water
and a heavy growth of briars. Here it was necessary to dismount and fix the ford in order to get
over. We crossed with some difficulty and some of
the soldiers got good and wet. We again turned to
our former direction, continuing through the valley
over good land, in places thickly grown with some
small trees which looked like junipers. Among them
there were some madroños which were larger, and
had fruit of the size of a large chick pea, although
it was not yet ripe. On the way we encountered two
arroyos, heavily grown with trees but without water.

At half past five we halted at a grove of oaks in which there was good pasturage for the animals but no water for them, and it was lucky for us that we had a little in a calfskin bag.—From the presidio 24½ hours.[1]

November 28.—At daybreak it was very clear, and before sunrise we saw an iris bow in the west. About seven o'clock we set out from the camp site toward the northwest, continuing through the same plain. The journey, although it has been no more than four and a half hours over a level road, has been very hard, for it has been difficult because of the thick groves of juniper and madroño trees, which I mentioned yesterday, although the groves were separated by patches of good land, grown with pasture and having good oaks and live oaks. We encountered three arroyos during the day, two without water and the other one containing it only in pools, but all three have a heavy growth of trees in their beds.[2]

At half past eleven we came to another deep arroyo, in which runs a good stream of water of about two bueyes. Its bed is thickly grown with cottonwoods, willows, sycamores, laurels, briars, and other trees unknown to us. Near the ford it has a grove of very high redwoods, and at about a hundred paces farther downstream another very large tree of the

[1] Camp was westward or southwestward of Santa Clara, evidently on Calabasas Creek.

[2] Stevens Creek, Permanente Creek, San Antonio Creek, and Madera Creek were all in the line of this day's march.

same redwood. It is visible for more than a league
before reaching the arroyo and from a distance it
looks like a tower. We crossed the arroyo, which
has very steep banks on both sides, and halted near
it at half past eleven in a plain which has good pasturage for the animals and many oaks and live
oaks.[1]

In all the day's march we have not seen a single
Indian, but we have seen many trails which cross the
plain and come down from the high sierra on the
north to the large estuary which we have in sight,
only a league from the camp. The point or end of it,
they say, ascends about two or three leagues above
this place. When we reached the arroyo, while seeking a ford along its banks the captain saw at a distance two Indians, who immediately hid and have
not permitted themselves to be seen again.—From
the presidio 29 hours.

The first expedition was in this same place, it
being the last one which they reached. They camped
here while the explorers were seeking the port of
Monte Rey on the 7th, 8th, 9th, and 10th of November, of '69, and on the 11th in the afternoon they
started back over the same road by which they had
come, along the beach.

To both the commander and me the camp site
appeared suitable for a mission, and the site nearest

[1] This arroyo where camp was made was San Francisquito Creek.
The crossing was at the site of Palo Alto, near the railroad bridge,
where the tall redwood (palo alto) mentioned by Palóu still stands.
For Portolá's stop here see Bolton, *Palóu's New California*, II, 220.

to the estuary or arm of the port of San Francisco. It enjoys many and good lands for raising crops, pasturage, firewood, timber, and water. Indeed, from this arroyo, although it flows very deep, since it comes down from the canyons of the high range, its water might easily be conducted for the irrigation of this plain. And besides this water it has other arroyos which descend from the hills and run on the surface of the land through the plain and go to empty into the estuary.

This place is distant from the mouth by which the estuary communicates with the sea of the gulf about half a day's journey, traveling light through the plain all grown with pasturage and oaks. The barks, entering the estuary and dropping anchor in it, would have this mission at hand and with ease the mission would receive succor from them. The place is in 37° 46′ north latitude, and its vicinity is very thickly peopled with large villages, whose inhabitants frequently come to the estuary to seek mussels and fish.

At two o'clock in the afternoon six heathen came to visit us from the nearest village, all without arms, and have been with us all the afternoon with the same confidence as if they were among their own people. They are very gentle and affable, have good features, and most of them are bearded. I made the sign of a cross on each of them, and they were very attentive to the ceremony although they did not understand it nor the purpose to which it was di-

rected. I spoke to them in the language of Monte
Rey a few words about God and Heaven, but, although they were very attentive, I was not satisfied
that they understood me, although when I talked to
them about other things it seems that they did understand me, and when they spoke I understood many
words, although I already knew that there were
many differences. I gave all of them their strings
of beads. Seeing the arrows which had been given
us by the village in the valley, they asked me where
I got them, and telling them that it was from the village nearby, I gave them to them, with which they
were very much pleased. They said goodbye, telling
me that they were going to notify the people of the
nearby villages, who next day would come and bring
us mussels, pinole, and atole. I thanked them for
this, telling them that we were starting early in the
morning, and later on would return to live with them,
to teach them what is necessary for their salvation.
They gave us to understand that they were much
pleased, saying that they all would assemble and
make their houses. With this they said goodbye.

Since this place is the nearest to the estuary, and
has everything necessary for a mission, to the commander and to me it appeared appropriate to erect
here the standard of the holy cross, which we did,
making it of two good beams (morillos). We set it
up on the bank of the arroyo near the ford where we
had camped, fixing in it our good hopes to found on
the same spot a church dedicated to my Seraphic

Father San Francisco, whom I name as intermediary in order that His Divine Majesty may grant that I may see it in my day, and that I may see reduced to our holy faith the great heathendom which inhabits this vicinity.

November 29.—We set out from the camp site a little before seven, for which reason and because of the great cold the heathen of yesterday had not yet appeared. We traveled northwest over the same plain or valley, which has good land and pasturage and is grown with oaks and live oaks. We have at the north, very close at hand, the great estuary or arm of the sea, and toward the south a high sierra covered with redwood trees, which are like cedar. At the foot of it there is a chain of hills with good land and pasturage and with groves of oaks and live oaks. In this way runs all the plain, in which in places are seen groves of live oaks. We encountered at each step very well beaten paths of heathen who come down from the sierra to the estuary, and I would gladly follow one of them in order to see what the estuary has to offer at its beach. Along this plain we traveled about two hours and a half, crossing some ditches of running water which come down from the hills and go to empty into the estuary, and which with little difficulty might be made use of to irrigate the good land of this plain.

Although this plain continues very nearly to the mouth of the estuary, without any interruption by sierra or hills, the commander, fearful of coming to some one of the many marshes in the neighborhood

of the beach of the estuary, decided to ascend the
hills and enter a narrow valley which is between the
hills and the high sierra toward the south (this being
the road traveled by the first expedition), in order
that in this way without hindrance or delay we might
reach the mouth of the estuary and examine it, taking on the return the road by the plain and keeping
as near as possible to the beach of the estuary.
On account of this decision we left the plain and
ascended the slope of a hill which offered an opening in order to descend with ease to the valley
mentioned.[1]

As soon as we started toward the range of hills,
we saw on the top of it a band of heathen, who immediately came toward us and appeared to be very
gentle and affable. All came up to me and without
the least resistance permitted me to make on them
the sign of the cross. I embraced them and gave them
some strings of beads, with which they were very
well pleased. The commander did the same. They
are very well formed and tall Indians. Many of
them are red and bearded, with long hair, all going
naked, now and then one of them having a little cape
on his shoulders, which does not reach below the
waist. Almost all of them carried in their hands
long poles like lances. They ascended the hill with
us, and from the top of it I saw a village on the floor
of the valley, near which was an arroyo of running
water. The houses are well made of grass, and are
inhabited by many people of both sexes and all ages.
The heathen traveled with us toward the village, but

[1] They turned into the hills in the vicinity of Belmont.

we turned aside, following the opening between the hills. We crossed the arroyo, which has a heavy growth of trees, and noticing that we were not going to the village, men and women came from it to see us and to accompany us.[1] These I likewise regaled with strings of beads.

We descended from the hills and entered a rather narrow valley which runs between a range of hills and the high sierra which is toward the south. It is thickly grown with oaks, live oaks, and red cedar. The bottom of it is nearly covered with a lake, a marsh, and arroyos, all grown with tules, and we saw in it innumerable geese. We immediately struck the same trail which the first expedition took, along the skirt of the range of hills. On it we encountered at each step arroyos of running water, from which, together with that which comes down from the sierra in other arroyos, are formed the lakes and marshes.[1]

In this valley we encountered four villages, inhabited by numerous people of the same kind as those who were accompanying us. In each one of them, because they were near the road, we halted a little while, in order to make friends with them and give them some beads. Their captains invited us to remain in their villages, but we thanked them and went forward, the number of our escorts increasing at each village. Among these people more than among the others I saw that they understand and speak many of the words of the language of Monte Rey.

[1] Crystal Springs Lake is in the valley where they entered it. San Andrés Lake still bears the name they gave the valley.

The women and children did not come near us very much, being more timid. But in one of the villages two old women came out to us on the road with their present of some baskets of atole and some tamales kneaded from their wild seeds. One of them, who according to what she said, was about eighty years old, told me that she was the daughter of the other one, who now could scarcely see and was unable to walk except when guided by a little boy who led her by the hand, and I understood that she had great-great grandchildren already full grown. I gave all of them some beads,[1] and the commander did the same.

We continued on our way until half past twelve, when we halted on the plain of a hill of the same valley where an arroyo of water passes, and where we had firewood and good pasturage for the animals.[2] The heathen of the villages which we passed on this journey accompanied us clear to the camp.

Among them there accompanied us a young fellow about twenty-five years old. He was fair, and with the bright red paint which he had on his face, his countenance was made pleasing. This fellow during nearly the whole journey stayed close by my side. I noticed that when he looked at me he began to weep, and when I asked him why he was crying he replied to me, although I did not understand him, and only

[1] The *Noticias* version adds, "after having made the sign of the cross on the old woman and those of her descendants who were present."

[2] The *Noticias* version adds, "not only in the large arroyo of the valley but also on a little arroyo which descends from the hills."

by his actions of putting his hand on his breast and motioning with the other hand forward did I understand that he wished to accompany me. I gave him a biscuit, thinking perhaps that his weeping was due to hunger. He ate a little and divided the rest among his companions who were the nearest to him, and not for this did he cease to give sighs from time to time. He arrived with us at the camp and remained with others until night, when they went to sleep at the village.

All the days during which they accompanied us in the neighborhood of their village he did not fail to visit us with these demonstrations of affability. Whenever he came he approached me, and raising my mantle, he covered himself with it, saying, "Me apam," "Thou art my father," the same words which the people of Monterrey use. He certainly melted my heart every time that he called me this, and I would gladly have taken him to Monte Rey, although it might be necessary to go without a mantle, but since it was not possible I consoled myself by telling him that I would return to live with them and would make him my son. He gave me to understand that he would be pleased, saying that they all would assemble and live with me. And for my part I immediately would have remained with them to prevent any one of them from dying in the meantime without holy baptism.[1]

November 30.—Before daybreak I said Mass, it being the Feast of San Andrés, for which reason we

---

[1] The last sentence is not in the *Noticias* version.

gave the name of that holy apostle to this valley,
since in the first expedition it remained without a
name because in it no village whatever was found,
whereas now, in so short a stretch, we have encountered five very large ones, from which it is inferred
that they easily move from place to place. While
the men were loading up, heathen already began to
come, among the first being my son, The Sorrowful,
who came to accompany us without being invited.

We set out from the camp site about seven
o'clock, although the thick fog prevented me from
seeing what time it was. We followed the same
valley, which runs in the same way, very leafy and
pleasant. About eight o'clock we encountered a village to which belong some of the heathen who were
accompanying us. They certainly served us greatly,
showing us the fords over the arroyos, which are
encountered very frequently, and with this aid we
were not delayed in seeking the fords. At half past
nine we emerged from the valley of San Andrés and
ascended some high hills. On a mesa between them
we encountered a fair-sized lake which is formed by
a small arroyo having plentiful trees and firewood,
and because we were now not very far from the
mouth of the estuary the commander decided to halt,
the journey having lasted two and a half hours.[1]

The camp site has toward the north a very high
hill, which I ascended with the commander in order

---

[1] Camp was at one of the small lakes between Baden Station and
the coast. The hills which Rivera and Palóu climbed after halting
were in Buriburi Ridge. From Belmont to this point the Skyline
Boulevard runs close to Palóu's trail.

to see the estuary, and we succeeded to our satisfaction especially with the arm of it which runs through the plain to the southeast. But the one toward the northwest we could not see, and even less the mouth, because the view was cut off by a high peak[1] which there is right in front of the hill. It appeared to me that the arm of the sea must be from twelve to fifteen leagues long from the mouth where it enters the Gulf of the Farallones to the end or point toward the southeast. Near the mouth it appeared to me about two leagues wide and it soon widens to about five leagues, so that it looks like a sea. Then it gets smaller and at the end it must be about a league wide. Its waters are as quiet as if it were a lake.

On this side toward the south where we are, its beach is dotted with little lakes, and little bays and arroyos which empty into it, and according to the tulares which I saw on the beach there may be many marshes. This being the case it will be difficult to reach the very beach, although by following any one of the well beaten trails of the heathen we shall be able to overcome this difficulty. It is the intention to do this on the return, when, leaving the road of the valley of San Andrés, we shall go through the plain of the estuary. From the hill we were not able to see clearly the beach of the estuary on the other side, because of the fog with which it was covered.

During the rest of the day there have been frequent visits of the heathen both from the villages

[1] San Bruno Mountain and San Miguel Hills.

which we passed through yesterday as well as from the beach of the estuary.[1] They dined at the camp, and I noticed in them great affection for our foods. I took advantage of this to make them like our company, telling them that in our lands we have an abundance of those very good seeds and those of the biscuit, which they are very fond of, much better than those which they have, and that I would return to live with them and would plant these seeds, and they would have them in abundance. It seemed to me that they understood me and that they were pleased, for they told me that they would assemble and make houses to live in.

At four o'clock in the afternoon a dense fog came up, very wet and cold, and I told the heathen to go to their village to sleep, so, taking some firebrands to warm themselves with on the way, they said goodbye. At night the fog got thicker, and the wind, rising from the west, converted it into rain, which lasted all night long, with a strong wind which gave us a very bad night.

December 1.—At daybreak it was raining and it continued until nine o'clock in the morning, when it again changed to a thick fog which continued until noon. Then the commander, seeing the day now clear, decided to climb the peak which we had in sight, in order to see the mouth of the estuary. On this errand he went with four soldiers, and I, with the rest, remained in the camp, but after two hours

[1] The *Noticias* version adds, "They were accompanied by The Sorrowful, of whom I spoke above."

he returned without having succeeded in seeing the mouth or even the estuary because of the thick fog with which it was covered.

About two o'clock nine heathen came to visit us, among them being two young boys of about fifteen years, whom I regaled with beads and a little biscuit, the commander doing the same. They remained until the hour for vespers, when we told them to go to the village. They asked if we were leaving, and when we told them not now, but next day if it did not rain, they said they would return in the morning, and then they said goodbye. This night it did not rain, but the northwest wind blew with such force that we could not sleep.

December 2.—Morning dawned cloudy and with a very cold wind. Nevertheless the captain went out on the same errand as yesterday. At twelve he returned to camp, telling me that he had been very near the mouth of the estuary, having been within half a league of it. He said that from the top of a hill he had succeeded in seeing the estuary clearly, and the mouth by which it communicates with the Gulf of the Farallones, and that it appeared to him to be about half a league wide. He said that near it on the side toward the Gulf there are three high rocks which are visible from a distance, and on the side toward the estuary in the same mouth an island, and behind this a gulf or bay, and that although there was a strong wind the water of the estuary was as smooth as glass. He noted likewise that the beach of the Gulf of the Farallones is not so wild as that of Monte Rey, for even with such a wind there were not many breakers. Likewise it appeared to him that the mouth of the estuary does not lie in the center of the gulf, but very close to the coast of the Punta de Reyes. From the top of the hill he viewed the land and saw that it would be easy to reach the mouth itself, and so he decided that we should not leave until we had succeeded in doing so.

During this journey the captain has noted that in the plain of the estuary there are no such winds as in the camp where we are, where, because of its altitude, they molest us greatly. For this reason he decided to descend to the plain, which we did, going about half a league nearer to the estuary, where we halted about half past four in a plain with good pasturage and through which runs a little arroyo of good water having firewood for our use.

December 3.—All night long it was raining on us, with a heavy wind, and it continued all the morning. In the afternoon, although the rain ceased, the very cold wind did not abate. Notwithstanding that the day was so raw, twenty-four heathen came to visit us, apparently from a different village than the rest which we have seen, although they speak the same language and use many of the words of the language of Monte Rey. They came with their presents of some tamales, more than a span long, with corresponding thickness, made from their wild seeds. They have good flavor and are very oily, and although ugly in color, being black like tar, I paid for them with beads. The rest of the afternoon we remained in camp, the heathen staying close to the fire and carrying such wood and water as was necessary for our use.

These Indians are of as good stature as the rest which I have already mentioned, most of them are bearded, and some of them are fair. Most of them carried for arms short lances with points of flint, worked as if they were of iron.[1] Before nightfall we told them to go to their village to sleep, but they replied that it was far away and that they would remain in the brush of the arroyo. The captain permitted them to do this, and taking some fire brands they went to find shelter. All night the wind continued very strong and cold.

December 4.—Day dawned with the same cold, stiff wind which prevented me from saying Mass. Although it was Sunday we remained without Mass, I being afraid that the light would go out. Although early in the afternoon the sun came out the wind did not abate. Nevertheless, the commander decided to go forward to get somewhat closer to the mouth, for the purpose of going to examine it as soon as the weather should permit. While they were loading up, the same heathen as yesterday came and I went with them to the fire and told them that we were going now, but that later I would return to live with them. They understood me well, and signified

[1] The *Noticias* version adds, ''the only difference being that they are smooth.''

that they were well pleased. I again gave them
beads and a little tobacco, and as soon as they
saw it they called it by the same name which they
use at Monte Rey, *Sahuans*. Then they began to
smoke, and I noticed in them the same custom and
ceremony as in all the others, the chief beginning to
smoke and then the rest. Passing the pipe around,
each one blew out mouthfuls of smoke toward the
sky, proffering some words of which I understood
only one, *Esmen,* which means "Sun." I said goodbye to them, crossing each of them, they being very
attentive to the ceremony, which they did not understand, none of them resisting. On the contrary,
those who were somewhat apart from me came close
to me. I consoled myself with this, since I could
not remain with them to learn the language in order
to instruct them and seal them with this holy seal
of sacred baptism.

We set out from the camp site at half past eight,
four of the heathen accompanying us without having
asked permission. The rest went toward the beach
of the estuary, which I understood they call *Auguas,*
being different from those of Monte Rey, who say
Calen. We traveled directly north, over medium
sized hills, crossing some valleys between them, in
which we saw three arroyos of running water without any growth of trees except a few small willows
and some tulares. After traveling an hour and a
half we encountered, not far from the trail which
we have mentioned, a dead deer partly eaten by a
wolf, by which the four heathen remained, asking

us for a fire to roast it with. Lighting the fire for them, we continued our way until eleven o'clock, when we halted on the slope of a hill, on whose skirt runs a little arroyo of water, forming a long lake which ends at the beach.[1]

While they prepared for us a mouthful to eat, the commander decided to go to examine the mouth of the estuary so that in case it should rain in the afternoon we should have accomplished this task. We set forth at twelve o'clock with four soldiers, all the rest remaining at the camp. Going to the northwest we crossed some hills and some arroyos which run between them and carry some water. Then came some large sand dunes, which we crossed with some difficulty in order to descend to the edge of the water at the beach of the Gulf, along which we traveled about half an hour straight north.

We now came to the cliff of a high hill which did not permit us to travel by the edge of the water which bathed the cliff. At the foot of the cliff, somewhat apart from it, there are some six rocks, three of them very large and sharp pointed. We saw them from a long distance, and from the sea they can be seen several leagues before reaching them. They form a triangle made by three peaks in which they end, which may serve as a sign for finding the mouth of the estuary. They are distant from it about a gunshot toward the south, and therefore they do not hide the entrance into the mouth.

[1] This was Lake Merced.

Seeing that the cliff prevented us from going along the beach we climbed the hill, which is of sandy land. When we had reached the top of it we saw the mouth, which is like a narrow channel, through which the great estuary of San Francisco enters the Gulf of the Farallones. Thus the end of the hill forms a wall or rampart of the channel, and on the other side, toward the north, a rampart is formed by a high sierra which ends in a cliff at the channel, whose face is of red stone and appears to have been sliced. This high sierra, which is very bare and without trees, runs to the west and ends in the Punta de Reyes, near which it is said is the Port of San Francisco.

The channel or strait is about half a league long from east to west, and from north to south it seemed to me that it was not more than a quarter of a league wide.[1] The channel is clear, without shoals or rocks, the two submerged rocks[2] which are in it being close to the cliff on the south side. We did not see any breakers in the strait or channel, but we were unable to ascertain whether or not it might be deep enough for large ships. For this it is necessary to explore it with a launch, but the estuary being so large ought to have depth enough. What we did notice was that in all the channel the sea is as smooth as glass, which is true of all the estuary which we saw from the cliff at the mouth. Toward the east in the mouth of the strait we saw an island of medium size,[3] but it does

[1] The *Noticias* version adds "in the narrowest place."
[2] Mile Rocks.   [3] Angel Island.

not impede the entry. Indeed, between it and the point of land on the south side there is formed a passage through which enters the arm of the estuary which runs to the southeast, and on the north side is formed another passage by which enters the arm which runs to the northwest. To us it appeared that each of these passages has the same width as the channel, a quarter of a league.

Behind the island we saw a large stretch of water which looked like a bay, with a beach which ends in the low land, although nearby there is a range of hills and a high sierra. Ships entering through the channel could anchor behind the island for shelter from the winds, for from the place where they begin to enter the strait they are free from breakers.[1]

Although I said that the land on either side of the channel or strait forms cliffs along the sea, this is not true of all the half league of its length, but it is true of the greater part, for on both sides it has low land with a beach, and so I judge that there will be no difficulty in crossing over with launches and loading and unloading or even in passing over horses to go by land to the Punta de Reyes,[2] and perhaps by the narrows of the channel it will be practicable to take them over led behind a canoe.

[1] The *Noticias* version adds, ''for they would now leave the Gulf of the Farallones, and even in this we noticed that there was little swell, for even after such heavy winds as have been blowing all these days and still continue up to today, we saw that the beach was quiet.''

[2] The *Noticias* version adds ''near which, it is said, is the harbor of San Francisco.''

I could not observe the latitude because we arrived at the mouth about one in the afternoon, but, considering the observation which the father preacher Fray Juan Crespi made on the 26th of March in the past year of '72, when he was opposite the mouth on the other side, about three leagues distant from the beach of the estuary, which according to his diary showed the latitude of 37° 54', I judge that it will be the same here, or if there is any difference it will be a matter of just a few minutes.

While we were on the cliff of the hill or point of land which on the south side forms the strait or channel of the mouth of the estuary of San Francisco, having in view the Gulf of the Farallones and the two points, Punta de Reyes and Punta del Angel de la Guardia, alias de las Almejas, which form it, as well as a heap of farallones which I saw clearly and which appeared to me to be within the Gulf, and are those which are most inclined to the south, I set the compass to map them, and they were to the west-southwest of me. The Punta del Angel or de las Almejas, distant from the mouth about four or five leagues, was directly south of me. Punta de Reyes, in which a high bare sierra ends, and which is distant more than twenty leagues from the mouth of the estuary, lay to the west-northwest of me, and it might serve for sailors who might wish to come to the mouth of the estuary.

Thus, starting at the Punta de Reyes, and steering to the east-southeast, they will strike the mouth of the estuary. Two leagues before arriving they will see the three large pointed rocks which are at the foot of the cliff and near them toward the north they will find the entrance. And from the farallones which lie more to the south, steering to the east-northeast, they will likewise reach it. I do not speak of the Punta del Angel, alias de las Almejas, on account of the short distance which it extends into the sea, for vessels will not approach it. Nevertheless, if from it they should wish to go to the mouth they must steer north, for from a distance they will likewise see these three rocks, and it might be that they would see them from this point, and arriving at them they will find the channel and will be able to enter it.

The coast which runs from the mouth to the Punta de las Almejas, which as I said is distant about five leagues, is a quiet coast running from north to south, and it has near the point a cove which forms something like a little bay, on whose beach there is a good lake of fresh water.[1]

The other coast, from the mouth to the Punta de Reyes, which is about twenty leagues, appears to run straight west-northwest, for I only saw about four leagues from the mouth a cove, with a beach which I saw clearly, and if in it there is anchorage, vessels will be able to take refuge there and be protected from the winds, especially from the west and northwest, from which it appears this cove is pro-

[1] The cove is at San Pedro Valley.

tected. For from the place whence we looked it appeared to be a bay with a beach, and if it is such it might serve as a place in which to await the rising tide or a favorable wind in order to enter and pass the half league of the strait to the estuary. In the high sierra of San Francisco which ends at Punta de Reyes we saw from a distance, within a clump of trees, a smoke which we judged to be a village of Indians.

Having now seen so close at hand the mouth or channel through which the estuary of San Francisco communicates with the Gulf of the Farallones, it has seemed to all of us that it must be about a quarter of a league wide, although seen from a distance it looks wider, for to the captain who saw it so close by its width appeared to be half a league. In view of this I was not surprised that to Father Fray Juan Crespi, who in the year '72 saw it from the other side of the estuary about three leagues from the beach, this mouth appeared to be three-fourths of a league wide, as he says in his diary. Moreover, from the place from which he mapped it, he was looking at the island in front of the mouth, and without doubt he saw the two arms which enter the strait or channel between the island and the two points of land, which doubtless are more than three-fourths of a league apart. But the mouth by which such a great volume of water enters the Gulf of the Farallones is not more than a quarter of a league wide. The other islands which the father mentions in his diary, and are shown on the map which he made, we could not see. No doubt they were hidden from us by the high cliffs of the strait. If God permits us to reach the other side of the estuary I will give an account of them.

Since this high, precipitous hill is the point of land which on this south side forms a wall or rampart for the strait or channel for the mouth of the estuary of San Francisco, whose waters bathe it, and since up to the present it has not been trod by any Spaniard or by any Christian whatsoever, it seemed well to the commander and to me to erect on its summit the standard of the holy cross, and we did this, forming it of two beams and planting it in a place where it may be seen from the beach.[1]

Having concluded the examination to our entire satisfaction, we returned to the place where we had left the camp, by the same road over the beach, the sand dunes, and the hills, arriving there at about three o'clock in the afternoon. On the beach we encountered the skeleton of a whale and a raft made of tule, of the kind the heathen use for fishing, although we did not see any heathen or any of their trails. But we did see many deer, encountering herds of six or eight of them together.

The commander, seeing that the weather is so rainy and that the ground because of the rain is becoming very soft, and that if the rains continue it will be impassable, especially with the animals which have just come up from Old California with the new

---

[1] The cross was erected at Point Lobos.

Photo by Bolton

The coast above Point Año Nuevo.

Photo by Bolton

Pescadero, a site "excellent for a large mission."

families, he tonight decided not to go forward, but to return to the presidio by the beach and by the same road that was taken by the first expedition in the year of '69, reserving until after the rains the exploration of the other side of the estuary and of the Rio Grande which empties into it.[1]

December 5.—In view of the decision of the captain to return by the beach to the presidio, we set out from the camp site about seven o'clock in the morning, going south and crossing hills of pure earth, covered with pasturage and with various canyons which have their arroyos of running water that form lagoons of various sizes. The journey has been one of six hours, including some stops which we made to permit the soldiers to hunt geese, on account of the many which at each step are encountered. They succeeded in killing some of them, but I could not taste them because it is Advent.

After traveling three hours over hills, we had to go down a very high one whose descent, besides being very long, was very steep. At the bottom of it we found the trail which the first expedition made five years ago, it being the plan to follow it as far as the presidio. At eleven o'clock we came to a large lake, among high hills, which ends at the beach of a little bay, distant about a league from the Punta del Angel, alias de las Almejas.[2] If the beach had permitted and a cliff had not cut off the passage, we

[1] The *Noticias* version adds, "notwithstanding that we had set out with provisions for forty days."

[2] The day's march was from the vicinity of Lake Merced to San Pedro Valley, where the lake was.

could have saved a long distance and would have been freed from the bad places which occur.

The lake forced us to make a detour of about half a league, for we saw ourselves obliged to approach the beach to cross by the sand dunes, and by the shore of the lake we entered the valley, halting at one o'clock in the afternoon in a canyon, near an arroyo, one of two which this valley has and by which the lake is formed.[1] This lake is grown with tules, and on its banks it has some willows and briar patches, and the same is true of the beds of the two arroyos. On the skirts of the hills there are some live oaks, although few. If this place had wood it would be suitable for a mission, for it is so near the mouth that by the beach it can be little more than three leagues distant, and the site has good lands and plentiful pasturage for cattle. Shortly after our arrival it began to get cloudy, threatening rain, although after all it ended in a mist or heavy fog, which lasted all the night and thoroughly wet the land.

December 6.—Morning dawned with the same damp fog which had lasted all night, and we set forth at the usual hour, about seven o'clock. As soon as we started from the camp we began to ascend high hills, and because of the wetness of the earth the trail was very difficult, and we encountered some very dangerous places, especially some slopes of very high and steep hills, so that on looking down I was horrified by their depth.[2] For this reason I trusted

[1] Camp was in San Pedro Valley, east of San Pedro Point.
[2] They were now crossing Montara Mountain.

more to my own feet than to those of the mule. After these hills and slopes we had to descend the steep grade of a hill, although it was of pure earth and pasturage. This over, we found ourselves very close to the beach of the Punta de las Almejas, so-called because of the many mussels which were obtained on this beach by the first expedition, with which they supplied the need which they suffered for lack of provisions. We then continued over a level road along the skirts of the hills, and then about a league by the edge of the water of the sea, until our way was cut off by cliffs along the skirts of the hills. We crossed four arroyos, so deep that we had to fix trails down and up their banks.

At two in the afternoon we came to a fifth arroyo. A little before reaching it we saw near the beach two heathen, who as soon as they spied us scampered to their village which they have in an arroyo. Then about fifteen heathen came out from it armed with bows and arrows. As soon as we came to them the commander made signs, inquiring why they came with bows. Then one of them, who no doubt was the chief, gathered up the bows and sent them by another person to the village. They asked us if we were going to halt there, and when we told them that we would stop on the other side of the arroyo, they showed us the descent, which is very steep and deep as is also the ascent. We halted near the cliff, which has good pasturage, although there is lack of firewood, but the heathen provided us with all that was necessary, carrying it from the canyons behind the hills.[1]

The village is built right in the arroyo on a high mesa something like an island, and from the plain neither it nor even the channel of the arroyo is visible. No doubt they live in this place in order to free themselves from the winds and cold, from which they are well protected. The village does not seem to be large, judging from the few houses which it has, as well as from the small number of adult people who permitted themselves to be seen, who did not exceed twenty. They remained in the camp the rest of the day, very ready to do whatever they were requested, bringing wood and water, the first one to volunteer being the petty chief. They speak very few words of the language of Monte Rey, and I understood almost nothing that they said. Only by signs did I learn that they have their village in the sierra and that they are camped in this arroyo only temporarily. We tried to ingratiate ourselves with them by glass beads and some little gifts which they greatly esteemed. The commander gave the chief a little piece of cloth which he greatly prized. The women and children did not come to the camp, but remained all the afternoon in sight, on the cliff, on the other side of the arroyo, which is where they have the path to go down to the village. A little before nightfall

---

[1] The arroyo was perhaps Pilarcitos Creek, and camp in the vicinity of the town of Half Moon Bay. From here the route was close to the beach all the way to San Lorenzo River, over Portolá's trail.

they were told to go to the village to sleep, which they did, asking us if we were leaving the next day.[1]

December 7.—In the morning it was misting the same as it had been doing nearly all night, and for this reason the march was suspended. About ten o'clock it stopped raining. The heathen now came with their presents of some large baskets of thick atole made of acorns and some large tamales made of their black seeds. The little chief brought a boy of his about twelve years old, whom I tried to please with glass beads and other little gifts, for which his father effusively expressed his thanks. The commander did the same. They remained at the camp all day, where they ate dinner, and I noticed a great liking for our foods. When they went back to the village the commander told them that we were going to leave next day and that if they wished to come with us to show us the fords of the arroyos they should come early. They volunteered gladly to do this and withdrew to their houses.[2]

December 8.—Before daybreak I said the Mass of our Sweetest Patroness of the Spains and of our Seraphic Religion. After this was concluded day dawned fair, with bright sunshine, so that we were able to set forth at the usual hour. While the men

[1] The *Noticias* version, besides adding several interesting items here, says, ''The chief or headman told us that he had known our captain since the first expedition, when he had accompanied him for a day's march.'' Rivera, it will be remembered, was with Palóu in 1769.

[2] The *Noticias* version here adds a whole paragraph regarding the natives of the country just passed through.

packed up the commander went to the village, and
from the cliff he called the heathen, inviting them to
go with us, and immediately the little chief came
with seven others, most of them carrying some pikes
for arms. A short time after leaving the camp site
we came to a very deep arroyo with most difficult
descent and ascent. We crossed it with much trouble,
and in doing so I got wet half way up my legs. Before going a league we came to a larger one, but we
forded it easily, following the heathen guides.

Having crossed the arroyo they conducted us
along high hills with steep descents and ascents.
With good intentions they took us off the trail of the
first expedition, directing us by another, which led us
to a very large village which we saw from the summit of a very high hill, up which they guided us. The
commander, noting the very rough descent and that
in front of us there was a very high sierra covered
with redwood, and that apparently it was impassable, and that at the foot of the high hill ran a large
arroyo heavily grown with trees, and that on the
bank of it on the skirt of the sierra there were many
people, saw the purpose of the Indians, and that we
were off the road which we ought to have followed.
In order to put a stop to the detour at once, he decided not to go to the village nor to descend to the
arroyo, but to turn to the south and descend from
the high hill to follow a valley which we saw between
the hills and the sierra in order to free us from the
roughness of the mountains.

As soon as the heathen guides saw that we were taking another road they stopped, acting as if chagrined. The people of the village came in a hurry to overtake us at the descent from the hill, and one of them who had a beard as long as the best hermit made us a speech. I understood not a word of it, but from the signs we were able to understand that he was inviting us to the village which, having had notice of us, had prepared much pinole and atole. We thanked him, saying that we were going by another road, because that sierra was very high and we would not be able to cross it, but that later we would return to their village. I regaled with glass beads him and all those whom we were able to reach. Then we said goodbye, leaving them apparently disconsolate, and the guides so discomfited that now they did not permit themselves to be seen.

We continued toward the south along the skirt of the hills, which, with the high sierra, form a narrow valley, and at half past ten we came to the arroyo of Santo Domingo, which the first expedition crossed, and since which time it has had this name.[1] To cross it was necessary to dismount and open a road and fix the descent and the ascent. Near it I saw some little houses of heathen, although without people, and we concluded that they must be in another village which they have on the beach which is distant only half a league.

[1] This was San Gregorio Creek.

We went forward by the trail of the expedition, and at twelve we came to the valleys of San Pedro Regalado, which have two large arroyos distant from each other about a league, both with large volumes of running water coursing through a heavy growth of cottonwoods, willows, sycamores, and live oaks. At both it was necessary to dismount in order to cross. Besides the two large arroyos, it has other fair sized ones which empty into the channels of the large ones, with whose waters with little labor it would be possible to irrigate the abundant land for raising crops which those valleys have. We likewise encountered in them some lakes with plentiful water and large tule marshes. There is an abundance of firewood and also of timber for building, especially red cedar, of which there are good groves of dense growth. To all of us this place appeared excellent for a large mission which would not lack anything necesary.[1]

Near the first of the two large arroyos we saw vestiges of a village with its cemetery, in which there were planted two very high, slim and straight poles, at the top of each of which there was hanging a cape made of grass of the kind the heathen use, this being a custom which they have in the burial of their chiefs. Having crossed the second large arroyo we

[1] The valleys of San Pedro Regalado were the valleys of Pescadero Creek and Arroyo de los Frijoles. There is still a lake near the mouth of the latter stream. Portolá crossed these creeks on October 24, 1769, on his way north. See Bolton, *Palóu's New California*, II, 207.

halted near it about three o'clock in the afternoon, in a plain grown with hazelbrush and with good pasturage, the march having consumed eight hours, including the detour which we made and the delays at the arroyos. During the whole journey there has been good sunshine, and it has become so warm that we have feared it will rain again soon.—From the estuary, 22 hours.

December 9.—Day dawned with a heavy frost, which congealed the water in the vessels. About seven o'clock we set forth from the camp site, by the road of the expedition, ascending and descending hills of pure earth and good pasturage but without firewood or timber, for only now and then in a canyon between the hills are seen live oaks and an occasional redwood. Between the hills we crossed arroyos with running water. At nine o'clock we came to a fair-sized valley in which we saw a very large marsh grown with tule, and crossed an arroyo with much running water where it was necessary to fix a ford and to cut off the trees in order to cross it. On its banks we found vestiges of an abandoned village with its cemetery and the stone which they use, with a pole set in it. Some of the soldiers said that this was the place where the first expedition found a large village with many houses, among them being a very large one, for which reason it was given the name of Ranchería de la Casa Grande.[1] Near the

[1] Casa Grande was on Gazos Creek or Whitehouse Creek. Portolá camped at the same place on October 23, 1769.

arroyo in a canyon between the hills we saw a dense grove of redwoods.

Having crossed this arroyo there appeared before us a very high and steep range of hills, and in order to go around it and not to test its roughness, the commander decided to turn to the west and descend to the beach. We did so, crossing some hills that were less rough, and in a short time we found ourselves on the edge of the beach. But the cliff with which the land ends would not permit us to travel along the edge of the water, and so it was necessary to travel along the skirt of the hills which, although it is all level and of good land, presented some arroyos to cross, whose ups and downs gave me some trouble because they were very steep.

At ten o'clock we came to a very deep arroyo whose descent is a cliff, making it necessary to make a winding trail in order to get down, and to cross it by the sand bar on the beach which affords a passage, for the purpose of following along the edge of the water, which is where the expedition traveled. We did so, but having traveled a good stretch by the beach the rising tide prevented us from continuing because already the water reached the cliff, and so it was necessary to go back in a hurry and climb up the cliff from the arroyo in order to halt by it and wait for low tide in order to cross the bad stretch. For this reason the journey has lasted only three and a half hours.[1]

---

[1] A long paragraph is added here in the *Noticias* version.

From this place on the cliff of the arroyo we have in sight and distant only half a league toward the north the Punta de Año Nuebo. This is the one which, together with the Punta de Pinos, which is at the south, forms the Gulf of Monte Rey, and above it is seen very plainly the high sierra of Santa Lucía. The Punta de Año Nuebo, which we have so close at hand, is a tongue of low land, rocks, and reefs of very slight elevation, but it extends a long way into the sea, and to sailors doubtless it would look very high because of the range of hills and sierras which it has very near by. But between this point and the range of hills there is more than a league of level land, which is the skirt of the range of hills which we have crossed today. This point Año Nuebo juts into the sea much farther than the Punta de Pinos, for which reason from the presidio and even from the Rio de Monte Rey the Gulf appears to be round like an O. But looked at from here the mouth is very wide, for from the Punta de Pinos to this one of Año Nuebo it must be from twelve to fifteen maritime leagues, and by land much more because of the deep pocket which the gulf forms. The Punta de Año Nuebo is in the latitude of 37° 5′, and from this cliff where I took its direction it lay west by northwest from me. All this afternoon we have been watching to see if the tide were falling, in order to be able to pass by the beach, but we have not noticed any change since morning.[1]

[1] Camp was on Año Nuevo Creek. Point Año Nuevo is still so-called.

December 10.—Early in the morning the captain
sent men to examine the passage along the beach,
and when they brought a report that they saw no
change since the day before, he decided to cross the
arroyo, ascending the cliff on the south side, then
following along the skirt of the high sierra as far as
he could and afterward traveling along the sierra in
the place where it might appear to be least rough,
since there is no other way for it. For the purpose
of examining the passage into the sierra he sent four
soldiers ahead and we set out from the camp site at
half past seven. Having traveled about half an hour
along the skirt of the sierra we met the four emis-
saries, who reported that we could descend to the
beach, which now permitted it and for which they
had made a path by which to descend from the cliff.
We came to this place, and as soon as I saw what
they called a path it seemed to me that it might better be called a very crazy ladder. I descended it
fearfully and had only the consolation that if I fell
from such a distance it would be upon the sand. We
all descended without the least injury, whereby we
were freed from the roughness of the sierra.

Then we traveled along the edge of the water,
and about nine o'clock we crossed on the same beach
the Arroyo de la Salud, so-called since the first expedition, because here so many who were gravely ill
with scurvy got well from a rain storm which fell
upon them. Just when they were in fear of death
they awoke relieved, and soon they found themselves

entirely well. Attributing this to a miracle, as an act of thanksgiving we said a *Salve* to Nuestra Señora de la Salud. Crossing the Arroyo de la Salud we followed the trail of the expedition not very far from the beach, over the high hills and along their sides, which were not very dangerous or rough, being of pure earth and grown with grass. At half past ten we reached the place which the expedition called San Pedro Alcántara.[1] This is a valley of fair width with good lands for raising crops, and through it run two arroyos and plentiful water with which all the land of the valley might easily be irrigated. The place has much firewood, timber for building, especially redwoods, and good pasturage for stock, and so it possesses everything necessary for a settlement. And in the neighborhood there is no lack of good villages, for although in the day's march we have not seen a single heathen, yet at each step we have encountered their well beaten trails which descend from the sierra to the beach, and in the same valley we saw the houses of a village, although without people, who we judged were in the sierra gathering acorns. The two arroyos of this valley, both of which empty into the sea, are about a quarter of a league apart at their mouths. Since they are very steep their downs and ups when we crossed them caused us a great deal of labor and obliged everybody to put his foot to the ground.

[1] Arroyo de la Salud was Waddell Creek, and San Pedro de Alcántara was Scott Creek. The latter has fine redwood groves.

Having crossed these arroyos we entered a spacious plain in sight of the beach, with good land and pasturage lying along the skirts of the hills. Although it is as level as the palm of the hand, we found in it four arroyos of running water, to cross which it cost us some labor, because their descents and ascents were so precipitous that in some of them it was necessary to go down on foot in order not to roll to the bottom. At half past three we halted at the fifth arroyo. It is very wide and has much water, from which is formed a large lake on whose shore we halted not far from the beach, having the advantage of good water, plentiful firewood, and pasturage for the animals.—From the estuary, 33 hours.

December 11.—Before daybreak I said Mass, which was attended by everybody, it being the Third Sunday of Advent, and at half past seven we set out from the camp site following close along the beach by the banks of the lake. By the sand bar we crossed the arroyo, which enters the sea with a good flow of water. Continuing along the skirts of the hills in sight of the beach over level land with mellow soil and with beautiful pasturage, after having traveled half an hour we crossed an arroyo with more than two bueyes of water which runs along the surface of the earth and with which it would be easy to irrigate the half league of the plain which we had previously crossed. This arroyo since the first expedition has been called Santa Cruz.[1]

[1] Arroyo Santa Cruz and San Lorenzo River still bear the same names.

Having crossed this arroyo we very soon came to the San Lorenzo river, which is very large and has a wide channel grown with cottonwoods, willows, sycamores, and other trees. Near the ford close to the sierra there is a grove of redwoods. This site is suitable not only for a town but for a city, lacking in none of the necessities all right at hand and in abundance, and with the advantage of being near the shore of the gulf, for it could be founded a quarter of a league from the beach with all these conveniences. Only stone is lacking, as is the case in all the rest of the sites, for it is the scarcest article, but it might be found in the canyons near the sierra. Within the grove of the river I saw some little houses of heathen, and although we did not see any heathen near or in the valley, we did see many of their trails with fresh tracks.

Having crossed the river we followed the road along mesas of good land and gradually leaving the beach until we were about a league from it. In traveling two hours we crossed three arroyos having plentiful running water, a heavy growth of trees in their channels, cottonwoods, sycamores, willows, and some live oaks. Their water, which comes from the heights, might be used to irrigate the mesas. Above the range of hills runs the high sierra, which has a heavy growth of redwoods.

Before reaching the third arroyo we saw some heathen. They did not hide, but on the contrary they stopped, and when we got near them as soon as I called they came up to us. I gave them glass beads and, grateful, they showed us the ford of the arroyo, whose descent and ascent were rather steep. On the banks of the arroyo we encountered other heathen whom we also regaled. These people apparently were hunting, for I saw two who were following a deer. The village is in the hills, on whose skirts we saw at a distance some people and smoke.[1]

Soon after crossing this arroyo we came to a larger one with deeper channel, in which we saw a village of a few houses made of tule. As soon as the heathen saw us descend to the arroyo they began to hide, some in the houses but most of them in brush of the arroyo. In crossing by the ford it was necessary to pass right close to the houses, by the very trail used by these people, but we saw nobody except a young fellow about thirty years old, and an old woman over eighty who welcomed us with much gabbling and a lighted firebrand.

We stopped for a while, until the pack train had crossed the arroyo, to see if more heathen might come out, in order to relieve their fear. But, seeing that they did not come out and that the old woman continued yelling, I shut her up with a string of beads, which she accepted and began to look at with admiration. She repaid the gift with the firebrand, which I accepted in order that she might not be offended. I likewise regaled the man and he gave me

[1] They were now in the vicinity of Aptos, where two creeks come together.

some acorns. I asked him what his name was and he replied with the same word that they use at Monte Rey, *Yuccs,* from which I inferred that if they do not speak the same language they must use many of its words. We climbed out of the arroyo, and as soon as the pack train had got across, the people who had hidden began to come out. Judging from the number which we saw it must be a small village.

We continued on our way toward the southeast over hills and little valleys heavily grown with live oaks, and in some level places we saw some lakes. Afterward we ascended a very high range of hills overgrown with redwoods, very high, thick, and straight. Along these hills and in their vicinity we saw groves of hazelnuts, although it had been recently burned and had not grown up again. On a hill not very far from the road which we were traveling we saw five heathen standing still, armed with bows and arrows. They were painted in such a way that from a distance they looked to me as though dressed in striped clothes. When we got opposite them I called them and gave them some strings of beads, and the captain did likewise. I asked these men some questions, but they either did not understand me or made believe they did not understand. The village, which is behind a hill, is very populous.

We traveled in the valley between the hills and in a little while came to a large lake which when the first expedition went through was called the Laguna del Corral[1] because it was used by the many sick men whom they then were carrying. To relieve them they were able to use the lake by setting up some poles and putting bars in a narrow place opposite it, thus forming a pasture in which to keep the animals at night. This served as some respite for the soldiers during the four days they stopped here, in which they gave communion and extreme unction to three of the soldiers who were most ill, besides others who continued the journey provided with the sacraments and in agonies on the road.

From the lake we continued to the southeast and entered a large plain, all of good land and pasturage and with some trees. After having traveled half an hour through it we saw not very far from the trail toward the east a large, dense grove of redwoods. At three o'clock in the afternoon we came to a large river which crosses the plain. It has a great volume of water and a wide channel heavily grown with trees. We crossed it and halted on the south bank, in the same place where the first expedition camped, since which time the stream has had the name of the Santa Ana, alias el Pájaro.[2]

Near the camp runs another growth of trees which ends at the river and appears to be the tree line of some arroyo which empties into it. To all of

---

[1] Evidently the lake now called Corralitos Lagoon. The next paragraph shows that it was passed by the explorers just before they entered "a large plain," such as lies between Corralitos Lagoon and Watsonville.

[2] The stream is still called Pájaro River. Camp was near Watsonville.

us this great plain appeared to be a site suitable for a mission, having all the conveniences of land, water, pasturage, firewood, and timber, and being distant from the beach about a league; and according to the many trails which cross the plain and run to the beach, no doubt there must be a large population which could be assembled, in addition to the large village which is at the Laguna del Corral.—From the estuary, 40½ hours.

December 12.—Early in the morning I said the Mass of our Lady of Guadalupe, which was attended by all. At half past seven we set out toward the southeast through the same plain as yesterday, which we finished crossing at eight o'clock, then entering some hills through an opening which we saw between them. In the plain there is a large lake of good water with extensive tulares, from whose water we saw thousands of geese emerge. We continued along the shore of the lake and entered a rather narrow valley between hills of pure earth and grass, with some live oaks that are not very large, all the floor of the valley being covered with lagoons of various sizes so that the entire valley looked like a lake, and obliged us to travel along the slopes of the hills. Having finished the valley we ascended some high hills, and having descended from these we found ourselves in the plain or large valley of Santa Delfina. We began to cross it at ten o'clock, and at half past twelve we arrived at the river of Monte Rey which we forded, halting on the bank in the same place where we spent the night of the 23d of last month, the day when we set out from the presidio.[1]

A league before we reached the river we saw near a lake some women who were gathering grass seeds and who as soon as they saw us scampered and hid in the brush, where we concluded they must have a village. On the beach we saw a smoke and in the grove along the river at nightfall we saw another fire, from which I infer that there are many people in the vicinity of the river who have not yet entered the mission, and whom it will not be practicable to move because of the river and of the mussels and fish which they have in the estuary, into which the river enters.— From the estuary, 45½ hours.

December 13.—At half past seven we set out from the river and took our way toward the presidio over the same road which we followed on going, and after traveling two and a half hours at a good pace we arrived at ten o'clock at the presidio of Monte Rey. —From the estuary, 48 hours.

I stopped here for a short time and then set out for the mission of San Carlos, where I arrived a little after eleven o'clock, finding the reverend father president and the father companions without any change in health. On seeing me they were delighted, but in a short time they joined me in the sorrow which I brought at not having accomplished the complete exploration of all the vicinity of the

[1] This day they crossed the hills south of Watsonville Junction, skirted Elkhorn Slough (the ''large lake of good water with extensive tulares''), and passed the vicinity of Del Monte Junction.

estuary of Our Father San Francisco and of the Rio Grande which flows into it, for the reasons which are set forth above.

We spent on the journey twenty-one days, in which we traveled eighty-nine hours, always at a good pace, that is, from the presidio to the mouth of the estuary forty-one hours, and from there to the presidio forty-eight hours, by the road which we traveled having made almost a circle.

Among the good sites suitable for missions which we have found in this journey my attention was called especially to six: two on going, by the road through the valleys, and four by the road along the beach which we traveled on the way back, since they have all things necessary for good settlements. They are the following:

By the Beach[1]

1. The Rio de Santa Anna, alias del Pájaro, distant from the royal presidio of Monte Rey seven and one-half hours. This river empties into the gulf of the presidio, and the settlement could be established very near the beach, in order that the Indians might enjoy the advantage of mussels and fish.

2. The Rio Grande de San Lorenzo, distant from the foregoing site seven hours, and from the presidio fourteen and one-half hours. This river empties into the same gulf, and the settlement might be

[1] In the *Noticias* version the remainder of the diary is summarized in one short paragraph.

placed about a quarter of a league from the beach, on the arroyo of Santa Cruz, which is some five hundred paces from the river.

3. The Cañada de San Pedro Alcántara, known by the soldiers as El Alto del Jamón. It is distant from the foregoing site six hours and from the presidio twenty. It empties into the same gulf, on whose beach the settlement might be placed. It is distant from the Punta de Año Nuebo three and one-half hours, and from the mouth of the estuary twenty-eight.

4. The Cañadas de San Pedro Regalado, distant from the foregoing site nine hours and from the presidio twenty-nine. These valleys empty outside of the gulf of Monte Rey four and one-half leagues beyond the Punta de Año Nuebo. The settlement might be placed on the second large arroyo about half a league from the beach. In the nineteen hours' journey from there to the mouth of the estuary, I did not see any place suitable for a settlement, for lack of timber and even of firewood, although in regard to land, water, and pasturage all the country which we traveled over has them in abundance.

By the Road Through the Valleys

5. The valley of San Pasqual Baylón, at the mouth of the Cañada de San Benito, distant from the presidio toward the northeast eight and one-half hours.

6. The plain of the great estuary of San Francisco, at the arroyo where the cross was erected, distant from the foregoing site about twenty hours and from the presidio twenty-nine. From the beach of the estuary it is distant about an hour; from the point or extremity of the estuary about three hours; and from the mouth by which the estuary communicates with the Gulf of the Farallones eleven hours by the road which we traveled through the Cañada de San Andrés. Following the plain of the estuary it might be some six hours' journey. It seems to me that this is the site nearest the mouth of the estuary on the side which we explored.[1]

These sites appeared to me to be those most suitable for settlements, because they have everything necessary and many heathen both in them and in their vicinity, for although right along the road we saw only those which I have mentioned in this diary, yet the many well beaten trails made by them which we saw caused me to believe that this country is very thickly peopled by them.

May the God Most High, Father of Mercies, grant that in my day I may see them congregated in missions in those sites or in others, and that no one of them may die without holy baptism, in order that

[1] Stated in terms of modern geography, the six sites recommended for missions by Palóu were (1) on Pájaro River near Watsonville, (2) on San Lorenzo River at Santa Cruz, (3) at Scott Creek, on the coast near El Jarro Point, north of Davenport, (4) on Pescadero Creek near Pescadero, (5) in Hollister Valley, near Hollister, (6) on San Francisquito Creek, at Palo Alto.

thereby may be increased the number of the children of God, and of the Holy Church and of the vassals of our Catholic monarch, and so I beg of the Divine Majesty. At this mission of San Carlos de Monte Rey, December 14, 1774.

FRAY FRANCISCO PALOU.

I certify that this is a copy of the original which is in the Secretaría de Cámara y Virreinato which is in my charge. Mexico, May 27, 1775.

MELCHOR DE PERAMÁS.

INDEX

INDEX

A

Acaguechis (Ajagueches, Axagueches), 55, 83, 195, 322, 325.

Agua Amarilla, 277, 278, 330, 333, 336, 345, 358, 359, 368. See *Laguna Salada*.

Agua Caliente, 124, 237, 375, 376, 387.

Agua Dulce, 25.

Agua Escondida, 6, 32, 35, 139, 156, 159, 256, 257, 317.

Aguaje de la Luna (Heart Tank), 28, 316.

Aguaje de la Purificación. See *Cabeza Prieta Tanks*.

Aguaje Empinado (Heart Tank), 27, 28, 30, 122, 154, 155, 235, 254, 255, 316.

Agua Salada, 25, 27, 153, 254.

Albino Tank, 32, 156.

Alburquerque, Duke of, Viceroy, 118, 231.

Alcántara. See *San Pedro*.

Alegría. See *El Carrizal*.

Almejas. See *Punta de las Almejas*.

Altar, El, presidio, river, and valley, 1–18, 33, 38, 70, 100, 134–145, 157, 209, 248, 309–311, 364.

Angel Island (Isla del Angel), 427.

Angustias, Las, 60, 63, 182, 273, 355.

Año Nuevo Creek, 443.

Año Nuevo Point. See *Punta de Año Nuevo*.

Anza, Juan Bautista, First Expedition to California, 1–392; from Tubac to Caborca, 1–14, 133–144, 247–249, 307–310; through the Papaguería, 15–32, 145–155, 250–256, 311–318; through the Yuma Country, 33–56, 156–175, 257–269, 319–325; across the desert, 57–84, 176–194, 270–281, 326–340; over the Sierras to California, 85–101, 195–211, 281–290, 341–349; to Monterey and back to the Colorado, 102–117, 215–230, 291–297; up the Gila and home, 118–130, 231–243, 298–306; diaries of, 1–243; equipment, 1–2, 134–135, 247–248, 309; reasons for going by Altar, 2–4, 136–137, 248–249, 310; speech to Palma, 40–41, 163–165; route of, 386, 388. (See the footnotes, maps, and illustrations, throughout).

Apaches, 3–11, 126–128, 137–143, 240, 242, 248, 260, 303, 305, 310, 381, 383, 389, 391.

Aquituni, 128, 242.

Aritoac (Aricurittoac), 301, 376.

Arivaca (Aribac, Aribaca), 4, 5, 138.

Arivaipa (Aribaipa, Aribaipia, Baipia), 15–20, 146, 250, 311, 312.

Arizonac (Arizona), 7, 49, 140, 170.

Arrastre, 16, 21, 25.

Arricivita, Fray Juan Domingo de, 392.